D0521938

SPEAKING OF CHILDREN
THEIR LEARNING
ABILITIES / DISABILITIES

Speaking of Children

THEIR LEARNING
ABILITIES / DISABILITIES

Careth Ellingson

HARPER & ROW, PUBLISHERS

NEW YORK, EVANSTON, SAN FRANCISCO, LONDON

1817

FIRST EDITION

Designed by Sidney Feinberg

Library of Congress Cataloging in Publication Data

Ellingson, Careth.
  Speaking of children.
  Bibliography: p.
  Includes index.
  1. Exceptional children—Education.   2. Educational
psychology.   1. Title.
LC3965.E44   1975   371.9′2   73–14256
ISBN 0–06–011178–X

75 76 77 78 79 10 9 8 7 6 5 4 3 2 1

For Della and Susan,
Without whom life would be sterile—and very dull

Contents

Part Four

Illustrations follow page 210

Prologue

In the "small hours," when we conceive our children, our thoughts rarely, if ever, include the future academic life of the yet unborn son or daughter. It seems so far away . . .

We cannot be faulted for this; the child is like a butterfly's wing—delicate, beautiful beyond description, and so very easily shattered. In the back of our minds, we are always aware of this fragility—but mother nature gives us optimism, an optimism that is almost always fulfilled. This book is about those children who do not quite fully fulfill their promise nor our optimism.

Among the most tragic sights on the education scene are the bright, alert children who are unable to learn in a standard classroom—the children who suffer the handicap known as learning disabilities.

No one knows for certain how many such children there are. Professionals in the field estimate, conservatively, that nearly 10 million children have a learning disability sufficiently severe to impede academic progress. The figure is staggering. The academic problems that these children present can be overwhelming. The waste of human potential if help is not provided is tragic.

All children are the responsibility of all adults. It is true, however, that the major portion of responsibility for any given child falls on his parents and teachers. Through the guidance of the home and the schools—and to a lesser degree of other institutions of society—the child is helped to develop into a civilized, educated member of the community. Even under normal circumstances, the process requires much of child and adult alike.

When we set up institutions and establish standards to educate and civilize our young, we try not to be rigid. We try to offer children opportunities to explore their own interests, talents, and aspirations. We try to motivate the learning process. We try to think of every child as an individual, rather than average versus nonaverage, normal versus abnormal. We try. We rarely succeed. The requirements of formal education, especially primary education, allow little room for those who do not fit readily into accepted classroom patterns.

Unfortunately, millions of children simply don't fit the patterns. These are the learning disability children. They have been called by many names both in clinical and layman's terms. Their disabilities and symptoms of disability take many forms, often very subtle or nonspecific. Although unable to function comfortably or securely in the normal classroom, these children do not need the full range of treatment required by those with the more severe and obvious handicaps. Through no fault of their own, they live in a world that makes demands that they are unable to meet.

What, exactly, are learning disabilities?

The United States Office of Education gives the following definition, a definition generally accepted at the state level throughout the country:*

"The term 'children with specific learning disabilities' means those children who have a disorder of one or more of the basic psychological processes involved in understanding or in using language, spoken or written, which may manifest itself in imperfect ability to listen, think, speak, read, write, spell, or do mathematical

* This definition is currently under advisement at the federal level; the goal is a *positive* expansion of of the guidelines for learning disabilities.

calculations. Such disorders include such conditions as perceptual handicaps, brain injury, minimal brain dysfunction, dyslexia, and developmental aphasia. Such term does not include children who have learning problems which are primarily the result of visual, hearing, or motor handicaps, of mental retardation, of emotional disturbance, or of environmental disadvantage."

Thus, we have guidelines: average or above intellect; no organicity to a degree that affects or depresses the intellect to less than average; no severe physical incapacities; no psychotic aberrations; and no environmental abuse.

This book is about children's learning *a*bilities and *dis*abilities. For it is not enough to inquire into the symptoms of disabilities if one does not understand ability—its nature, components, and functioning. This is particularly true of learning disabilities because the children affected are often so very close to the accepted norm. It is possible for a child to go through his entire academic life performing inefficiently, consistently underachieving his actual potential, without ever being recognized for what he is—learning disabled. Some day, after he has left school, someone, a statistician most probably, will label him a functional illiterate. The tragedy is that the label will be accurate.

Learning disabilities cross discipline lines—psychology, a number of specialized medical fields, and education. An individual case can be unbelievably complex. For this reason, more than a thousand pieces of clinical literature were studied for this book. Many professionals were consulted for guidance. As far as possible the concepts of the literature have been translated into more readable language. This has not, however, always been possible or desirable. Too simplistic an approach to the multidiscipline professional language of learning disabilities would, in the long run, be a disservice to the reader. Anyone who confronts effectively any field of endeavor must know the language of the professionals involved. Without this knowledge, clinical language can become a barrier to understanding. Footnotes and reference citations have been kept to a minimum to ease the flow of what is, in some instances, rather technical data. Only the directly quoted reference material bears the author's name. It is inherent in this work that those persons referred to are beyond question in their professional credentials.

The book is divided into four major sections. The first section is devoted to normal development and to learning processes. It touches lightly on how development and the learning process may be disrupted or delayed.

The second section discusses the dysfunctions: how to identify them; the major different patterns that learning disabilities can present; what distinguishes the various characteristics of learning disabilities.

The third section is devoted to helping the child by utilizing the educational processes, management, behavior modification, and chemotherapy. This section ends with a case study of a clinical school that portrays how all these components juxtapose in favor of the child.

The fourth and final section contains a preliminary screening section for parents and classroom teachers who feel that they might have recognized a child in these pages.

Parents who read this book should first think about their own goals. No matter what dreams we have for our children, the primary goal for us all when thinking of our offspring should be an efficiently functioning adult. We want our sons and daughters to grow up healthy and whole. We want them to acquire the abilities and skills that will allow them to earn a living, live productively and happily. None of us can, nor should be, satisfied with an end product that is intelligent but semi-illiterate.

Experience has shown that once parents realize that their child has a problem, that he is not just being "bad-tempered, lazy, or deliberately dumb," they will make every effort to find professional help. These pages will help parents toward a first concrete awareness of what may be a vague, uneasy sensing of a problem, or it may lead them to the very real knowledge that their child has a learning disability. Every parent with a young child can discover here what may be a potential threat to his child's future. With or without a learning disability, this information is important to your child.

Since this is just one book and there are millions of involved children, the information contained here must be general in nature. *Every child is an individual and as such needs individual analysis and help.* Seek out professional assistance if you have a problem. Do not use these pages and the information contained in them as anything more than a guide to understanding. You would not be reading this if you were not concerned and aware. So, carry this attitude the next step—go to qualified professionals. You will find them in schools, hospitals, colleges, universities, mental health and guidance clinics, private and public facilities.

Do this for your child.

Careth Ellingson
Coral Gables, Florida

Part One

*Knowledge is not a reflection of reality
but the result of active interaction between
the subject and its environment.*

—Bärbel Inhelder,

writing in 1968 about the theories of Piaget

1

"We just had a baby!" are some of the happiest words that can be said. A child is the product of human mating—a living organism that combines the sum total of his ancestors, his natal life, and the successful completion of his arduous journey from the womb to earth air. All these help make him the unique individual he is going to become.

In a book that is primarily concerned with learning, it may seem strange to discuss a child's conception and his genetic heritage. What possible *lasting* effect could these factors have on a 6- or 14-year-old sitting in a classroom so many years past the moment of mother and father's conceiving him.

For some children, the answer is everything.

The way in which a child develops and matures physically, neurologically, chemically, mentally, and emotionally has a direct bearing on his later academic performance—on the efficiency with which he functions.

A child's ancestors determine his genetic inheritance. Heredity, coded through the chromosomes, offers familial characteristics and chemical efficiencies/inefficiencies—physiological strengths and weaknesses—for such diverse matters as blood type, blue eyes, allergies (or at least the propensity toward certain allergenic reactions), even an appendix with a tail. This inescapable genetic heredity is ours for our entire lifespan and beyond, even though an endless range and variety of genetic backgrounds may be joined by two biological strangers marrying and reproducing the species.

We are all born with half of our future children's genes; the other half comes from our marriage partner. Naturally, as generations pass, some characteristics of genetic origin are cancelled by this joining of strangers; others are reinforced. From what is available, Mother Nature picks and chooses.

When humans mate, one male sperm travels a difficult path to fertilize one female egg. This single sperm is composed of twenty-three chromosome pairs. The female egg is composed of nutrients and a nucleus. This nucleus also contains twenty-three chromosome pairs. When sperm joins egg, and each unfolds its chromosome pack, we have the beginning of a new human being, a normal fetus which carries forty-six chromosomes. At this point, both mother and father have made their total contribution to the biological heredity of their child. From now on, everything that happens to the developing fetus is a direct contribution of the internal (womb) or external environment.

What, exactly, are chromosomes? The composition is: atoms into molecules, molecules into deoxyribonucleic acid (DNA), DNA and structural proteins into genes, genes into chromosomes. This sequence is the secret of the universe, the building materials of all life. DNA is basically extremely stable and is the coding or programming molecule for genetics. The carrier for this coding is ribonucleic acid (RNA).

Atoms, molecules, genes, chromosomes, DNA, RNA—the whole of a living organism—in this case, the human being, has a *chemical base* upon which environmental nutrients and heredity interact. This is important to remember. Throughout the learning process chemical action and interaction dominate.

At each step of the process of re-creating life from the living, there are dangers, over most of which we have no control. Science already knows, for example, that each of us possesses about eight harmful genes of varied severity. Perhaps if we bred ourselves like racehorses with careful attention given to compatible bloodlines, we could eventually outbreed genetic mistakes. However, since our sex lives are not controlled by outside handlers, this, of course, will never happen. And if it did happen, what sort of human would we have in the long run? The guess would be nothing desirable. We breed racehorses for strength, stamina, configuration, and so forth. We create children out of love, in spite of nature's need to propagate the species. Nature pushes us to procreate, but intellectually we usually want our children. The love men and women have for each other, and the love and desire they have for their progeny, overrules nature's inherent demand for genetic engineering of the species.

■

Our first opportunity to define in personal terms a child's development is at birth. We can see, hear, and feel the wiggly bundle that has come into our lives. Our reactions are not scientific; they are emotional. The parent only knows and cares that the baby looks normal, sounds normal, and feels normal. But within this new, small body a scientific pattern of development has already begun. This development is dynamic. It is an active, positive, and palpable sequence of events.

Development may be defined as growth (physical and physiological), maturation (anatomical, neurophysiological, and chemical), and learning (experience, training/education, observation, exercise/repetition).

Even though birth is the point at which we truly "take over" our children's lives, the manner in which this environmental "takeover" affects the individual child for good or for ill has been modified by his genetic background and *in utero* experiences.

In utero experience begins early; by the fourth week of gestation, the embryo has a primitive heart, eyes, lungs, and the beginning development of a nervous system.

An especially significant stage of prenatal neurophysiological growth occurs by approximately the fourth month of fetal life. A substance called myelin appears. Myelin is composed of complex lipoproteins and neurokeratin protein. When speaking of myelin, scientists refer to its formation, development, and maturation. Myelin maturation has proved to be an accurate yardstick for measuring normal development. It is pinkish-white in color, fatty, and waxy-looking. Compacted normally in the human body, it gives color to the brain and spinal cord "white matter" as opposed to the "gray matter" found in the cortex. (Thus, the cortex may be considered to be nonmyelinated.) As one of its functions myelin sheaths our nerve fibers. An example of a demyelinating disease (nervous tissue breakdown) is multiple sclerosis. Science does not yet know how myelin growth commences in the body. It is known that myelin can be destroyed and that its destruction can be fatal. Two such destroyers are carbon monoxide and tetraethyl lead.

Myelin is still incompletely formed at birth in a full-term, nine-month baby, except in the brain stem and the center of the spinal cord. The maturation of myelin proceeds from the brain stem (at the base of the skull) down and outward from the spinal cord. An infant's abilities also grow downward and outward, in the manner of a cross. Starting with sucking, the infant goes through successively more sophisticated stages of development and ability—the beginnings of visual and auditory processing, bowel and bladder control—on to talking. Myelination is, for the most part, completed in the brain between two and three years of age. However, the process is ongoing in the brain until somewhere around age sixty.

The single most important aspect of the myelination process is that it can be either arrested or abnormally slowed in its maturation. Because the myelination process progresses at a different rate of maturation in different parts of the body, arrested or slowed myelination may affect children differently.

Obviously, myelination is extremely important to the nervous system, and it is the nervous system that is responsible for all maintenance and control of body and mental functions. The system has two main divisions: the peripheral nervous system (PNS) and the central nervous system (CNS).

The function of the nervous system begins with *neurons,* individual cells that are responsible for the transmission of electrical impulses. These impulses carry stimuli (information) to and from the body. Input is carried by dendrites; output by axons.

There is an interdependent action between the peripheral and central nervous systems. The peripheral nervous system is divided into the autonomic and the somatic, with the autonomic portion again divided into the parasympathetic and sympathetic systems. These autonomic systems are primarily concerned with visceral functions, smooth muscle activity, and glandular secretions.

The somatic portion of the peripheral nervous system is concerned with sensori-motor functions. A sensory, or afferent, nerve takes impulses *to* the central nervous system; a motor efferent nerve takes impulses *from* the central nervous system to the peripheral system.

The central nervous system consists of the brain and spinal cord. Here, bundles of axons are called tracts, and collections of neurons are called nuclei. It should be remembered that a great deal of the language of education today is based on the use of the terms "tracts" or "pathways." This terminology did not evolve by accident. As you can see, there was a sound neurophysiological basis for bringing these terms to education.

The CNS and PNS interfunction through the synapses—the chemical junctions between two neurons. The synapses are the transmitters of the nervous system. Although they do not touch, the neurotransmitted information jumps the synaptic cleft to continue its journey to, from, or within the nervous system.

A summation of this aspect of human development would be that the nervous system baseline is chemical and characterized by the transmission of stimuli by electric impulse(s); a chemical inadequacy or imbalance, or an electrical "short-circuit," can contribute to a learning disability.

■

The *difference in potential* between human babies and animal babies lies in the brain. At birth, an animal's brain has already reached almost its total potential for size, output, and capacity for experience. This is not true of humans. Because of our convolutional brain growth, which allows intellectual development, we are able to reason, analyze, and originate. A healthy intellect is capable of new learning from birth until the day we die.

Normal intellectual development goes through structured periods with each period laying the foundation for the next. Less than two decades ago, it was generally an accepted hypothesis that a newborn infant was a neuter entity. That is to say, he was not functioning beyond elimination, feeding urges, and the automatic or internal body functions of heartbeat, breathing, reaction to heat or cold, etc. Supposedly, the infant had no capability for reaction to outside stimuli; external factors had no genuine effect on a newborn infant.

Medical research has since proved this theory wrong. From birth, an infant can and does react to its environment in rapid, progressively sophisticated stages.

A few days from birth, after the birth amniotic fluid is gone from the middle ear, a baby can hear. There is evidence that this hearing is not limited to just loud noises. He may shortly be able to discriminate the direction from which a sound comes and even the pitch of the sound. Thus, if Mother walks into the room talking to the baby, he may well turn his head toward her.

A newborn, 4 to 8 weeks old, can *see* as well as any adult. What he can't do is *sort* what he sees.

There is even some evidence that infants who are only a few weeks old begin embryonic language formulation. Granted, this "pre-speech" activity is confined to gestures and facial expressions and rudimentary speaking in the form of movement of lips and tongue.

Cognitive and memory processes begin in an infant at about 8 weeks.

The intellectual development of our children—a development unique to our species—is of prime concern. Piaget, the noted Swiss child psychologist, divides this intellectual development into four periods: sensori-motor, preoperational thought, concrete operations, and formal operations. These periods, or plateaus, have substages that may be called schemas. For example, during the sensori-motor stage, an infant acquires a sensori-motor scheme of grasping. One can observe a baby grasp and handle many objects, all of which have one thing in common—they are amenable to grasping. Even though the objects grasped may differ in configuration, size, color, or whatever, a baby can grasp them and does. The grasping schema corresponds to the common property of the objects or, even more simply put, confers this common property (graspable) on the objects. Thus, as Piaget says, "If the stimulus could not be assimilated, it would not constitute a biological stimulus; it would simply not exist for that particular organism."

If a baby didn't have a particular structure—nerves, tissue, fingers, bones, muscles, thumb, forefinger—he not only could *not* grasp but would not *want* to grasp. Sharks or pigs do not possess the physical properties with which to grasp a ball. Therefore, they not only cannot grasp but do not want to. A human being has within himself not only the ability but the *natural proclivity* to grasp and pick up objects.

Thus our intellectual development starts with pure reflex and by the age of about 12 has progressed to the ability to think abstractly. Quite a journey for the brain, but a journey which takes place within the framework of ourselves as human beings. We expect our children to develop and learn because we know that they can.

The first stage, from birth to about 2 years of age, is called the sensori-motor period of development. It might well be called discovery through manipulation. The child learns to manipulate objects, move about physically, and to initiate events. He learns that objects have a permanence, even when taken from his immediate environment. His perceptions slowly become organized. But everything is still externalized. He has no ability to ascribe internal and symbolic representations of time, space, and shape to his life. He sees, he acts, without conceptual curiosity or knowledge of results. Because he lacks internal imagery and language he does not understand that inanimate objects have no life. He is all action without the ability to formulate the concept of reaction, or the results of his actions.

The sensori-motor growth period of a child is not all that is happening to him while this neurophysiological activity is progressing. He is also developing psychologically. A child's emotional development at this stage may be quite fragile due to the necessary interaction between his emotional growth and his sensori-motor progress. Everyone has a body image concept, a personal mental image of their body and how it "fits" into the immediate environment.

If a parent disrupts or destroys, even for a few minutes, a child's body image concept it may have serious consequences, most especially if the child in question is suffering a sensori-motor growth lag.

For example, if you toss your baby up in the air, you are disrupting his accustomed figure–ground perception, perception still in its formative stages. The tossing may be tolerated by the child, even to the point of learning to like it. In other words, he adjusts, which is normal. But, if you accidentally drop him, he may survive the fall without any signs of physical damage but the emotional damage may be severe or extremely slow in healing.

There are, of course, other forms or causes of emotional damage that may interact with the child's sensorial and psychological growth. Even though very young, a child who faces constant frustration because he is unable to "do" what he feels ready to "do," unable to talk so that his wants are met, unable to move at will to an objective, is prey to deep-seated feelings of frustration and inadequacy. These feelings can bear unpleasant fruit as the child continues to develop. Like the rock starting down the snow-covered mountain, the whole thing grows bigger and more out of control, until, finally, we are dealing with an enormous snowball, a snowball all out of proportion to the original rock. The problem also is now all out of proportion to the original cause. Thus, an unrecognized maturational lag, emotional disruption, or organic inadequacy will suddenly have a societal impact. Why? Because the child is not functioning at the same level as his peer group and he has reached the age where it has begun to show. Of course, his failings will not be quite so evident during the early levels of his next developmental stage as they will be later in school, but they are there just the same.

The second plateau or stage of development is called preoperational thought. From age 2 to about 7, perceptions become functional at a practical level. Language development begins. The child is able to activate *mentally* his sensori-motor schema. He is not only beginning to acquire language but also imagery and internal representations of his heretofore external world. Though he can now follow a sequence of events through to conclusion, he cannot yet reconstruct the sequence in reverse. This is due to his inflexible approach. His thinking is irreversible. He categorizes life according to his own perceptions, not those of the adults surrounding him. His thinking is totally *egocentric;* he cannot assimilate or grasp another person's point of view.

Here again, emotional nutrients are invaluable. If, for instance, an event shatters the child's emotional environment, his language development may suffer. And, if language development does not proceed at the proper rate, how then can he function efficiently in a classroom? It must be recalled that this period of development is from 2 to 7 years of age, and by that time he is in school.

Since his mental processes are, at this stage, egocentric and irreversible, it is important that his *perceptions,* upon which are built his imagery, memory, and eventual conceptual strength, be accurate. Cultural and emotional nutrients should be rich and full to round out his development for the next stage.

From age 7 to about 11, the child enters the period termed concrete operations. Concrete ideas have formed and he can apply logic to these ideas. Mastery of length, mass, and volume, and the concept of conservation of these, come to all children in the same sequential order with the total concept becoming stable by about age 11 or 12. A child can then understand that 12 inches on a ruler can be the same as 12 inches on a piece of rope, or, that when water in a glass that is short and wide is poured into a tall, narrow glass it does not change in quantity, thus acquiring the conservation concept. Though he is now less egocentric and is able to reverse his thought processes, his generalizations and abstractions are still based on events and objects that are concrete.

His ego-self concept of body imagery is firmly grasped although a serious emotional blow can still be devastating—death of a parent or close friend, for example, a new marriage partner or divorce for his parents—anything that seriously disrupts his stable environment or his still egocentric "self."

The final stage of intellectual development is called formal operations. From age 11 on, the adult powers of reasoning, abstraction, and symbolization gradually emerge. The half-grown child can now begin to challenge adults by using logical arguments. He can draw implications from a situation and can reason hypothetically. What he has been taught about the mores of our society—social conduct, morality, social justice—begin to become clear to him. And, often, much to parental chagrin, he begins to pick and choose what mores he thinks are right or usable.

Within the framework of Piaget's four levels, there are many specific milestones at the practical level that we may expect a child to reach at a given age. (See Developmental Milestones at the end of this chapter.) However, development at this practical level can be, and often is, uneven. A lag of a week or acceleration of a week for any given task still falls within the range of normal development. Children pass from plateau to plateau in a slowly integrated manner. There is no abrupt change from one stage of development to the next.

As the infant moved from reflex action to intelligent behavior, his primary source of new knowledge was experimentation. He learned five perceptual basics of the world: proximity (nearness/ farness), separation (apartness), order (succession), enclosure (surrounding), and continuity.

With these perceptual basics come the beginnings of memory storage. As the child actively sought out new experiences and intellectual activity, he layered new data onto his past instinctive knowledge and acquired concrete knowledge. Physiologically, his eye, hand, and motor coordination went from primitive to sophisticated. His environment influenced his innate desire and drive for development. For academic purposes he reached the stage of *readiness*.

Maturation plus adequate experience equals readiness.

Developmental Milestones: Check Your Child

ONE MONTH OLD (4 weeks)

	Early	Usual	Late
Avoids annoying stimuli			
Both hands held tightly fisted			
Can follow toy to midline but not past it			
Clenches hard as toy touches it			
Cries in response to definite stimuli			
Decreases activity and looks at examiner			
Drops at once toy put into hand			
Grasping not related to vision			
Holds head up when supported			
If held sitting, lets head sag			
Indefinite stare at surroundings			
Lifts head when startled			
Likes light			
Makes noises in throat			
Nursing skills integrated			
Pulls hands, grasps, stretches			
Reflex nursing skills developed			
Responds negatively to unpleasant experience			
Responds positively to pleasant experience			
Sees toy only when brought in front of eyes			
Sensitive to: feeling			
tone of voice			
touch			
Tears			
Watches and follows briefly			

TWO MONTHS (8 weeks)

	Early	Usual	Late
Alert expression			
Can follow dangled toy past midline			
Definite direct regard			
Eyes follow moving persons or things			
Holds head erect but it bobs			
Interested especially in red and orange			
Notices loud noises, color, movement			
Occasional smile			
Pattern sucking in nursing			
Repeatedly lifts head to 45° when on abdomen			
Responds to people and experiences			
Retains toy briefly if put in hand			
Several kinds of vocalization			
Shows preference			
Single vowel sounds: ah, eh, uh			
Slow to notice toy held over chest midline			
Smiles back if you nod head and talk to him			
Turns from side to back			

Developmental Milestones: Check Your Child

THREE MONTHS (13 weeks)	Early	Usual	Late
Concentrates on examiner			
Coos, chuckles			
Enjoys brightly colored items, candlelight			
Eyes fixate (true convergence)			
Follows toy or person's hand, side to side			
Glances at toy when put in hand			
Grasping integrated with vision (eye-hand)			
Head bobs forward if held sitting			
Holds hands open or loosely closed			
Holds hands up to look at			
Holds head up sustainedly when prone			
Holds toy put in hand with active grasp			
Lifts head and chest			
Prompt regard to toy dangled midline at chest			
Pulls at clothes			
Recognizes bottle			
Shows purpose			
Symmetric posture of head and body is seen			
Vigorous body movement			

Early	Usual	Late	FOUR MONTHS (17 weeks)
			Brings hands together in front of chest
			Can control head
			Coos, chuckles, laughs, babbles, crows
			Gets excited, breathes heavily in play
			Head steady, set forward, when sitting
			In prone, holds head at 90°, looks ahead
			Initiates smile when people stand by him
			Looks at toy in hand
			Loud laughs
			Makes sounds at will
			Prone, lifts head, by using hands or forearms
			Reaches purposefully for objects
			Rolls side to side
			Scratches fingers, clutches at clothes
			Seems to understand gestures, facial expressions
			Sitting, follows moving object
			Symmetrical postures predominate
			Takes object momentarily if held near hand
			Waves arms, moves body at sight of toy
			When on back, takes toy to mouth

Developmental Milestones: Check Your Child

FIVE MONTHS
(21 weeks)

	Early	Usual	Late
Accepts one object handed to him			
Brings both hands toward toy			
Elements of decision			
Fixates intensely			
Has command of eyes			
head			
Looks for toy dropped in sight			
Much disequilibrium			
No head lag, pulled by hands to sitting			
Pushes whole chest off of bed when prone			
Rolls over back to front			
Rolls over front to back			
Smiles at self if close to mirror			
Smiles spontaneously			
Squeal—high pitched			
Sucking stimulated by seeing object			

SIX MONTHS
(26 weeks)

Early	Usual	Late	
			Accepts strangers
			Differentiates between strangers and family
			Grasps foot when lying on back
			Grasps with whole hand
			Grunts and growls
			Initiates "conversation" with toys or people
			Picks up and palms small toy—all finge
			Puts toy in mouth
			Reaches
			Rolls from back to front, pulls arms out
			Sits with minimal support on hard surface
			Smiles and talks to self if near mirror
			Vocalizes consonant and vowel ma, da ga

Developmental Milestones: Check Your Child

SEVEN MONTHS
(30 weeks)

EIGHT MONTHS
(34 weeks)

Item	Early	Usual	Late		Early	Usual	Late	Item
Aims mouth at cup								Adjusts slowly to new situations
Bangs toy up and down								Afraid of strangers
Can accept two objects								Bites and chews toys
Controlled movement of lips, mouth, tonque								Can sit erect on a hard surface 10 minutes
Distinguishes: between meanings of voices family's and stranger's voices								Creeps
								Crys for food when he sees it
Enjoys people								Easily over excited
Feeds self a cracker								Easy shifts between crying and laughter
Feet to mouth when lying on back								Holds two toys a long time
Has color preferences								Imitates others
Lifts head if on back								New awareness of distance and location
Likes high chair								Persists in reaching for toys out of reach
Likes rhythm (pat a cake)								Picks up one toy, then another
Manipulating increases								Prone, can pivot in a circle with arms
Notices details								Sits up
Picks a toy up in each hand								Stands up
Reaches out, pats self, if close to mirror								
Selectiveness appears								
Self contained—plays alone								
Stands if chest held under arms								
Vowel sounds in series								

Developmental Milestones: Check Your Child

NINE MONTHS (40 weeks)	Early	Usual	Late
Does a good job of feeding self a cracker			
Drops 1 of 2 toys to pick up 3rd			
Has depth perception			
Holds own bottle, picks up if dropped			
Holds toy number 1, plays with toy number 2			
Imitates cough, tongue, click			
Interest in motion			
Knows own name			
Mama, baba, dada—no meaning			
Picks up tiny objects—lint, crumbs			
Pulls to sitting position			
Sits alone, changes position, no falling			
Sits up without help from lying down position			
Unwraps block			
Varied vocalizations			
Waits for food without crying			

Early	Usual	Late	TEN MONTHS (44 weeks)
			Demands more of mother
			Goes to prone position without falling
			Holds out toy to someone: does not let go
			Identifies places and goes to them
			Increased radius of action
			One other word
			Plays nursery game if asked
			Plays nursery game if you do it first
			Pokes with index finger
			Pulls self to a standing position
			Puts toy in cup but does not let go
			Reaches for image of toy in mirror
			Responds to situations as a whole
			Says mama and dada and means it
			Shy at first with strangers
			Smiles while watching or playing
			Stands and lifts one foot up and down
			Stands at chair without leaning against
			Stands at least 5 seconds holding on
			Steadily and indefinitely sits erect

Developmental Milestones: Check Your Child

ELEVEN MONTHS
(48 weeks)

	Early	Usual	Late
Emotions come and go			
Holds furniture and walks around it			
Holds interest			
Looks a person over: face, then head to toe			
More crying, less smiling			
More fearful			
Picks up raisin with thumb and fingers			
Puts toy in box if shown, does not let go			
Sits up from lying down position—no help			
Takes toy out of box or cup			
Takes toys one place to another intentionally			
Tendency to elevate arms			

ONE YEAR
(52 weeks)

Early	Usual	Late	
			Active
			Bangs two cubes together
			Drinks from a cup
			Eats from a spoon
			Enjoys applause, laughter, socialization
			Gives affection
			Good natured
			Hands toy upon request
			Helps in dressing (pushing arm in sleeve)
			Lets go of toy into hand of another
			Offers toy to own mirror image
			Perceives emotional expressions
			Persistence in reaching
			Plays with several small objects at a time
			Rooting and sucking only evident if hungry or asleep
			Says two or three words plus mama and dada
			Sensitive to people
			Stacks two blocks
			Voluntary release of object
			Walks with support—holding one hand

Developmental Milestones: Check Your Child

THIRTEEN MONTHS

	Early	Usual	Late
A beginning in throwing a ball			
Fights over toys			
Imitates behavior			
Imitates scribble			
Imitates vocalization			
Intentionally grasps two tiny toys, one hand			
Looks where he is asked			
Plays pat a cake moving own hands			
Pulls at others' hair or clothes			
Puts toy into box if you point and ask him to			
Some self feeding			
Stands alone momentarily			
Suspicious of all			
Takes a few steps alone, falls headlong			
Walks hanging onto furniture			

FOURTEEN MONTHS

Early	Usual	Late	
			Grasps with skill and confidence
			Handles cup himself
			Indicates wants
			Prefers places and objects to new fac
			Reaches straight out parallel to midl
			Spreads hands out parallel to midlir
			Stands alone well

Developmental Milestones: Check Your Child

FIFTEEN MONTHS	Early	Usual	Late	Early	Usual	Late	EIGHTEEN MONTHS
Can put five or six small toys in container							Affectionate
Climb, clambering, try again							Begins to use either hand crossing mid-line
Demands own way in everything							Can walk upstairs if hand is held
Eager to go places							Climbs into adult chair
Enjoys noise							Drinks well
Gets up in middle of floor and walks							Eats with a spoon, still spills
Helps turn pages in picture book							Hugs and loves doll or animal
Holds or carries objects in either hand							Impetuous
Imitates smoking, coughing, sneezing							Impulsive
Interested in own sounds							Independent
Less fighting over toys							Individual play
Likes to bend over and look between legs							Interest in chores
Listens							Likes to be read to
More aware of playmate							May use 5 10 words
New fear							Points to picture of object asked for
No longer creep or crawl							Pokes with sharp objects
Pats pictures in book							Rarely falls when walking
Picks up raisin with thumb and index finger							Runs stiff legged
Plays ball with another							Temper tantrums from fatigue
Points							Toilet trained daytime
More self feeding							Tries to hand cup to mother
Stacks three blocks							Turns book pages 2-3 at a time
Start, stop, go							Walks or crawls pulling string toy
Strong gross motor drive							Whole arm movements
Takes off shoes, hat, mittens							
Talks jargon							
Throws toys out of pen							
Walks well							

Developmental Milestones: Check Your Child

TWENTY-ONE MONTHS	Early	Usual	Late
Takes a favorite object when he goes to bed			
Accident prone			
Afraid of strangers			
Aware of people—their rights and and possessions			
Conscious of adult disapproval			
Enjoys household activities			
Increased span of attention			
Increased visual appreciation			
Less impulsive			
Less independent			
More demanding of adults			
More responsive to adults			
New awareness of room and contents			
Responds "no" for "yes"			
Scribbles spontaneously			
Sense of possessiveness about his property			
Takes off coat, shoe, socks, pants			

TWO YEARS (24 months)	Early	Usual	Late
Asserts superiority			
Can keep eyes on ball			
Can reach in curves or angles			
Closes eyes at times and hits nose			
Crosses midline			
Dawdling			
Engages in parallel play			
Fits one thing into another			
Four block tower			
Helps with housework—errands, puts toys away			
Hides toys			
Improved eating			
Insists on finding own way going around corners			
Is fond of small objects			
"It's mine!"			
Kicks ball forward			
Knows if picture is upside down			
Looks and then acts			
Looks for missing objects			
Many fears			
Opens doors			
Proud of new clothes			
Puts things together			
Recognizes familiar pictures			
Responds to two requests			
Rivalry			
Self-centered			
Sometimes fears large objects			
Takes things apart			
Throws a ball			
Uses some space words (where, there)			
Uses two and three word sentences			

Developmental Milestones: Check Your Child

TWO YEARS, SIX MONTHS
(30 months)

	Early	Usual	Late
Alarmed by movement toward him			
Chooses between opposites			
Demanding			
Eyes diverted, fail to return to object			
Fears of space			
Grasps strongly			
Lured by movement in space			
Possessive			
Restricted range of visual adjustment			
Selfish			
Throws ball overhand			
Unmanageable by direct approach			
Uses verbs, nouns, adjectives, adverbs			

THREE YEARS
(36 months)

Early	Usual	Late	
			Alternates feet on stairs
			Feeds self
			Jumps in place
			Knows own sex
			Puts on shoes
			Rides tricycle
			Uses simple form board
			Uses preposition, pronouns
			Visual fears predominate

THREE YEARS, SIX MONTHS

	Early	Usual	Late
Copies a circle			
Dresses self with supervision			
Eight block tower			
Plays cooperative games			
Responds to three commands			
Washes and dries hands			

Developmental Milestones: Check Your Child

FOUR YEARS

	Early	Usual	Late
Anxious to please and conform			
Buttons			
Copies a cross			
Counts three objects			
Exaggerates			
Goes on outside errand, no crossing of street			
Laces shoes			
Pesters younger siblings			
Plays cooperatively with other children			
Shows independence in out-of-bound behavior			
Skips on one foot			
Teases older siblings			
Tension overflows (stress, stomach ache, urination)			

FIVE YEARS

	Early	Usual	Late
Can name penny, nickel, dime			
Colors within boundaries			
Copies a square			
Counts ten objects and fingers			
Draws a man using eight body parts			
Dresses and undresses with no assistance			
Has outgrown fears of unreal			
Is more gentle			
Likes directions — needs time and leeway			
Little tensional overflow			
Sentences without evidence of enunciation decay			
Shows interest in letters			

2

"My child starts first grade next week." Another happy communication—we hope.

In 1911, John Dewey said, "Education may be defined as a process of continuous reconstruction of experience with the purpose of widening and deepening its social content, while, at the same time, the individual gains control of the methods involved." A very tall order to face a very small 6-year-old.

A child enters the world of formal education to learn, to acquire knowledge that he can use. The process is a complex one, and it is necessary to know how it works in order to understand how the ability to learn can be disrupted. Young and old alike receive stimuli through the same channels: eyes, ears, movement, and touch. Educators refer to these pathways as Visual (V), Auditory (A), Kinesthetic (K), Tactile (T), and shorten the whole thing to V. A. K. T., with K and T often combined and named Haptic.

When we say "learning" we tend automatically to equate *ability* to learn with intelligence. However, the scientific interpretation of the term "intelligence" has, over the years, come to mean "higher level of abstract thought processes." For a 6-year-old child sitting in a classroom, the actual degree of his intelligence (with the exception of a handicap so severe as to be out of the purview of this book) is not the key to his efficient learning during the early stages of formal education.

While it may be startling to realize that a youngster does not need primarily to call upon his intellect, per se, to cope with the first few grades of school, it is true. As we have seen, it is not until about age 11 that a child enters the formal operations stage of intellectual development. Until then, what he does need is efficient central and peripheral nervous systems that are effective in handling input (decoding), processing (association), and output (encoding) of information. His learning pathways must give him accurate reception of percepts. His brain must properly give attention to, associate, synthesize, sequence, and store the received perceptual stimulus. Then, he must be able to use the data successfully for verbalization, reading, spelling, writing, penmanship, and mathematics (quantitative language). Without conquering these basic skills, the child cannot and will not learn effectively. The whole—input, processing, and output—must flow smoothly, automatically, with no disruptions.

If his learning tools, the brain and neural system, are competent a child will be able to perform at least the first of the two basic forms of learning—*receptive.*

Receptive learning is primarily concrete learning: the child absorbs specific factual data—for example, "The Declaration of Independence was signed in 1776." Receptive learning is the basic form of learning until about the sixth or seventh grade. If a child's learning systems are efficient, he will progress in elementary school regardless of his future potential for discovery learning.

If a child is *able* to go the next step, to *discovery* learning, he will begin to learn how to form concepts. This is exactly what the term "discovery learning" implies. When varied or incomplete material is presented, the student conceptualizes either an answer or a theoretical implication. A child's time spent in receptive learning serves as the base upon which his conceptual building blocks are laid.

Learning, receptive or discovery, is a step-by-step process, complex, interwoven, and multilevel. It begins with the *input* of information, which is then *processed* and finally expressed in various ways as *output.*

Input

Educators define learning tasks in terms of behavioral objectives. The most immediate classroom behavioral objective that a parent or teacher ordinarily becomes aware of is reading. Since the general public often considers reading as an eye-oriented function, let us begin there.

One of the essential elements of reading is "visual perception." The phrase seems to refer to the act of "seeing." However, visual perception has nothing to do with the eyes as organs of vision. Perfectly healthy eyes can fail to produce correct or complete perception. A vision problem, due to eyes that function imperfectly, may be corrected with glasses, but the child may still have perceptual problems.

It has been estimated that nearly three-fourths of our knowledge is acquired visually—that mankind is "eye-minded." Obviously, then, efficient visual perception is necessary to the successful act of reading, just as reading is necessary to learning.

Frostig describes and analyzes the five areas of visual perception. Included in this analysis is a brief description of how the various perceptual areas affect a child's learning abilities.

Perception of Position in Space

Perception of position in space may be defined as perception of the relationship of an object to the observer. Spatially, a person is always the center of his own world and perceives objects as being behind, before, above, below, or to the side of himself. A child with disabilities in his perception of position in space is handicapped in many ways. His visual world is distorted, he may be clumsy or hesitant in his movements, and he has difficulty in understanding what is meant by the words designating spatial position, such as in, out, up, down, before, behind, left, or right. His difficulties become most apparent when he is faced with academic tasks, because letters, words, phrases, numbers, and pictures appear to him distorted and confusing. To give the simplest and most frequently encountered example, a child with difficulties in perceiving the proper position of an object in relation to his body is likely to perceive b as d, p as q, on as no, 24 as 42, and so on. This, of course, makes it difficult for the child to learn to read, write, spell, and do arithmetic.

Perception of Spatial Relationships

The perception of spatial relationships is the ability of an observer to perceive the position of two or more objects in relation to himself and in relation to each other. This ability to perceive spatial relationships develops later than, and grows out of, the simpler one of perceiving the position of an object in relation to one's body. Perception of spatial relationships is more complicated than the other perceptual processes. Disabilities in the perception of spatial relationships make impossible the proper perception of the sequence of letters in a word, so that a child may read the word "string" as "stirring," or spell it "siturg." In attempting to solve arithmetic problems, he may be unable to remember the sequence of processes involved in problems of long division or fail to perceive the relative position of the digits in problems of multiplication. A myriad of other tasks, such as model making, map reading, understanding graphs, and learning systems of measurement, to name a few, may be equally difficult for him.

Perceptual Constancy

Perceptual constancy is the ability to perceive an object as possessing invariant properties, such as shape, position and size in spite of the variability of the impression on the sensory surface (sensory surface = eyes, ears, hands, nose). This means that where constancy of shape is concerned, two or three-dimensional forms are recognized as belonging to certain categories of shapes, whatever their size, color, texture, mode of representation, or the angle seen by the perceiver. A person with adequate perceptual constancy will recognize a cube seen from an oblique angle as a cube, even though the retinal image differs from that presented by the cube when seen squarely from the front.

Three aspects of objects besides shape that may be visually perceived as constant are size, brightness and color.

Size constancy is the ability to perceive and recognize the actual size of an object regardless of factors that may change its apparent size. For example, a person familiar with the standard-size football perceives one that is a field's length away as being the same size as if it were in his hands, despite the diminutive retinal image.

Brightness constancy involves the ability to judge the lightness or whiteness of an object regardless of the amount of light reflected by it. A piece of white paper is perceived as white, even though the light that illuminates it may be unusually dim or bright.

Color constancy involves the ability to recognize colors regardless of background or conditions of illumination.

There is, as yet, no conclusive theory of how visual constancy is developed and of how or why different stimuli arouse the same percept, but obviously learning and experience are important factors. Of these four aspects of visual constancy—shape, size, color, and brightness—the first two are the most important for a person's adequate orientation in his environment. A color-blind person is only minimally handicapped, and even a totally blind person who has learned to judge size and shape through other than his visual senses can recognize his environment and adapt his actions to it. On the other hand, adequate perception of shape and size, whether obtained through visual experiences or through kinesthesis and touch, is essential if a person's physical surroundings are to appear relatively stable and predictable to him. A child with poorly developed shape and size constancy is not only likely to be made anxious by the general unreliability of appearances of his world, but he will also have major academic difficulties. Although he may learn to recognize a number, letter, or word, when he sees it in a particular form or context, he may be quite unable to recognize the same symbol when it is presented in a different manner. Such a child is constantly deceived by his senses. A word he knows well in one form or color or size or type of writing, or in conjunction with certain other words, may appear new to him when presented in another form, color, size or context. For a child with such a disability, learning to read, to work with symbols in any way, is most difficult.

Visual–Motor Coordination

Visual–motor coordination is the ability to coordinate vision with movements of the body or with movements of a part or parts of the body. Whenever a sighted person reaches for something, his hands are guided by his vision. Whenever he runs, jumps, kicks a ball, or steps over an obstacle, his eyes direct the movement of his feet. In such everyday activities as getting dressed, making a bed, carrying a tray, entering a car, or sitting down at the table, the eyes and the whole body work together. The smooth accomplishment of nearly every action depends upon adequate eye–motor coordination. This visual–motor coordination is also important to space perception and planning motor sequences. A child with defective or poorly developed visual–motor coordination is indeed handicapped in trying to adjust to the varied demands of his environment. Though his academic learning may be less affected by a disability in the visual–motor area than by disabilities in other areas of visual perception, he will certainly have difficulty in learning how to write.

Figure–Ground Perception

To understand figure–ground perception and its importance, it is essential to remember that we perceive most clearly those things to which we turn our attention. The human brain is so organized that it can select from the mass of incoming stimuli a limited number of stimuli, which become the center therefore of attention. These selected stimuli—auditory, tactile, olfactory and visual—form the figure in the person's perceptual field, while the majority of stimuli form a dimly perceived ground. For instance, a little girl bouncing and catching a ball in a play yard has her attention directed to the ball, which is the figure in the scene she perceives. Since other features of the play yard—sandbox, teeter-totter, flower bed, toy pail—are not the focus of her attention, they form the dimly perceived ground, of which she is probably only sufficiently aware to avoid colliding with them. The figure is that part of the field of perception that is the center of the observer's attention. When the observer shifts his attention to something else, the new focus of attention becomes the figure, and the previous figure recedes into the ground. If the little girl puts down her ball and picks up the pail instead, the pail becomes the figure in her field of vision and the ball becomes part of the ground. Another important fact with regard to the figure–ground perception is that an object cannot be accurately perceived unless it is perceived in relation its ground. The little girl would be unable to perceive the exact position of her bouncing ball and would have great difficulty in catching it if she did not see it constantly in relation to the ground formed by the surface of the play yard and adjacent objects. An observer can accurately judge the distance of an object, its size and even its shape only if he perceives it in the proper relationship to its ground. A child with poor figure–ground discrimination of perception characteristically appears to be inattentive and disorganized. This is because his attention tends to jump to any stimulus that intrudes upon him—to something that moves or glitters or is brightly colored, for instance—no matter how irrelevant it may be to what he should be doing. Alternatively, his difficulty in screening out obtrusive stimuli may prevent him from separating himself from a particular stimulus, even though he ought to shift his attention to some other figure for purposeful activity. The child may be unable to draw a straight line between boundaries because one of the boundaries captures his attention and he directs his pencil towards and along it. Other difficulties arise in transferring the focus of attention from one stimulus to another and results in scanning problems. A child with poor figure–ground perception will appear to be careless in his work because he is unable to find his place on a page, skips sections, cannot find the word he is seeking in the dictionary, and is unable to solve familiar problems when they are presented on crowded pages, since he cannot pick out the relevant details. A typical complaint about such children at home and at school is that they seem unable to find anything, even when it is right in front of their noses.

Since adequate visual perception encompasses an automatic sense of horizontal spatial relationships, the development of laterality and directionality is a prerequisite. Laterality is the inner sense of one's own body symmetry. It is the ability to know automatically, from *within* one's self, leftness, rightness, or two-sidedness. It allows a child to perform smoothly with either hand or leg, or eye as he chooses. There is also a subconscious selection of left or right ear for hearing.

Directionality is the projection of laterality into space, the awareness of left, right, up, down, in front of, and behind, in the environment around us. With maturation, a child develops an awareness of the relationship between the position of an object and that of another object or to himself: "The chair is to my left, the table is to my right, therefore, as the objects face me, the chair is to the right of the table."

When laterality and directionality are functioning properly, we have horizontal spatial relationships that are usable.

The next step in visual perception is *Gestalt* and the resultant closure. They are the end result of visually perceiving the parts to make a whole.

The theory of *Gestalt* is that the whole is greater than the sum of its parts, the concept of form wherein an object is not perceived as component parts but rather as a complete entity or whole. We cannot read, spell, write, or do mathematics without *Gestalt*. Completed *Gestalt* is imperative if a child is to formulate words or problems.

Closure, which is the result of *Gestalt,* gives visual unity. Thus, the ╱─╲ come together to form an A. And the formulation of this A is not disturbed by other letters before or after the A, or, as in the case of Figure A, if pieces or parts of the overall whole are missing.

The lines are organized into a word instead of being viewed separately.

Even if we have *Gestalt* and closure, our percepts (what we perceive) can still trick us, given the right situation, as in Figure B.

The second most used pathway of learning is the auditory (aural) channel. As with visual perception, auditory perception should not be confused with auditory acuity. Acuity is the physiological act of hearing—of being aware of pitch and sound level. As with the eyes, the ears, as organs of hearing, may have some organically based malfunction which can affect the ability to hear. Such a situation requires not only medical attention but also consideration in the classroom. But it is not the same thing as the inability to receive auditory messages accurately.

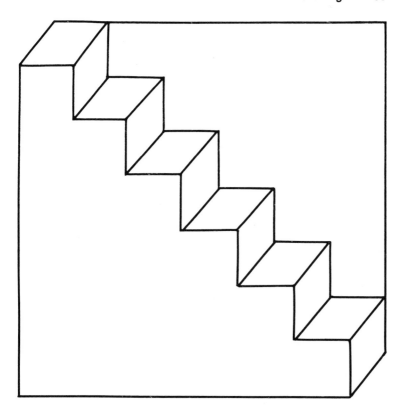

The staircase changes as a whole when we focus on the near edge of the middle step.

Our aural sense has an automatic figure–foreground and back-ground–selective mechanism. This mechanism enables us to select priorities for the simultaneous processing of aural data. We can tune out the useless environmental noise to attend to what is important. This selection is necessary for efficient auditory reception.

Auditory reception includes two main functions: attention and discrimination. A child must "attend" to the language and he must be able to discriminate between the different and very often tiny variables of sound in our language. He must, for example, be able to discriminate between "pit" and "pet" or "where" and "pear."

From auditory reception flows the next step, which is auditory perception. Aural perception is an awareness of and ability to interpret language. If a child cannot properly perceive language as it is spoken to him, he cannot efficiently relate language sounds to the written symbols that are the representation of language. Language stimuli are unique and possess properties not associated with other kinds of aural material such as environmental sound stimuli. As with visual perception, auditory perceptions require aural *Gestalt* and closure.

Adequate auditory perception can sometimes be a tricky thing. For instance, a child may have fairly efficient aural percepts until he encounters a stressful situation; then the percept simply doesn't register or gets scrambled. Fatigue or overloading could have the same affect. Most of us, when we are tired, may have some trouble either with attending to language or understanding exactly what is said without great conscious effort. For a child whose aural channel is inefficient, perceptual strength can be very fragile.

While auditory association is, technically speaking, a function of the processing stage of learning rather than the input stage, it is best discussed here. Aural association means that a child has the ability to relate spoken words in a meaningful way, the sorting and association of concept from the spoken word.

Aural sequencing is a temporal process. Literally, this means hearing a sequence of sounds in time. The memory, or retention, of these symbol–sound sequences is what allows us to hear the *formed* words. The process works in this order: (a) symbol–sound sequencing, (b) words in order, (c) sentences in order, and so on.

Without symbol–sound sequencing ability, a child cannot reproduce (vocalize) words correctly and he cannot spell. Without symbol–sound sequencing *memory,* a child cannot follow directions given orally. "Take out your book, turn to page ten, read the page, and answer the questions on page eleven." Literally, without efficient aural sequencing, language is an incoherent and useless noise to a child.

■

Lesser known and lesser used in the standardized classroom are the opportunities for learning through the haptic system (kinesthetic and tactile) of the body. Tactile refers to our cutaneous (skin) or touch sensory system; kinesthetic refers to our body and joint (muscle) movement system.

Here we have a valuable addition to the learning process. As a learning tool, haptic sensations must not be confused with vital and gnostic sensations. Vital sensations are largely unconscious and have to do with the automatic regulation of visceral events. Gnostic sensations are those such as vibration and position which require analysis and interpretation by the receiver.

Our muscle-sense, or proprioceptive system, is sensori-motor oriented and, as such, plays a major role in a child's earliest learning attempts. Even standing upright is a proprioceptive act of learning. There are two basic forms of muscle control: gross and fine. Gross muscle control includes such motions as walking, moving arms, wrists, and waist. Fine muscle control, however, is a different matter. For our purposes, we will confine the discussion to the fingers. If his fine muscle control is good, a child is able to "flutter" his thumbs and index fingers in a rapid rhythmic movement. If a child's rapid rhythmic movements are slowed or faulty, he will, for example, have problems with his penmanship.

Muscles and skin working with our nervous system form our haptic system. Gibson states that the haptic system is composed of five subsystems: (a) cutaneous touch gives perceptions to the skin and deeper tissue without movement; (b) touch–temperature refers to the combination of skin stimulation and vascular dilation or constriction; (c) touch–pain refers to the registration of pain; (d) haptic touch is the movement of the joints along with stimulation of the skin and deeper tissues; (e) dynamic touch is muscular exertion in combination with stimulation of both the skin and the joints.

To understand how valuable the haptic system is to learning, imagine yourself totally encased in a neutral material with only your eyes and ears exposed. You have cut off two main avenues of sensory input with a resultant deprivation that grays or tones down the world to an uncomfortable level. The sensations of touch and coordinated movement are not only fun but can be an integral factor to learning.

Let us review what is stimulated in the body when the haptic system is activated, regardless of whether the stimulation is passive or self-initiated. The organs that receive stimulation through the haptic system are called *mechano*receptors. Returning to Gibson, he tells us that these *mechano*receptors are located throughout the body in: (a) the skin and deeper underlying tissue; (b) the muscles and tendons which attach muscles to bone; (c) the skeletal joints and connecting ligaments between all movable bones; (d) the blood vessels; and (e) the hair cells located in the semicircular canals, utricle, saccule, and cochlea of the inner ear.

Haptic stimuli may be thought of as "mechanical energy" (created by the stimuli to the haptic system) that the *mechano*receptors convert into electrical energy. This electrical energy is then transmitted along the neural pathways to the brain.

Processing

Visual, auditory, and haptic input must be *processed* through the nervous system and in the brain to elicit any form of response. This V. A. K. T. processing is integrated and multilevel, at least it should be.

At first, a child's whole world of learning is based solely on perceptions. These perceptions are the various stimuli he receives through his eyes, ears, sense of smell, touch, taste, and body movements. A stimulus will trigger an automatic "attention response" whereby the incoming stimulus sets off electrical impulses which travel along specific pathways of the neural system. Naturally, these electrical impulses do not "look like" or resemble the original stimulus. This electrical flow must not be interrupted or mispathed. If it is, then the initial stimulus is misinterpreted in the brain. Sometimes, one will hear that a child seems to have "short-circuits," a reference to this electrical impulse process and the necessary synaptic cleft "jump."

Before a child can have an automatic "attention response" he must "pay attention," which is a more deliberate act. Attention allows a child to select from the environment a piece of data (stimulus) regardless of any distracting influences that may also be present. A child attempting to copy A, B, C will first concentrate on the A alone and be only peripherally aware of the B and C. Then, he is able to move on to the B with the A and C receding into the background. In a classroom, receptive learning is somewhat like the old mule joke, "First you have to get his attention."

Even though a child may have adequate attention, he must also have an *attention span,* a length of time during which he can hold his attention to one task. Attention span varies with every individual, and the span time may be affected by such factors as age, motivation, and the task at hand.

For instance, a baby will grasp an object to stick it in his mouth. However, a sudden noise will interrupt his attention (of object going to mouth). The infant is receiving multisensori stimuli (object to mouth *and* sudden noise), and he is too young to simultaneously attend to both visual–motor and auditory stimuli; so the object will be stopped halfway to his mouth thus he can attend to the noise. Later, if he happens to see the object again, its journey may be resumed.

In a classroom, a child who does not have an adequate attention span may be distracted by something so insignificant as a bit of dirt on his paper or by a truck rumbling past outside.

A child must also have an internal consistency for his learning. If, for example, a child's visual perceptions do not offer him "constancy"—an A always looking like an A, no matter what type style or in what word he sees it—he cannot use that A. And if this A is not stable, or constant, for him it will also have an emotional effect. He goes through his daily life feeling internally insecure. This internal insecurity can then set up a reflex action wherein even if the A begins to stay consistent (acquires constancy), he doesn't feel safe trusting his perceptions.

Constancy directly affects *coding*. This coding is not that of the biological or automatic type, but rather the conscious effort to code or sort our lives and, for learning, our language. For language, we code similar or like sounds—fat, cat, sat, hat. Or, we may classify similar things—apple, pear, banana, all fruit or all food.

■

None of these processing activities are usable to a child without association, memory, and automization. These follow one from the other in order.

Association establishes the connection of new information with what is already stored in the brain and allows for the recall of data from this brain storage.

There are certain associative laws that one should become familiar with. *Temporal contiguity*—sensations, ideas or movements that occur close together in time, or at nearly the same time, tend to become associated with each other. *Repetition (frequency)*—ideas that occur together repeatedly tend to become associated with each other. *Similarity*—ideas whose referents are similar tend to become associated with each other. *Recency*—associations that were formed recently are easiest to remember. *Vividness*—the more vivid the associative experience, the stronger the associative bond.

Association is the key to memory and automization.

Memory is brain storage. There is considerable scientific evidence that memory is a cellular or organic process which is chemical in nature, linked directly to DNA and RNA. Although DNA is a genetic material, it is vital to the formation of specific kinds of RNA. In turn, RNA directs the formation of proteins. These proteins consist of organized sequences of amino acids. Amino acids are involved in the metabolism and formation of neurotransmitters.

Short-term and long-term memory involve direct chemical activity in the nervous system and brain, as well as association, repetition, perception, and motivation.

Piaget believes that there are three levels of memory and that each level is based on different human functional accommodations—recognitive memory, having as its functional base perceptual schemes; reconstructive memory, having as its base imitation; and evocative memory, having imagery as its base.

Although chemical in nature, and therefore complex, the process whereby a *short-term* memory trace of an event is laid down in the brain is an everyday, almost moment-to-moment happening. A telephone number is given for a callback, we look at the number and dial, the party answers, and we immediately lose the memory of the number.

If, however, the number called results in some startling news or the person calling is important enough to us personally, we may very well put the number automatically into our memory storage system. This storage system may be activated in two other ways: (1) repetition—we must call the same number several times; (2) association—we can associate the number or conversation with another event which calls it to mind.

Memory retrieval from storage depends upon association. Often, a simple clue will suffice to activate the retrieval system, the first digit of the telephone number, for example. It may also take the name, business, and a clear view of one's relationship, good or bad, with the person to be called to set the retrieval system in operation. The smooth, effortless operation of the retrieval system is called automization.

A child must have full powers of retrieval or automization. Even though this process is primarily seen in the *output* or encoding of a child at work who is successfully using what he has learned, automization starts with the input stimuli. It must then go through processing to the point where the stimulus is so thoroughly settled in the associative tracts and the memory that it can be called up for use with only a minimum of conscious effort on the part of the learner.

■

As a child matures, he reaches a stage of processing at which he can begin forming concepts. He has layered perceptual learning into his brain; that is, he has accumulated a body of knowledge on which he can draw. At this point, he can take multiple or incomplete data and conceptualize an answer or theory. He is able to pull the parts together to form a whole, or he is able to receive only partial data and still formulate a whole. Sometimes, this whole may be, for him, something new or heretofore unknown.

It is easy to understand that, if a child has the potential ability for conceptual strength, he *must* receive and process percepts correctly, else he stays at the concrete or preoperational-thought stage of development rather than moving on to formal operations. Thus, if perceptions are incomplete or inaccurate, or if the percepts are not processed efficiently, it follows that a child's ability to conceptualize will be damaged or even nonexistent.

Output

No amount of input and processing does any good if a child cannot use what is learned. He must have the ability to communicate in a manner that can be received by others. The child must be able to verbalize, to read, to spell, to write, to offer penmanship, and to use quantitative language (mathematics). The reality of learning is the use of language.

What is language? Language has sound, meaning, and structure. It is a means of communication which involves vocalized sounds (speech), expressed in definite forms (words), and arranged according to specific rules (grammar).

Language requires a multitude of skills—directionality, sequencing, closure, blending, part-to-whole, to name a few. It is not necessary here to go into a detailed breakdown of language and the rules that govern it. What is important is to understand that language is fundamentally a symbol–sound thing. The alphabet provides the symbols, each symbol has a sound, and the sound changes as the various symbols are combined and sequenced.

Our alphabet (symbols) are incomplete geometric forms; they are portions of squares, triangles, circles, and straight lines. As a child learns, he takes these geometric designs, effects *Gestalt* and the resultant closure, sequences the symbols in the correct left to right direction, blends the achieved association of sound, and *voilà!*—he has a word. He has gained the first step toward all classroom learning. It has been said that no one is truly proficient in a foreign language until he can think in it. For a new learner, reading, spelling, and writing (the formalization of English) is a foreign language.

For output a child must *encode* or express the language. Bush and Giles give short, to-the-point definitions of the basic forms of expression of the language provided by adequate encoding.

Verbal Expression (vocal encoding). The ability to express ideas in spoken language.

Manual Expression (motor encoding). The ability to express ideas in meaningful gestures.

Grammatic Closure (auditory–vocal automatic). The ability to predict future linguistic events from past experience.

Auditory Sequential Memory (auditory–vocal sequencing). The ability to remember and correctly repeat a sequence of symbols just heard.

Visual Sequential Memory (visual–motor sequencing). The ability to remember and reproduce a sequence of visual stimuli.

Successful perceptual motor skills. The ability to use the gross and fine muscle movements smoothly.

■

Admittedly, the *input, processing,* and *output* abilities as discussed here are but a skeleton, with little embellishment, of the entity known as cognition. Every year science adds to our knowledge of how our brain and body work in rapport to gather, glean, and use learning. The "how" of learning has been under debate for a very long time. The debate has often centered on the relative importance of nature versus nurture, heredity versus environment. Recent discoveries about the chemistry of the brain have made this simplistic argument obsolete.

Cognition is the means whereby data are transmitted, transformed, reduced, elaborated, stored, recovered, and used. This is true whether the data are academic, environmental, or social.

Although many body functions may be thought of as passive (heartbeat, digestion, etc.), cognition requires, even unknowingly, the active participation of the person. From birth, we sort, select, organize, and reorganize stimuli both at the conscious and subconscious levels. We know that a child cannot learn without association and we know that concepts and associations change as new percepts are laid down. We also know that some people never achieve true conceptual strength.

The Russian psychologist Luria tells us that cortical functioning in mankind during the processing of information through the eyes and ears is dynamic (active), investigatory, and selective.

If learning were not dynamic, we would never move forward; if it were not investigatory, we would never achieve abstract thought; and, if it were not selective, we would go mad! Learning, whether it is receptive or discovery, is information. The input, processing, and output of information is a patterned neurochemical event.

A human being is really just a bunch of chemicals held together inside skin. But what a marvel! Computers have not yet been built that can match the processing abilities of our brain and nervous system. No other living thing on earth is as physiologically sophisticated and complex, yet we can be incredibly fragile. All of us, even the very brilliant, have strengths and weaknesses, areas of efficiency and inefficiency. Those of us who have inefficiencies in areas where "they don't show" can live without ridicule from our fellows.

For those whose inefficiencies "show," life and learning can be very, very tough.

Part Two

3. Evaluation and Dysfunction

These children are as handicapped by the ignorance surrounding their problem, as by the problem itself.

Frances K. McGlannan

3

We have seen how a child develops and learns. These processes are innate and systematic. Sociologically speaking, in the United States, technically dedicated as we are to the concept of the "norm," any interruption, no matter how slight, of natural growth and cognitive development is labeled abnormal. "Abnormal" is too harsh a word to apply to any of our fellows, let alone a small child who suffers a minimal learning disability. This rigid categorizing of normal/abnormal is too concrete, too final, to be really useful to any of us.

The problem is that this negative categorization has not served well the needs of a child in a classroom. Because of this, there has been a strong movement to obliterate the use of any label with regard to any individual child. This movement was initiated in the field of mental retardation when it was determined that a label can sometimes become a self-fulfilling prophecy.

Other areas of education have become supporters of the premise that labeling is an unnecessary burden to a child. Primarily, this support has come from educators who are unhappy with etiological labels which are based on physical or medical causes of handicaps. These labels do not tell the educators how to teach the child. *Etiological* labels, however, are necessary for homogeneous grouping. This type of homogeneous grouping is vital to scientific research, for without research we would not have the progress and change that is so necessary to knowledgeable education.

Alternatives to general labeling must be found, workable alternatives, not just stopgap solutions. A classification system based on cognitive functioning is needed that would be universally meaningful to evaluators, teachers, and parents alike. In biology, for example, subclassification within a species is a cornerstone of science. It is possible to classify, rather than label, most children who suffer a learning disability. By knowing about and understanding learning pathways and how learning stimuli activate each person's brain and nervous system, we can, through the use of psychometric evaluations, write prescriptive profiles and efficiently group for, teaching, those with learning disabilities. What all this really means is that with the help of various diagnostic tools, a teacher can learn which strengths and weaknesses a child has, which classroom behavioral task objectives the child is able or unable to achieve, and thereby decide which teaching techniques may be used to help him achieve specific goals.

Evaluation often begins in the classroom when the teacher screens her students for ineffective or inefficient functioning. If a school is really up-to-date, it will offer formal screening instruments for use in this assessment at the kindergarten and/or first-grade level. This initial classroom screening by the concerned teacher is an act that might not only change a child's life but in the long run may save it. Delay in the discovery and treatment of learning disabilities can set a pattern of failure and frustration that can wither the very soul of a human being.

If a child screens poorly, he is sent to the school psychologist or, failing this, the parents are informed that he should be tested by an outside source.

The cornerstone of evaluation is psychometric testing, but evaluation is much more than just tests. Evaluation is multidisciplinary. Evaluation considers the child as a whole organism and as such researches familial history, perinatal life, birth, development, environment, emotional stability, nervous system functioning, and mental abilities. Because of the broad range of factors that must be investigated on a *multidisciplinary basis* (neurology, endocrinology, pedagogy, for example), the question of terminology can be the single most confusing problem that a parent meets.

Every discipline has its own terminology and when we cross discipline lines the meaning and use of a word can change entirely. Let's take two examples: behavioral objective and encoding. The term "behavioral objective" came from the field of psychology and was originally used in connection with the behavior modification techniques developed by that discipline. Today, *behavioral objective* as used in education also means a classroom learning goal.

The term "encoding" came from the field of biology and in this discipline means the laying down within the brain and nervous system of a memory or knowledge of a specific stimulus. In education, the same term means the ability to use the data (output) and *de*coding means input.

In this book, the term "behavioral objective" is always modified by the words "classroom" and "task." This is necessary because of a later discussion on behavior modification, which will carry no modifying words. The term "*de*coding" means input, and "*en*coding" means output. It was necessary to make a choice so that the terminology used would be consistent. The reader must be aware, therefore, that certain terms chosen for use here may have an alternate meaning in popular use in other publications or in other geographical areas. Careful attention was given to employing the most commonly used terms and to define these terms. However, what may be considered by one professional to be a very precise descriptive phrase may to another be "mushy" or imprecise. Workers in the field of learning disabilities have long been calling for a standardization of terminology, but such standardization continues to be difficult, since there are so many subtle facets of the problem and so many involved disciplines. All terms used within each discipline are basically correct; the problem seems to lie in precisely defining the nuances of meaning. Often, when using a certain term here, an attempt has been made to give another integrated definition in parentheses to clarify the issue for the reader.

■

Evaluation can be, for a parent, expensive, time-consuming, and sometimes frustrating. It introduces an unknown and complicated event into our lives. The first step is to form at least a preliminary judgment as to whether a particular child will be well served by the evaluation process. After this decision is made, there are certain rights and responsibilities that a parent has to the child, to himself, and to the persons performing the evaluation.

It is important that both parent and child enter a testing situation with proper attitudes. It is very possible that all your fears about your child are unfounded. Whether they are unfounded or not, parents should remember several basic "do's" and "don'ts" after they have decided in favor of evaluation and before they enter the test situation.

First, no matter what a parent feels may or may not be wrong with his child, he should not attempt to develop preconceived ideas of what the problems may be. It is on *professional* evidence alone that the diagnosis must be based. Home diagnosis can *never* be satisfactory. There are certain preliminary judgmental steps that a parent may take (see Screening Instruments and Checklists), but these steps are only for the purpose of identifying the child who may need testing. Screening is like the tip of an iceberg: it brings the submerged need for evaluation to your attention.

Second, don't surprise the child with testing. If it is a younger child, a simple explanation is all that is necessary: "Tomorrow we are going to meet a nice man/woman who will have some games for you and who will ask you some questions." The older child usually knows that he has a problem, so a simple statement of fact is all that is really necessary: "Tomorrow we will try to find out what the problem is and how to solve it." Do not frighten the child, no matter what his age. Do not make him feel as if his whole world hangs in the balance. Do not make him feel that he must perform well or else this will be another case of failure for him.

Cancel the appointment if the child does not feel well or was sick the night before. Do this even over the objections of the examiner. Remember that evaluation can be a commercial operation and you may meet resistance to cancelling an appointment. An ethical professional examiner, however, will *not* want to test your child if he is not feeling his best.

Tell the examiner, *before the evaluation,* if the child is taking any form of medication. *This is extremely important.*

Don't lie to the examiner, either by omission or commission, when relating the family history, the child's problems, behavior, and attitudes. Full and complete knowledge of all relevant facts is the surest pathway to accurate diagnosis.

A psychiatrist, Dr. Barry Kaplan, says, "Often, a youngster is first brought to us because the parents have decided that their child has a 'learning block.' It may take up to five sessions with the child and his family to dig out the truth. This consumes our time and the family's money, both too valuable to waste. These are the parents who refuse to face reality and accept psychometric testing. This evasive tactic serves no purpose except to place an additional and unnecessary burden on the child."

A perennial question concerns the age at which testing should be done. The answer, as with remediation, is the earlier the better. Parents should initiate evaluation early and should always keep a record of where the child has been tested so that it will be possible to refer to the results in succeeding years.

Every parent has the right to ask *first* what areas the contacted facility will test or evaluate. Most facilities have what is called a "primary test battery," and it is this battery that you should inquire about. A listing here of the many fine instruments available today is relatively unimportant, with one or two exceptions which will be discussed later. What is important in learning disabilities is the areas of functioning that are to be tested. An evaluation for a suspected learning disability should cover:

COMPLETE ANALYSIS OF THE CHILD'S BACKGROUND. This will include a *medical* history with emphasis on pregnancy, perinatal problems, childhood illnesses and/or accidents; and a *developmental history* with emphasis on the child's attainment of expected milestones. *Family information* should emphasize family interrelationships and genetic information. The *school history* should stress preschool and primary school experience, whether this experience was positive or negative for the child, and the child's *social relationships* with emphasis on immediate peer group interaction. All previous academic and medical referrals should be supplied. This information is supplied by both the parents and professionals, who have seen the child prior to the immediate evaluation situation.

INTELLECTUAL TESTING. This must be done on an *individual* basis, not with a group IQ instrument.

EVALUATION OF PROCESSING DYSFUNCTIONS. This should include an analysis of the child's modality strengths and weaknesses.

EDUCATIONAL EVALUATION. The emphasis here is on task analysis.

During the evaluation procedure, the examiner will make observations and notations of the child's emotional growth and behavioral displays.

It is the responsibility of the parent to make certain that all these areas are being evaluated. Always be aware of the fact that what the examiner discovers about your child and his areas of handicap will be the key to the remediation of the child's problems.

It is customary for a facility to quote a flat fee for a primary battery. This fee should include your parent conference at which a full discussion of the results of the examination are given (diagnosis and protocol), recommendations made for adjunct referrals to concerned disciplines (a neurologist, for example), and specifics of the child's academic needs offered (learning profile).

Every parent has the right to inquire about the examiner's qualifications, his background, the degrees he holds, and his experience. A parent also has the right to inspect the examiner's formal credentials; in some areas, this may be extremely important. Many states have no system of professional licensing and issue only standard commercial or occupational licenses. An individual's claim that he does "psychological or psychometric evaluation" does not guarantee that he is adequately trained and fully qualified to do so. This rule also applies to those private non-clinical schools that offer a "reading clinic diagnosis." Far too often this "reading clinic diagnostician" is a teacher who, although well qualified to teach in a classroom, is not qualified to evaluate at the level that is needed in learning disabilities. Often, this offer of service is based on the growing awareness among private schools that learning disabilities can be a grand source of extra income.

Those who are qualified examiners will not object to a parent's questions; others are likely to be evasive. If you find yourself in a questionable situation, leave. Don't waste your money and your child's efforts.

Once satisfied that a professionally competent diagnosis will be made, the parent has the continuing responsibility to follow through on all referrals that are made by the examiner. These may be in the fields of neurology, pediatrics, endocrinology, ophthalmology, psychology, audiology, or optometry. If you do not follow through, you are getting only half a loaf. Decisions for outside referrals are made on the basis of the examiner's discoveries about the child through evaluation. The entire evaluation process builds like a pyramid for the child's benefit.

Eventually, everything that should be reviewed is examined and a complete diagnostic picture emerges. It is fairly standard procedure for the evaluator to act as the coordinating agency for all referrals, although sometimes it is the child's pediatrician who performs this service. All referral sources send and receive reports, and these reports are considered to be confidential and will not be released to any persons who are not designated by the parents and not professionally qualified.

Once diagnosis is accepted, fully confirmed with facts and data, and a program for remediation is begun, faith and trust must take over. No matter what the problems may be, the remedial facility must always have supportive help from the home environment. If a learning disabled child has to fight his parents' destructive attitudes, as well as his academic problems, the child is wasting his strength in nonproductive activity.

A major pitfall for many parents is the cost of evaluation. In every field, the price of goods and services increases when the purchaser needs something that is not standard. This rule holds as true in the field of education as it does in business. In spite of inflation, there are reasonable limitations, however, to this cost. The parent must investigate and become aware of what are the average price limits in his geographical area.

A parent should be equally suspicious of the low-cost and the exceptionally high-cost facility. It is possible for a facility to use its evaluation techniques to insure enrollment of students. It is always a safe question to ask of any facility, "What percentage of your student enrollment comes from your evaluation department?" If the figure is high, 60 percent to 80 percent, for example, then there is the definite possibility that you are going to receive what is euphemistically called "an enrollment diagnosis."

The following is a rough breakdown of the four sources a parent usually has available to him for evaluation.

PUBLIC FACILITIES. These are frequently the lowest in price. They are usually very cooperative in aiding the parents with the necessary referrals to other disciplines. Parent conferences are not usually of long duration or too detailed. The public and mental health clinics are an excellent place to start. Most public facilities offer a sliding fee based on family income.

UNIVERSITIES AND COLLEGES. The price range here can be from zero to very high. Often, they are the only source (outside of the public school guidance counselor) that a parent has available for testing. One must always remember that a portion of the examination may be administered by students in graduate school, working with a qualified director guiding their activities. Cooperation for multidiscipline referrals is usually limited to those universities that are deeply involved in research. The parent may be absolutely certain of an ethical situation.

PRIVATE FACILITIES. Cost is generally high, upward of $300. The evaluation battery should be quite complete and the parent conference detailed. A good rule of thumb for choosing is their referral sources. Do the local medical doctors, public schools, universities and colleges refer to them? Listen to determine if you are getting a "sales pitch," or if the services offered are being professionally explained to you without a sense of pressure.

PRIVATE INDIVIDUALS. The range here is extremely wide and difficult to stabilize. One of the best examiners in the country charges $40; one of the worst, $250. Ask your pediatrician, school officials, or other parents for an opinion of the individual in question.

The purpose of the cautions set forth here has not been to give you the impression that evaluation is a "buyer beware" situation. Generally speaking, it is not. In any rapidly expanding field, and learning disabilities most certainly falls into this category, there are those individuals who will take advantage of parents' fear of the unknown and their concern for their child. This is true no matter what the endeavor may be; we have unethical attorneys, landlords, and practitioners in every field.

As recently as ten years ago, testing and evaluation was a risky thing for parents. Today, it should not be. The workers in this field have pushed our knowledge further than could possibly have been imagined a decade ago. We all owe a great deal to the professionals who have dedicated their time and talents to the learning disabled.

■

To understand the interaction between tests, let us look at three major instruments: the WISC-R, ITPA, and Detroit, as they are called in psychometric shorthand.

To administer the WISC-R, the examiner must be especially qualified and at the graduate level. The Detroit and the ITPA may be administered by the classroom teacher.

The *Wechsler Intelligence Scale for Children–Revised* (WISC-R) is an instrument designed to measure Intelligence Quotient (IQ). It is divided into two sections, Verbal and Performance, each section containing what are called subtests. These subtests are designed to test the abilities of the child in specific areas. Each section, Verbal and Performance, gives the examiner an IQ score for that section. The total of the two sections is then mathematically reduced to what is called a Full Scale IQ.

Any instrument that tests intellectual capacity tests the *current capacity* of the individual. It has been demonstrated that with early and proper remediation of deficit areas, it is possible to raise some subtest scores.

Regarding the nature of intelligence and the determinants of intelligence test achievement, Dr. David Rapaport comments: "When a subject takes an intelligence test, his performance represents his efficiency of functioning then and there. This may or may not be an adequate sample of his general efficiency, or, in other words, of the intellectual assets potentially at his disposal. His present life-situation, or even present testing situation, may temporarily encroach upon and diminish his efficiency. On the other hand, the store of intellectual assets potentially at his disposal is not necessarily a final and unchangeable characteristic. The environment in which he grew up, including home, region, and country, with its barrenness or stimulating character, had its influence. The degree of schooling and the profession chosen may have expanded or constricted the development of the endowment and range of efficiency. An emotional or organic disturbance may have caused an arrest or setback of the level of efficiency. Thus, in the intelligence test performance, a number of influences interact, yielding the results obtained."

An exact IQ figure is not usually given to the lay public. Rather, the IQ is translated into Percentile Rank of Population. A chart of the classification of intellectual level, IQ range, and percentile of the population who fall into these classifications would be:

Class	Range	Percent of Population
Defective	69–and below	2.2
Borderline	70–79	6.7
Dull–Normal	80–89	16.1
Average	90–109	50.0
Bright–Normal	110–119	16.1
Superior	120–129	6.7
Very Superior	130–and above	2.2

Examiners consider one of the most significant results that they can receive from the WISC-R is an imbalance between the Verbal and Performance scores. This may indicate dysfunction, which in turn will depress the overall Full Scale Score. They can then look at the individual subtests to discover the specific areas of strengths and weaknesses in the individual being tested.

Formal testing instruments are standardized for specific age levels. For example, the WISC-R is one of the series of Wechsler Scales and is designed to test children between the ages of 6 years to 16 years, 11 months. For other age groups, there are the Wechsler Pre-school and Primary Scales of Intelligence (WPPSI) and the Wechsler Adult Intelligence Scale (WAIS).

The following breakdown demonstrates the task demands of the various WISC subtests.

WECHSLER INTELLIGENCE SCALE FOR CHILDREN—W.I.S.C.

VERBAL SUBTESTS

INFORMATION

MEASURES—range of information acquired both in the home and at school. It requires associative thinking and general comprehension of facts.

INFORMATION (*Continued*)

TASK DEMAND
  Focus auditory attention.
  Hear and comprehend question.
  Have the background information
    available through past experience.
  Recall the information.
  Have the necessary vocabulary.
  Make a vocal response.

EMPLOYS
  Auditory Discrimination
  Associative Memory

DEPENDS ON
  Cognition
  Conceptual–Vocal

SIMILARITIES

MEASURES—both abstract and
    concrete reasoning abilities
    and the ability to form verbal
    concepts.

TASK DEMAND
  Focus auditory attention.
  Hear and comprehend question.
  Have the necessary vocabulary.
  Understand the concept of "alike"
    or sameness.
  Have conceptual ability.
  Make a vocal response.

EMPLOYS
  Convergence

DEPENDS ON
  Auditory Discrimination
  Auditory Memory
  Cognition
  Associative Memory
  Conceptual–Vocal

ARITHMETIC

MEASURES—the child's ability to
    solve arithmetic word problems
    which are figured mentally with-
    out the aid of pencil or paper. It
    shows practical knowledge of com-
    putational facts and concepts.

TASK DEMAND
    Focus auditory attention.
    Hear and comprehend question.
    Retain auditory information.
    Have necessary computational facts
        and concepts.
    Translate word problem into
        correct numerical operation.
    Sustain concentration.
    Solve problem mentally.
    Make a vocal response within time
        limit.

EMPLOYS
    Auditory memory
    Associative memory

DEPENDS ON
    Auditory Discrimination
    Sensory Integration (block
        problems)
    Cognition
    Conceptual–Vocal

VOCABULARY

MEASURES—the child's verbal
    resources. It evaluates his
    ability to understand words and
    his general range of ideas
    and information.

TASK DEMAND
    Focus auditory attention.
    Hear and comprehend the question.

VOCABULARY (Continued)

Have past experience with the word.
Translate the word into a mental
    picture of the object or
    concept.
Be able to describe the object
    or concept.
Make a complex vocal response.

EMPLOYS
    Cognition
    Conceptual–Vocal

DEPENDS ON
    Auditory Discrimination
    Associative Memory

COMPREHENSION

MEASURES—practical information and
    a general ability to evaluate past
    experience. It shows use of common
    sense and judgment.

TASK DEMAND
    Focus auditory attention.
    Hear and comprehend question.
    Use judgment and common sense.
    Think of multiple answers or reasons.
    Make a complex vocal response.

EMPLOYS
    Social comprehension
    Conceptual–Vocal

DEPENDS ON
    Auditory Discrimination
    Cognition
    Associative Memory
    Divergence

DIGIT SPAN

MEASURES—rote sequential memory
    for digits, as well as mental
    manipulation and concentration.

TASK DEMAND
    Focus auditory attention.
    Hear the digits.
    Remember the digits.
    Note the sequential order.
    Remember the sequential order.
    Understand the concept of
      "backwards."
    Synthesize and reverse the digits.
    Retain digits until reversed.
    Make a vocal response.

EMPLOYS
    Auditory memory

DEPENDS ON
    Auditory Discrimination
    Auditory Sequencing
    Vocal Repetition

PERFORMANCE SUBTESTS

PICTURE COMPLETION

MEASURES—perceptual and con-
    ceptual ability, the ability to
    visualize essential from non-
    essential detail, and long term
    visual memory.

TASK DEMAND
    Hear and comprehend instructions.
    Focus visual attention.
    Understand concept of "missing."
    Recognize objects.
    Discriminate details.
    Visualize "completed" objects.
    Sustain concentration.

PICTURE COMPLETION (*Continued*)
>   Determine essential missing part.
>   Make vocal response.

EMPLOYS
>   Visual discrimination

DEPENDS ON
>   Visual Closure
>   Cognition
>   Associative Memory

PICTURE ARRANGEMENT

MEASURES—the ability to see a
>   total situation based on visual
>   comprehension, temporal sequence,
>   and "social intelligence."

TASK DEMAND
>   Hear and comprehend instructions.
>   Focus visual attention.
>   Achieve concept from demonstration.
>   Visually discriminate details of
>   pictures.
>   Reconstruct situations.
>   Visualize temporal sequence.
>   Place pictures motorically.
>   Do above within time limits
>   (extra speed earns additional
>   points).

EMPLOYS
>   Visual discrimination
>   Visual sequencing
>   Sensory integration
>   Evaluation

DEPENDS ON
>   Cognition
>   Associative Memory
>   Social Comprehension
>   Manipulation

BLOCK DESIGN

MEASURES—the ability to perceive,
  analyze, synthesize, and reproduce
  abstract designs. It involves visual–
  motor coordination plus sustained
  concentration.

TASK DEMAND
  Hear and comprehend instructions.
  Focus visual attention.
  Achieve concept from demonstration.
  Analyze design pattern.
  Retain visual image of design.
  Achieve concept of bicolor
    block usage.
  Visualize individual blocks within
    the total design.
  Have adequate eye–hand coordination.
  Place blocks motorically.
  Evaluate product for correctness.
  Do above within time limits
  (extra speed earns additional
    points).

EMPLOYS
  Visual closure
  Convergence
  Evaluation
  Manipulation

DEPENDS ON
  Visual Discrimination
  Cognition

OBJECT ASSEMBLY

MEASURES—visual–motor coordination, synthesis of concrete forms,
  spatial orientation, and flexibility in working toward a goal.

TASK DEMAND
  Hear and comprehend instructions.
  Focus visual attention.

OBJECT ASSEMBLY (Continued)

> Visually perceive puzzle pieces.
> Recognize whole from the parts.
> Have adequate body imagery.
> Sustain concentration.
> Have adequate eye–hand coordination.
> Make motoric response.
> Evaluate product and have flexibility
>   to modify if necessary.
> Do above within time limits
> (extra speed earns additional points).

EMPLOYS
> Visual closure
> Cognition
> Manipulation

DEPENDS ON
> Visual Discrimination
> Associative Memory
> Convergence
> Evaluation

CODING

MEASURES—nonverbal organization
> and memory. Requires association of
> symbols, psychomotor speed, visual–
> motor dexterity, and flexibility in
> new learning situations.

TASK DEMAND
> Hear and comprehend instructions.
> Focus visual attention.
> Perceive and discriminate the
>   numbers and designs (symbols).
> Recognize the numbers.
> Achieve concept from demonstration.
> Remember number/symbol combinations.
> Sustain concentration.
> Have adequate pencil manipulation
>   skills (small muscle control).
> Make motoric (drawing) response.
> Combine speed and accuracy as

CODING (Continued)

score equals the number
done correctly within
time limit.

_____

EMPLOYS
Visual memory
Associative memory
Copying

_____

DEPENDS ON
Visual Discrimination

The scaled average of subtest scores is 10. How high above or below this mean a child's scores fall is significant to the examiner. In the hypothetical scoring sheet shown as an example one can readily see how the performance section has depressed the Full Scale score.

Verbal		_Performance_	
Information	8	Picture Completion	9
Similarities	15	Picture Arrangement	9
Arithmetic	10	Block Design	5
Vocabulary	16	Object Assembly	7
Comprehension	16	Coding	8
*(Digit Span)	8	†(Mazes)	

Verbal Scale IQ	118
Performance Scale IQ	84
Full Scale IQ	101

* Not included in Verbal score but useful diagnostically.
† Not usually given.

The subtests work in combinations to test six overall areas of functioning.

Picture Completion Block Design Object Assembly	Spatial	Comprehension Similarities Vocabulary	Conceptual
Coding Digit Span* Picture Arrangement	Sequencing	Block Design Object Assembly	Perceptual organization
Information Comprehension Similarities Vocabulary	Verbal compre- hension	Arithmetic Digit Span	Freedom from distractibility

* Also Aural Sequencing.

The *Illinois Test of Psycholinguistic Abilities* (ITPA)* is a series of tests which examine the individual's *language age* with regard to input, processing, and output. The basis of this approach is that language, or rather language acquisition, has two primary levels of organization: *representational* level, which involves the meaning or significance of linguistic symbols (alphabet), and the *automatic-sequential* level, which involves the retention of linguistic symbol sequences (words) and the execution of the automatic habits chain (input, processing, output). In the ITPA the representational level tests auditory and visual decoding (*input*), auditory–vocal and visual–motor association (*processing*), and vocal and motor encoding (*output*). The automatic-sequential level tests automatic auditory-vocal and sequential auditory-vocal and visual motor performance.

The norm that is used for these tests is the individual's *chronological age* and the scores are given in *language age* which reflects the differences in what we expect versus what the child is capable of doing. Again, the scores may change as the child receives help. A possible scoring sheet for the ITPA is shown on page 72.

* An abbreviated edition is in press.

ILLINOIS TEST OF PSYCHOLINGUISTIC ABILITIES

AUDITORY RECEPTION

MEASURES—ability to comprehend
the spoken word.

TASK DEMAND
Focus auditory attention.
Hear and comprehend question.
Have the necessary vocabulary.
Relate the noun to the verb.
Make simple "yes–no" vocal response.

EMPLOYS
Auditory discrimination

DEPENDS ON
Cognition
Associative Memory

AUDITORY CLOSURE

MEASURES—ability to perceive
a whole word when only some of it
is heard.

TASK DEMAND
Focus auditory attention.
Hear word components.
Have the necessary vocabulary.
Recognize word from given components.
Make vocal response (complete word).

EMPLOYS
Auditory Closure
Vocal Repetition

DEPENDS ON
Auditory Discrimination

AUDITORY SEQUENTIAL MEMORY

MEASURES—retention span for
    digits and the ability to
    correctly repeat a sequence of
    auditory symbols.

TASK DEMAND
    Focus auditory attention.
    Hear the digits.
    Remember the digits.
    Note the sequential order.
    Remember the sequential order.
    Make a vocal response.

EMPLOYS
    Auditory sequencing

DEPENDS ON
    Auditory Discrimination
    Auditory Memory
    Vocal Repetition

VISUAL RECEPTION

MEASURES—ability to gain
    meaning from visual symbols. It
    requires comprehension of
    pictures based upon common
    concepts.

TASK DEMAND
    Hear and comprehend instructions.
    Focus visual attention.
    Achieve concept from demonstration.
    Recognize the sample picture.
    Comprehend the essential character
      of all pictures.
    Associate concept or function with
      visual cue.
    Remember the sample.
    Discriminate between visual stimuli.
    Make a motoric (pointing) response.

VISUAL RECEPTION (*Continued*)

EMPLOYS
Visual discrimination
Pointing

DEPENDS ON
Cognition
Associative Memory
Convergence
Social Comprehension

VISUAL CLOSURE

MEASURES—ability to recognize
a complete object from an incomplete visual presentation. It
involves visual discrimination and
perceptual interpretation.

TASK DEMAND
Hear and comprehend instructions.
Focus visual attention.
Achieve concept from demonstration.
Retain image of the stimuli object.
Recognize the whole from the part.
Make motoric (pointing) response.
Do above within time limit.

EMPLOYS
Visual closure
Pointing

DEPENDS ON
Visual Discrimination

VISUAL SEQUENTIAL MEMORY

MEASURES—ability to correctly
reproduce a sequence of unrelated
visual symbols. It involves visual
reception and visual-motor expression.

TASK DEMAND
Hear and comprehend instructions.
Focus visual attention.

VISUAL SEQUENTIAL MEMORY (*Continued*)

Achieve concept from demonstration.
Perceive and discriminate the designs.
Remember the designs.
Note the sequential order.
Remember the sequential order.
Make motoric (manipulative)
    response.
(Some children name the designs
    and remember the sequence
    vocally.)

EMPLOYS
Visual sequencing
Manipulation

DEPENDS ON
Visual Discrimination
Visual Memory

AUDITORY ASSOCIATION

MEASURES—ability to organize
    and relate spoken words in a
    meaningful way. Requires the
    production of analogies or
    opposites.

TASK DEMAND
Focus auditory attention.
Hear and comprehend sentence stem.
Have the necessary vocabulary.
Understand concept of verbal
    analogies.
Identify the critical relationship.
Recall the appropriate answer.
Make a vocal response.

EMPLOYS
Auditory closure
Divergence

AUDITORY ASSOCIATION (Continued)

DEPENDS ON
    Auditory Discrimination
    Cognition
    Associative Memory
    Conceptual–Vocal

VISUAL ASSOCIATION

MEASURES—ability to organize
    and relate concepts presented
    visually. Requires the formation of analogies.

TASK DEMAND
    Hear and comprehend question.
    Focus visual attention.
    Achieve concept from demonstration.
    Recognize pictures.
    Achieve the desired analogy.
    Recognize the essential relationship.
    Make a motoric (pointing) response.

EMPLOYS
    Cognition
    Convergence
    Pointing

DEPENDS ON
    Visual Discrimination
    Sensory Integration
    Associative Memory

GRAMMATIC CLOSURE

MEASURES—ability to auto-
    matically use the often repeated
    expressions of standard speech.

TASK DEMAND
    Focus auditory attention.
    Hear and comprehend sentence stem.
    Perceive and comprehend visual cues.
    Have the required language pattern

GRAMMATIC CLOSURE (*Continued*)

    through past experience.
    Associate the appropriate language
      to the verbal and visual cues.
    Make a vocal response.

EMPLOYS
    Auditory closure
    Sensory Integration

DEPENDS ON
    Auditory Discrimination
    Visual Discrimination
    Conceptual–Vocal

VERBAL EXPRESSION

MEASURES—ability to express
    ideas in spoken words. It involves
    vocabulary, command of language,
    and experience at describing.

TASK DEMAND
    See and feel object.
    Recognize object.
    Have familiarity with the object
      through past experience.
    Gain concept, through demonstration
      of all the scorable dimensions
      (label, color, composition,
      function, major parts, etc.).
    Remember the dimensions.
    Have the necessary vocabulary.
    Make a complex vocal response.

EMPLOYS
    Tactile
    Divergence
    Evaluation
    Conceptual–Vocal

DEPENDS ON
    Visual Discrimination
    Sensory Integration

VERBAL EXPRESSION (*Continued*)

Cognition
Associative Memory

MANUAL EXPRESSION

MEASURES—ability to express
ideas through gestures.

TASK DEMAND
See picture and/or hear the name
of object.
Recognize object.
Have familiarity with the object
through past experience.
Gain concept, through demonstration,
that he should demonstrate the
use of the object manually.
Have the coordinated use of the arms
and hands.
Make motoric response.

EMPLOYS
Gross motor
Conceptual-motor

DEPENDS ON
Visual Discrimination
Auditory Discrimination
Sensory Integration
Cognition
Associative Memory

SOUND BLENDING

MEASURES—ability to synthesize
the separate sounds of a word and
produce the integrated whole word.

TASK DEMAND
Focus auditory attention.
Hear word parts.
Have the necessary vocabulary.

SOUND BLENDING (Continued)

Blend sounds to form whole words.
Make a vocal response.

EMPLOYS
Auditory discrimination
Vocal repetition

DEPENDS ON
Auditory Closure

PROFILE OF ABILITIES

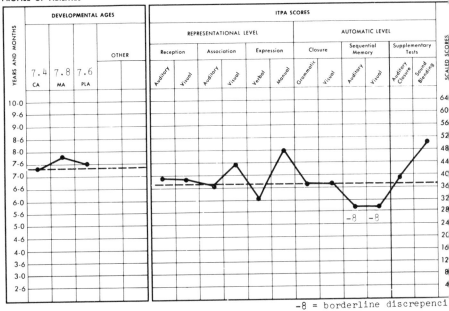

-8 = borderline discrepenci

The *Detroit Tests of Learning Aptitude* are also a developmental language test and the scores are received in *plus* or *minus* *age* versus chronological age. This instrument is relatively flexible in that its various subtests can be used to examine preschool through high school students. The teacher may choose which of the nineteen subtests she wishes to use for a particular student.

The usual number given is nine to thirteen. The characteristics of eleven of the possible nineteen subtests are shown, as follows.

DETROIT TESTS OF LEARNING APTITUDE

PICTORIAL ABSURDITIES

MEASURES—visual attention and discrimination of essential from nonessential details. It requires reasoning, comprehension, and verbal fluency.

TASK DEMAND
Focus visual attention.
Hear and comprehend instructions.
Have familiarity with the situations involved, through past experience.
Discriminate details of the picture.
Recall "correct" visual image from memory.
Select detail which is incorrect.
Make a complex vocal response.

EMPLOYS
Social comprehension

DEPENDS ON
Visual Discrimination
Visual Closure
Cognition
Associative Memory
Conceptual–Vocal

MOTOR SPEED AND PRECISION

MEASURES—fine visual motor coordination and speed. No memory is required but pencil skills are necessary.

TASK DEMAND
Focus visual attention.
Perceive circles.

MOTOR SPEED AND PRECISION (Continued)

Understand the concept of
staying "inside" the circle.
Coordinate visual and kinesthetic
cues.
Have adequate pencil skills.
Sustain visual concentration.
Have adequate muscular stamina.
Make motoric (drawing) response.

EMPLOYS
Kinesthetic
Drawing

DEPENDS ON
Visual Discrimination

AUDITORY ATTENTION SPAN
FOR UNRELATED WORDS

MEASURES—immediate rote memory
for words and the ability to
correctly repeat an unrelated
sequence of auditory symbols.

TASK DEMAND
Focus auditory attention.
Hear and discriminate the words.
Remember the words.
Note the sequential order.
Remember the sequential order.
Make a vocal response.

EMPLOYS
Auditory memory

DEPENDS ON
Auditory Discrimination
Auditory Sequencing
Vocal Repetition

ORAL COMMISSIONS

MEMORY—auditory attention and
    retention and the ability to
    follow directions involving
    gross motoric responses.

TASK DEMAND
    Focus auditory attention.
    Hear and comprehend the commissions.
    Remember the commissions.
    Note the sequential order.
    Remember the sequential order.
    Have ability to walk and use hands.
    Translate auditory directions into
        the corresponding motoric acts.
    Coordinate visual and kinesthetic
        cues.
    Make a motoric (gross motor)
        response.

EMPLOYS
    Kinesthetic
    Gross motor
    Conceptual–motor

DEPENDS ON
    Auditory Discrimination
    Auditory Sequencing
    Auditory Memory
    Visual Discrimination
    Sensory Integration
    Cognition

SOCIAL ADJUSTMENT A

MEASURES—practical information
    and a general ability to
    evaluate past experience. It
    shows use of common sense,
    judgment, and indicates the
    child's social and cultural
    background.

SOCIAL ADJUSTMENT A (Continued)

TASK DEMAND
Focus auditory attention.
Hear and comprehend question.
Have familiarity with the social
situation involved, through
past experience.
Use judgment and common sense.
Make a complex vocal response.

EMPLOYS
Social comprehension

DEPENDS ON
Auditory Discrimination
Cognition
Associative Memory
Conceptual–Vocal

VISUAL ATTENTION SPAN FOR OBJECTS

MEASURES—immediate recall of an
unrelated sequence of visual
symbols. It involves visual
reception and vocal expression.
Sequential order is not
required.

TASK DEMAND
Focus visual attention.
Hear and comprehend instructions.
Perceive and discriminate objects.
Recognize the objects.
"Name" the objects from the visual
cue.
Remember the objects (visually or
vocally).
Note the sequential order.
Remember the sequential order (not
required but as aid to memory).
Make vocal response.

EMPLOYS
Visual memory

VISUAL ATTENTION SPAN FOR OBJECTS (Continued)

DEPENDS ON
    Visual Discrimination
    Visual Sequencing
    Cognition
    Vocal Repetition

_____

ORIENTATION

MEASURES—practical information,
    judgment, and time and space relationships.

_____

TASK DEMAND
    Focus auditory attention.
    Hear and comprehend questions.
    See and comprehend visual cues.
    Have background information
        available through past
        experience.
    Recall the information.
    Have the necessary vocabulary.
    Have laterality and directionality.
    Be aware of body parts.
    Have knowledge of time factors.
    Make verbal response.
    Make motoric (gross motor) responses.

_____

EMPLOYS
    Kinesthetic
    Gross motor

_____

DEPENDS ON
    Auditory Discrimination
    Sensory Integration
    Cognition
    Associative Memory
    Conceptual–Motor
    Conceptual–Vocal

_____

MEMORY FOR DESIGNS

MEASURES—ability to copy designs
    both with visual cues and from

MEMORY FOR DESIGNS (Continued)

> memory. Involves visual and
> auditory reception and motor
> expression.

TASK DEMAND
> Focus visual attention.
> Hear and comprehend instruction.
> Perceive designs.
> Analyze the designs as to shape,
>   etc.
> Remember the designs.
> Have adequate eye–hand coordination.
> Have adequate pencil skills.
> Make motoric (drawing) response.

EMPLOYS
> Visual memory
> Copying

DEPENDS ON
> Visual Discrimination
> Visual Closure
> Evaluation

**AUDITORY ATTENTION SPAN
FOR RELATED SYLLABLES**

MEASURES—immediate rote memory for
>   sentences and the ability to
>   correctly repeat a meaningful
>   sequence of auditory symbols.

TASK DEMAND
> Focus auditory attention.
> Hear and discriminate the words.
> Comprehend the sentence.
> Note the sequential order.
> Utilize sentence meaning as an
>   aid to remembering words and
>   sequential order.
> Remember the sentence.
> Make a vocal response.

**AUDITORY ATTENTION SPAN FOR
RELATED SYLLABLES (Continued)**

EMPLOYS
>Auditory sequencing
>Vocal repetition

DEPENDS ON
>Auditory Discrimination
>Auditory Memory
>Cognition

VISUAL ATTENTION SPAN FOR LETTERS

MEASURES—recognition and recall
>of an unrelated sequence of
>visually presented letters. It
>involves visual reception and
>vocal expression. Sequential order is required.

TASK DEMAND
>Focus visual attention.
>Hear and comprehend instructions.
>Perceive and discriminate letters.
>Recognize the letters.
>"Name" the letters from the visual
>>cue.
>Remember the letters (visually or
>>vocally).
>Note the sequential order.
>Make vocal response.

EMPLOYS
>Visual sequencing

DEPENDS ON
>Visual Discrimination
>Visual Memory
>Vocal Repetition

ORAL DIRECTIONS

MEASURES—integration of
>visual and auditory cues, the
>ability to retain and follow

ORAL DIRECTIONS (*Continued*)

>   complex directions, and eye–
>   hand coordination.

TASK DEMAND

>   Focus auditory attention.
>   Hear and comprehend directions.
>   Focus visual attention (page
>   very "busy").
>   See and discriminate visual cues.
>   Remember the instructions.
>   Recognize the visual stimuli.
>   Associate verbal directions to the
>   visual stimuli.
>   Have number ability.
>   Understand such terms as
>   bottom, over, cross out,
>   first, triangle, etc., as
>   well as letters and numbers.
>   Have adequate eye–hand
>   coordination.
>   Make motoric (drawing)
>   response.

EMPLOYS

>   Auditory sequencing
>   Sensory integration
>   Drawing
>   Conceptual-Motor

DEPENDS ON

>   Auditory Memory
>   Visual Discrimination
>   Cognition

The entire range of Detroit subtests may be broken down into the following categories of mental faculties.

Pictorial Absurdities
Verbal Absurdities
Social Adjustment A
Orientation
Social Adjustment B
Disarranged Pictures
} Reasoning and comprehension

Motor Speed and Precision
Oral Commissions
Orientation
Oral Directions
} Practical judgment

Verbal Absurdities
Verbal Opposites
Free Association
Likenesses and Differences
} Verbal ability

Orientation
Memory for Designs
Disarranged Pictures
} Time and space relationships

Oral Commissions
Number Ability
} Number ability

Auditory Attention Span
   for Unrelated Words
Oral Commissions
Auditory Attention Span
   for Related Syllables
Oral Directions
} Auditory attentive ability

Pictorial Absurdities
Pictorial Opposites
Visual Attention Span for Objects
Memory for Designs
Visual Attention Span for Letters
Disarranged Pictures
Oral Directions
} Visual attentive ability

Motor Speed and Precision
Oral Commissions
Memory for Designs
Oral Directions
} Motor ability

A child, for example, may be -2^3 or $+1^9$. This means that the child is functioning at minus two years, three months *below* his chronological age, or one year, nine months *above* his chronological age.

The three tests that have been described illustrate the range and variety of such instruments and show how areas of deficit may be double-checked by the examiner. Many hundreds of tests are available to the examiner. Some—for example, the Wepman Auditory Discrimination Test, the title of which is self-explanatory— test only specific areas.

It is usually necessary to use a *minimum* of six instruments for a single *primary battery* which will test intellect, processing, and academic achievement levels. For a *secondary* battery, if one proves necessary, the evaluator may choose upward of ten additional testing instruments.

The evaluator may also *screen* for neurological development. This involves checking the child's gross and fine muscle control, gait, and posture (balance). If there is any question in the examiner's mind, he will make a referral to a neurologist.

■

Everyone has yet other facets to his mental functioning, in the sense of the total learning effort in addition to input, processing, and output.

All learning effort is modified by what are known as cognitive styles.

The *cognitive styles* affect the way in which a person uses his intellect. It affects, either positively or negatively, the efficiency of intellectual functioning. The sum total of an individual's cognitive styles are powerful factors, not only in the classroom but throughout life.

Learning disabled children often display one or more combinations of the counterpoints to the preferred cognitive styles. The first style related is the preferred; the second, or counterpoint, is intrusive to learning productivity.

REFLECTION-IMPULSIVITY. A child who has a reflective cognitive style has a long reaction time to stimuli and makes fewer errors. The impulsive child has a short reaction time and makes a large number of errors. The impulsive cognitive style offers little critical evaluation of the information or the available alternatives that the information may represent. It has been shown that there is a high correlation between habitual speed of decision impulsivity and the error factor.

FIELD INDEPENDENCE-FIELD DEPENDENCE. This cognitive style reflects the child's ability to separate figure-ground, to take a specific item (figure) from the field in which it is embedded (ground). Is the perception general and diffuse or is it structured and analytic? The field independent person is able to easily isolate the figure from the ground. A field independent child is more emotionally stable and displays better impulse control. Field dependent students will often demonstrate high activity levels and can be expected to respond to what is *for them* the most compelling part of the stimuli field, regardless of the intended primary stimulus.

FLEXIBLE CONTROL-CONSTRICTED CONTROL. This cognitive style concerns attention and the ability to focus on relevant stimuli while ignoring distracting and/or contradictory stimuli. A constricted control of attention does not allow the child to inhibit his incorrect verbalizations.

AUTOMIZATION. Again, the chain of automatic habits for encoding, processing, and decoding in addition to the ability to respond rapidly and easily to repetitive tasks without fatigue and overuse of attentional energies occurs. Children who are poor in concentration, low in persistence, and easily distracted by extraneous stimuli have a less efficient, and less effective, response to repetitive tasks and are therefore considered to be weak automizers.

Other aspects of cognitive styles that may have a bearing on the learning process have been identified and studied. David P. Ausubel relates these as: "Intolerance for ambiguity (tendency toward premature closure); intolerance for unrealistic experience; leveling–sharpening; need for simplification (skeletonizing, rationalizing); explication and importing of detail in memory (embroidery); vividness of memory; long-term or short-term memory; memory for particular kinds and sense modality of experience; constriction or flexibility in problem-solving. Other possible and suggested aspects of cognitive style include strategy preferences and problem-solving (focusing or scanning; whole or part hypotheses); strategy preferences in processing, acquiring and organizing information; memory for details or concepts; integration versus compartmentalization in memory; degree of openness to new information after closure is achieved."

■

The "behaviors" that a child has within him can also bring dire results in the classroom learning process and the social milieu. These "behaviors" may emerge from emotional and/or physical, especially neurological, causes. These "behaviors" can be severely intrusive factors to the learning process. Whatever the etiological causes, they must be dealt with, even if the involvement is only awareness on the part of the teacher or parents.

The one behavior that has stimulated the most recent public discussion is hyperactivity/hyperkinesis. Although these two terms are used in the public media interchangeably, they are not quite interchangeable since an accurate definition of each would indicate differences not only in degree but in the potential for future continuance.

Hyperactivity could easily be translated into the word "energy," excessive energy. The difference between just childhood energy and hyperactive energy is that the latter is excessive. It is excessive to the point of intrusion upon the task at hand. A child who lacks control of himself to the point of hyperactivity cannot attend to stimuli in an organized manner.

Hyperkinesis has a different quality about it; the child appears more "driven." There is an intensivity about the child's activity that is not present in hyperactivity. The hyperactive child may, as he matures, be taught some inner controls for his excessive activity while the hyperkinetic child will have many of the same *surface* symptoms but will also have a deeper and more prolonged control problem. The hyperkinetic child will, to the onlooker, often appear tense and rigid. Sitting still, for instance, requires such effort from *within* the child that, even though he may succeed, the effort will cost him dearly.

Both hyperactive and hyperkinetic children may need the aid of chemotherapeutic agents.

There is an opposite to the *hyper* termed *hypo*. The *hypo*active or *hypo*kinetic child functions *below* the expected levels of activity. Cases of this kind are not too frequently recognized. They do, however, exist and this behavior can present an equally serious deterrent to the learning process. Lassitude or ennui in any child should always be suspect and should have immediate medical diagnostic attention.

Rigidity is the inability to take a new course of action or to adjust to a new situation. Often learning disabled children suffer so severely from rigidity that just coming into a room where the furniture has been moved can disrupt their whole day; or, moving from one task to another in the classroom requires such an expenditure of effort on their part that it is self-defeating. By the time the child has made the switch, he is unable to function with any learning energy.

Clutter is something that parents especially notice. It is nervous speech that bursts from the child, accompanied by frequent omissions of words and sound substitutions. There is a possibility that children will clutter not only verbally but mentally as well when attempting to think.

Emotional lability is a behavior that "shifts" the child emotionally from one feeling to another, often with a rapidity that can be startling to adults. One minute the child is placid, the next he is an emotional whirlwind.

Impaired *social perceptions* indicate a nonverbal and nonemotional disturbance in the child's understanding of his environment and those who people his world. The child does not learn from the actions and expressions of others what he must do. Impaired social perceptions are especially treacherous for teenagers. They have great difficulty "reading" their peer group to determine what is required of them.

Low frustration threshold is relatively self-explanatory. This child is susceptible to the slightest pressure whether the source of pressure is environmental or academic. He gives up.

Impulsivity, which has already been discussed as a cognitive style of learning, is also a behavior in that a child will react to his environment, especially the hazards of the environment, in an impulsive manner. This is the child who, no matter how many times he has been told, and even though he is old enough to understand fully, will still dart out in front of a car after a ball.

Distractibility is the inability of a child to focus his attention on a task for more than a very short time. Sometimes this distractibility factor is so severe that the attention span is only a few seconds long.

Anxiety is a state of mind that we all have, at one time or another. A child who lives in a constant state of barely suppressed anxiety will test poorly, will be struck dumb if the teacher asks a question that he is unprepared at the moment to answer, even though he may well know the information. Anxiety can be a continuous state of agony that the child cannot verbalize because, naturally, he does not know what it is—he knows only that he is vaguely fearful and that sometimes the feeling becomes so strong that he cannot control it.

Perseveration is the uncontrolled repetition of an activity. A child writing a word with an *n* on the end may go on and write *nnnnnnn* all the way across the desk top. He may hammer a nail long after the nailhead has disappeared into the wood. Sometimes, the perseveration becomes so severe that the child's whole body will become involved in the arm and hand movement so that he will begin to rock in cadence with the perseverative gesture.

Conceptual disorganization under stress is, generally speaking, what it sounds like. The problem arises here, though, with the child who has limited conceptual capacities. When these limited capacities become disorganized because of stress, he is unable to function at the level which is expected of him while he is under control.

Overreaction to error may not seem very tragic. But if a child's life is filled with errors because of his handicap, this can become a rich source of energy dissipation.

Explosive behavior is just what it says. The child's behavior literally explodes into the world. He is often considered pugnacious by his peer group. His parents can be bewildered. Often, these children have damaged conceptual abilities and very poor inferential reasoning.

Catastrophic reaction involves the whole child. His body and mind react to a situation in a totally uncontrolled manner. He flails his arms, stomps his feet, screams his rage, rushes his body into total movement. The pleasant child becomes an instant nightmare with a force that affects his total immediate environment.

When reviewing these behavior descriptions it is readily seen that a child may display a combination of the behaviors described, and the term applied to an individual child by one professional may be used differently by another professional. Many of these behaviors, with the exception of the most severe, intertwine with each other and disrupt the different classroom behavioral task objectives.

■

Learning disability children have clusters of inefficiencies or disabilities. The term "learning disability" is not exactly accurate because there is really no such thing as a singular "learning disability." The singular term is used for grammatical convenience. What is accurate is that a "child has learning disabilities" and is therefore learning disabled. The clusters of disabilities are evidenced by inefficiencies, or dysfunctions, when a child attempts to reach certain expected and necessary classroom behavioral task objectives. From child to child the clusters of dysfunction can appear in different combinations according to the type and extent of the handicap, but the majority of learning disability children fall into two major categories: specific or global.

A *specific* disability is usually language-centered. The classroom task behavioral deficits and unfavorable learning characteristics are most noticeable in reading and spelling. Naturally, disabilities that affect language—i.e., reading and spelling—will of necessity lead to problems in all the other areas which are dependent upon these two skills.

A *global* disability usually involves multiple processing dysfunctions coupled with maladaptive behavior.

One of the most interesting and, for parents, confusing aspects of the differences between a specific and a global disability is that although a global case may seemingly have *more* problem areas, an individual child may have areas without deficit that are surprising. For example, one of the primary categorizing or cluster points of a *specific* disability is the inability to read. Yet, a child with a global handicap may appear to read quite well. The difference is that the child with the specific disability will, once he learns to read, be able to use this skill more effectively.

Each division, specific and global, may be subdivided. Here, however, we will concentrate on dyslexia, complex dyslexia, minimal neurological dysfunction, and minimal brain damage because these are the most prevalent disabilities. These are etiological and/or *medical* terms; for example, dyslexia refers to a specific language disability. In many communities and educational circles, these etiological terms have had descriptive behaviors and learner characteristics ascribed to them so that in effect they have served, to a degree, as a classification system. An educator who says a child is a "dyslexic" is not attempting to label the child but rather is using a form of verbal shorthand. There are broad patterns for each of the major divisions and their subcategories, and it is these broad patterns that reveal the general clusters of disabilities.

■

In modern society, dependent as it is on the printed word, those who cannot read easily, smoothly, without giving the act a second thought, are cut off irrevocably from most of the normal channels of learning and communication. A child with average or above intelligence who suffers from a specific language disability cannot function in today's world because he cannot learn to read efficiently.

Dyslexia, the medical term for specific language disability, may be defined as lack of ability or inability to read. The most widely accepted definition of the nature of dyslexia was given in 1960 at the Johns Hopkins Conference on Dyslexia. The conference defined Specific Dyslexia as a genetic, neurological dysfunction, uncomplicated by other factors. This means that a child who has a Specific Language Disability inherits from his parents, grandparents, or a preceding generation, certain factors which play a special role in his reading problems, and these factors lead to a basic malfunction or immaturity of the processing functions of his neural system.

The result of this neural-system inefficiency is that the child has distorted perception of written symbols (the alphabet). These faulty percepts primarily affect his symbolic sequencing, speech patterns, auditory and symbolic association, grammar, handwriting, spelling, and automization.

Specific dyslexia is the least severe of the disorders on the continuum of learning disabilities. A child with uncomplicated, genetic dyslexia is the closest to an average child in the classroom, even though he is not functioning at a level appropriate to his chronological age. Although learning disabilities as a handicap affect millions of school-age children, the incidence of dyslexia is believed to be only about 3 percent to 5 percent (perhaps even only one percent to 3 percent) of these millions.

The history of medically recognized dyslexia may be traced to 1896, when an English physician, Dr. James Kerr, cited a severe and specific learning disability in some children who were otherwise intellectually capable.

In the Scandinavian countries genetic or "family" dyslexia has long been recognized by both the medical profession and school authorities. A great deal of the original medical research was done in Denmark by Dr. Knud Hermann of the University Hospital of Copenhagen. Dr. Hermann, in his book *Reading Disability* and in other published works, helped to clarify the concept of "family dyslexia" and the fact that it can be inherited.

In 1950, Dr. Bertil Hallgren of Stockholm published a massive work on specific dyslexia, pulling the then current literature together and adding detailed research findings and observations of his own. The result was an extremely comprehensive study on the whole of inherited dyslexia. Later, the brilliance of Edith Norrie's teaching methods was added to the work of Hermann and Hallgren. Today, because of these workers and others, Scandinavia is fortunate in having recognized the dimensions of the problem and in having developed a demography of the disability. Even more important, however, is the fact that dyslexia is recognized for what it is—a genetic disability that can be treated with success—and no social stigma is attached to the victim. Since the 1950s and 1960s, the clinical literature in both Europe and America has trebled and trebled again.

What exactly are these familial characteristics that can lock an otherwise seemingly bright, normal child into a specific learning disability, a learning handicap that seems to have affected such well-known figures as Da Vinci, Einstein, and Churchill?

The clinical literature states that a number of characteristics are likely to appear, not only in the child himself but in his family tree—in his parents, grandparents (maternal and fraternal), his aunts, uncles, and siblings.

The first cluster of significant characteristics is left-handedness, ambidexterity (undeveloped laterality), spatial and language disorders. In the simplest, most general terms, the questions that should be asked concerning the family tree are: Did father have trouble in the early grades of school? Does mother's sister stutter? Is grandfather's handwriting still barely legible? Is brother a southpaw? Does mother or father still have to stop for a moment to ponder which is the left or right turn, especially when either is overtired or under stress? Can the child swim like a fish but is unable to pick up a dime easily? Does 20-year-old sister still knock over glasses at the dinner table?

Of equal importance is a second cluster of indicators: Families who demonstrate an allergenic history to foods or chemicals. (Asthmatics in the familial relationship should be considered.) Families with an overall poor medical history (this naturally does not include malnutrition). The emphasis here is on *hyper* and *hypo*glycemia (glucose intolerance), petit mal, or thyroid imbalances.

The final cluster of indicators, although still equally important, falls into the category that is called "clinically significant" and as such is usually only touched upon by those persons involved in research and uppermost clinical education. These indicators are hair color and twins. The evidence suggests that those families who report red or bright sandy-red hair also may have some tendency, if combined with other familial characteristics, to have a higher incidence of specific language disabilities.

Perhaps most influential of all the familial characteristics is the "twinning factor." Families with the "twinning factor" in present or preceding generations show a definite propensity toward specific learning disabilities. In a controlled pilot study, a significantly higher rate of twinning in the case families was reported. This higher twinning rate, as opposed to the average United States population norm for twin births, was more than 2½ times the normal rate. The norm for twin births is 1 in 88; the subject families registered 1,618 births (three generations) and 69.2 percent of the families reported twin births—284 percent higher than the expected rate.

When searching the family history for familial characteristics, it is necessary always to bear in mind the disqualification (or qualification) of a family member by reason of divorce, death (unregistered births), or adoption.

The uncomplicated, specific, language centered disability (dyslexia) encompasses the following general overall picture (protocol).

The child is *above average* in inferential reasoning (abstract thought), large muscle coordination and balance, short- and long-term memory for events. His general appearance is usually good.

He is *average* in expressive (oral) language, spatial reasoning, quantitative language (mathematics).

He has a *developmental immaturity* that can be evidenced by difficulty in sequencing of geometric forms, right–left orientation and body–image reversal; impaired social perceptions; a low frustration threshold; figure–ground confusion; immature speech patterns; and weakness in ocular control. His dominance and laterality have not been established by the expected age level.

In the area of classroom behavior, there is *some degree* of hyperactivity, rigidity, and emotional lability, with a *moderate degree* of impulsivity, distractibility, and anxiety. He will test poorly.

His cognitive learning style is primarily *field dependent.*

His verbal comprehension is *minimally impaired.*

He is definitively *impaired* in short- and long-term memory for sequencing and recognition of symbols, reading, grammar, handwriting, automization, small muscle coordination, position of symbols in space (reversals), eye–hand coordination, auditory association, and association of symbols. His perceptual motor match is impaired and his rapid rhythmic movements are slowed.

He is *seriously impaired* in auditory memory for sound–symbol association, sequencing of symbol–sounds, spelling, and expressive (written) language.

Depending upon his age, there may be a *mild* to *moderate* emotional overlay directly proportionate to unproductive classroom years.

The dyslexic's assets for future productivity lie in his conceptual strength which will, with proper help, eventually come to the forefront so that the prognosis for the future for this type of specific language disability is *good.*

The next step along the continuum of specific learning disabilities is complicated or complex dyslexia. The children with complex dyslexia do not fulfill the Johns Hopkins definition "uncomplicated by other factors." These are the children who are confronted by the full range of possible familial characteristics and who have also suffered some form of organic trauma or insult.

A trauma is an injury to the organism, usually brought about by mechanical means. An insult is a nature-precipitated affront to the organism involved. Either insult or trauma can be the result of any of the many minor or major problems which may arise during the perinatal period, at birth, or afterward. Often, the incident was so minor that it escaped notice. In fact, many times, the exact incident is never successfully identified either medically or in the minds of the parents of the child.

Although it seems unlikely that an incident that could go unnoticed could thrust a child so much deeper into the manifestations of a learning disability, unfortunately, this is often exactly what happens. Why? The answer to this question seems to lie in the vulnerability of this child. He is more vulnerable to *results* of trauma or insult—the "something" that for another child born of a different genetic background would probably not have had an effect. The "something" does not usually cause demonstrable neurological damage, but it does *compound* the child's genetically based language disability. This compounding, or plus factor, causes an intensification of the child's disabilities. This is why it is called *complex* dyslexia.

This child will be *above average* in large muscle coordination, short- and long-term memory for events, and usually have good general appearance. There may be a history (often documented) of perinatal or early childhood trauma that can be evidenced by "soft signs."

He will probably be *average* in balance, expressive (oral) language, and spatial reasoning.

He has a *developmental immaturity* which may be evidenced by difficulty in sequencing of geometric forms, figure–ground confusion, right–left orientation, body-image reversal, crossing the body mid-line, immature speech patterns. Dominance and laterality will not have been established by the expected age level.

There will be *some degree* of perseveration and conceptual disorganization under stress.

He will be *minimally impaired* in inferential reasoning (abstract thought), quantitative language (mathematics), ocular control, verbal comprehension, and social perceptions.

He will evidence a *moderate degree* of hyperactivity, emotional lability, and distractibility.

His cognitive learning styles are *field dependent, rigid* and *impulsive.*

He has a *low* frustration threshold.

He is definitively *impaired* in eye–hand coordination, reading, and automization. Small muscle coordination is also impaired and rapid rhythmic movements are slowed. There is a *high degree* of anxiety and he will test poorly.

This child is *seriously impaired* in short- and long-term memory for sequencing of symbols, recognition of symbols, position of symbols in space, association of symbols, sequencing of symbol–sounds, handwriting, grammar, spelling, perceptual motor match, expressive (written) language, auditory association, and auditory memory for symbol–sound association.

Given proper and early help, for the complex dyslexic the prognosis for reaching future potential is *moderately guarded.*

Genetically based specific language disabilities have a much higher incidence among male children. There also seems to be a difference in degree of overall disability; the males will, and do, run the gamut from mimimal to severe. The females, when young, only touch opposite ends of the spectrum and seem to be either minimal *or* severe. But a seeming degree of minimal disability in girls can be treacherous. A girl who is minimally handicapped will probably be able to achieve adequately most behavioral task objectives in the early classroom experience. But, when she becomes a teen-ager, many times her disabilities will surface with greater force in the social milieu as well as in the classroom. High school classroom work requires stronger conceptual strength and more adroit learning skills; the females will maintain good verbalization but evidence incompetencies in quantitative language, comprehension, and reasoning abilities.

With either males or females, a genetically based learning disability is not a "disease." It does not strike every male child of every generation. There is not, nor should there be, any social stigma or genetic "impurity" attached to what is a *remediable reading handicap caused by a maturation lag.* With the dyslexics, we are dealing with proven achievers; the basic parameters are different from those for other forms of learning handicap; they are generally considered to be high on the phylogenetic scales and as such are above-average children. Yet despite this fact, because of their problems they perform below average.

These children, who have the intelligence and conceptual ability to overcome their processing inefficiencies, are sensitive to their surrounding world. They seem to have an "inner awareness" that is unique. Because of this sensitivity, their ego is easily battered by school failure. They are particularly susceptible to the acquisition of emotional overlay. Teen-agers who have not received satisfactory supportive measures, both academic and social, are beset by a sense of frustration, failure, and unhappiness that can be crippling.

■

A familial history of language disorders is not pertinent to a diagnosis of neurological dysfunction or minimal brain damage.

No parent can foresee that they will have a child with a neurological involvement. The advent of such a handicap is totally beyond our ability to predict or avoid. Most certainly, the event should not be devastating to the family unit. Millions of adults are leading full, productive lives in spite of such a handicap. In considering long-range goals for the child, immediate academic success is not as important as slow, careful, and loving guidance. The child needs to be helped to achieve inner controls for his sensitivity and overreaction to the necessities of daily life.

We are again discussing children who demonstrate average or above intellectual potential, but who as the result of trauma or insult to the organism are unable to achieve their potential. These children can function effectively if correct academic guidance is used and if they are taught the necessary inner controls for the usually accompanying minimal to severe maladaptive behavior.

When speaking of children with minimal neurological impairments, Clements refers to them as those children "with certain learning or behavior disabilities ranging from mild to severe, which are associated with deviations of function of the central nervous system. These aberrations may arise . . . from biochemical irregularities, perinatal brain insults, or other illnesses or injuries sustained during the years which are critical for the development and maturation of the central nervous system, or from other organic causes as yet unknown."

No attempt is made here to list all the possible sources of trauma or insult. One child's trauma may result in dysfunction; for another child the same trauma may result in injury. The major medical differentiation is the degree of presenting handicap and medical proof. Very often the "why" or "when" of trauma, either for dysfunction or damage, is never known. From the time an embryo is conceived until death at any age, we are all subject to the possibility of brain injury. It is believed that approximately two-thirds of the involved children suffered "something" unfavorable during fetal life.

Aside from their learning and behavior inefficiencies, these children usually suffer from one other problem. Very often they do not display any visible handicap and, as with most things that are not clearly displayed, their parents do not become aware of their problems at an early age. This time lag can be crucial.

Even though these children have intellectual capacities which fall within the range of normal, the neurologically involved child is unable to use percepts to achieve concepts in the automatic interaction that is necessary to abstract thought processes. When an individual is incapable of, or has impaired, inferential reasoning, he is unable to function in his environment at the level that is expected of him. The individual functions, or attempts to function, on faulty or inconsistent data. As a consequence, he may behave inappropriately, which, in turn, results in punishment.

The child with a minimal neurological dysfunction will often have an *above-average* incidence of electroencephalographic abnormalities in his family history. There may also be documented evidence of a perinatal or childhood trauma, and neurological "soft signs" will be diagnosed.

His general appearance will usually be *average,* and his dominance and laterality can be established at approximately the normal age level.

He will be *minimally impaired* in expressive (oral) language, short- and long-term memory for events, spatial reasoning, position of symbols in space, recognition of symbols, verbal comprehension, auditory association, and inferential reasoning. He will have immature speech patterns, a confused body image, and minimally impaired balance.

This child will have a *moderate degree* of weakness in ocular control, figure–ground confusion, hyperactivity, perseveration, social imperceptions, and catastrophic reactions. Anxiety will cause him to test poorly.

He will be *impaired* in reading, grammar, auditory memory for symbol–sound association, short- and long-term memory for sequencing of symbols, quantitative language (mathematics), eye–hand coordination for symbols and geometric forms. His rapid rhythmic movements are slowed. Other areas of *impaired* functioning are: large and small muscle coordination, association of symbols, expressive (written) language, sequencing of symbol–sounds, auditory memory for words, handwriting, and automization.

His cognitive learning styles are *field dependent, rigid,* and *impulsive.*

He has a *low* frustration threshold.

He will have a *high degree* of emotional lability, distractibility, and overreaction to error.

His efficiency in perceptual motor match will be *seriously impaired.*

The minimal brain damaged child is similar to the child with neurological dysfunction, but . . . he has confirmed organicity, soft and hard signs. His general appearance may be slightly *below average.*

His speech patterns may be only *minimally impaired.*

He will be *impaired* in inferential reasoning (abstract thought), large and small muscle coordination, laterality development, ocular control, and social perception. His sequencing of geometric forms and symbols, auditory associations, expressive (oral) language, automization, and verbal comprehension are also impaired. There is confused body imagery.

His cognitive learning styles are *field dependent, rigid, impulsive,* and *constricted.*

He has a *low* frustration threshold.

There can be a *high degree* of hyperactivity or hyperkinetic behavior, perseveration, explosive behavior, catastrophic reaction, and distractibility.

He may be *seriously impaired* in the areas of perceptual constancy, eye–hand coordination for symbols and geometric forms, perceptual motor match, auditory memory and association for symbols and words, spatial reasoning, reading, grammar, handwriting, expressive (written) language, spelling, quantitative language (mathematics), short- and long-term memory for information, and balance. His rapid rhythmic movements will be *seriously impaired* as will his sense of position in space.

■

Another aspect to be considered is the possibility of a "dual etiology." An individual may, for example, have acquired a severe emotional overlay. This overlay may be so deep and of such a long duration that it then becomes the dominant handicap and as such must be remediated *first*. In such a case, the protocol of learning disability drops to a secondary status and does not rise again until it is felt that the child's psychological problems have been alleviated to the point where learning can become effective.

In reviewing the characteristics of children's learning disabilities it must always be remembered that there are as many degrees and combinations of these dysfunctions as there are children. The continuum sets only rough parameters; it is in no way a concrete profile of any individual child.

It is possible to list the *general* clusters of characteristics that may be found in a given substrata of learning disabilities, whether specific or global. The fairly detailed breakdown of characteristics given in the text and displayed on the four charts should not be overwhelming. In keeping with the goals of this book, it is necessary to offer such a *composite* to the reader. However, an *individual* child does not evidence *all* the manifestations or specific degrees of the different characteristic clusters.

A MODEL CONTINUUM OF BEHAVIORS AND CHARACTERISTICS

SPECIFIC

Specific Language Disability

(dyslexia)

Degree	General appearance	Familial history of language disorders	Inferential reasoning (abstract thought)	Balance (posture)	Large muscle coordination	Short and long term memory for events	Spatial reasoning	Expressive language (oral)	Quantitative language (mathematics)	Ocular control	Laterality and dominance not established	Right-left orientation	Sequencing of geometric forms	Figure-ground confusion	Immature speech patterns	Low frustration threshold	Social perceptions	Body image reversals
Seriously Impaired																		
High Degree of Impaired																		
Moderate Degree of Impaired																		
Minimally Impaired																		
Some Degree of Difficulty Imm.																		
Developmental Imm. turity Evidenced by																		
Below Average										◇	◇	◇	◇	◇	◇	◇	◇	◇
Average							◇	◇	◇									
Above Average	◇	◇	◇	◇	◇	◇												

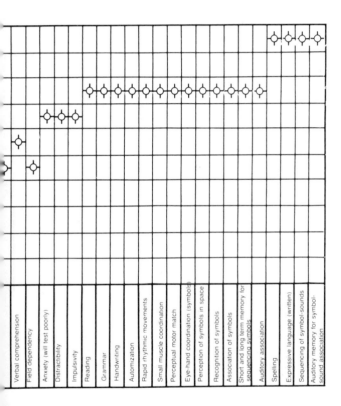

	Verbal comprehension	Field dependency	Anxiety (will test poorly)	Distractibility	Impulsivity	Reading	Grammar	Handwriting	Automization	Rapid rhythmic movements	Small muscle coordination	Perceptual motor match	Eye-hand coordination (symbols)	Perception of symbols in space	Recognition of symbols	Association of symbols	Short and long term memory for sequencing symbols	Auditory association	Spelling	Expressive language (written)	Sequencing of symbol-sounds	Auditory memory for symbol-sound association

The author gratefully acknowledges the use of these charts that were formulated by Frances K. McGlannan; 1800 case studies supplied this data and the patterns identified are for a teacher training module.

A MODEL CONTINUUM OF BEHAVIORS AND CHARACTERISTICS

SPECIFIC

Specific Language Disability + Trauma or Insult

(complex dyslexia)

Characteristic	Seriously Impaired	High Degree of Impaired	Moderate Degree of Impaired	Minimally Impaired	Some Degree of Developmental Immaturity Evidenced by Difficulty in	Below Average	Average	Above Average
General appearance								◇◇
Familial history of language disorders					◇			
Inferential reasoning (abstract thought)							◇	
Balance (posture)							◇	
Large muscle coordination								◇◇
Short and long term memory for events								
Spatial reasoning							◇	
Expressive language (oral)					◇		◇	
Quantitative language (mathematics)					◇			
Ocular control					◇			
Laterality and dominance not established						◇		
Right-left orientation						◇		
Sequencing of geometric forms						◇		
Figure-ground confusion			◇			◇		
Immature speech patterns						◇		
Low frustration threshold								
Social perceptions								
Body image reversals					◇	◇		
Hyperactivity				◇◇				
Rigidity				◇				

Anxiety (will test poorly)

Distractibility

Impulsivity

Reading

Grammar

Handwriting

Automization

Rapid rhythmic movements

Small muscle coordination

Perceptual motor match

Eye-hand coordination (symbols)

Perception of symbols in space

Recognition of symbols

Association of symbols

Short and long term memory for sequencing symbols

Auditory association

Spelling

Expressive language (written)

Sequencing of symbol-sounds

Auditory memory for symbol-sound association

Incidence of Peri-natal or early childhood trauma

Cannot cross mid-line

Perseveration

Conceptual disorganization under stress

A MODEL CONTINUUM OF BEHAVIORS AND CHARACTERISTICS

GLOBAL

Minimal Neurological Dysfunction

Characteristic	Above Average	Average	Below Average	Developmental Immaturity Evidenced by: Difficulty Up... / Some Degree of	Minimally Impaired	Moderate Degree of	Impaired	High Degree of	Seriously Impaired
General appearance	◇								
Familial history of language disorders									
Inferential reasoning (abstract thought)									
Balance (posture)						◇			
Large muscle coordination				◇					
Short and long term memory for events				◇					
Spatial reasoning				◇					
Expressive language (oral)					◇				
Quantitative language (mathematics)						◇			
Ocular control					◇				
Laterality and dominance not established									
Right-left orientation									
Sequencing of geometric forms									
Figure-ground confusion					◇				
Immature speech patterns				◇					
Low frustration threshold					◇				
Social perceptions					◇				
Body image reversals								◇	
Hyperactivity									
Rigidity					◇		◇		
Emotional lability								◇	
Verbal comprehension									
Field dependency					◇				

Grammar
Handwriting
Automization
Rapid rhythmic movements
Small muscle coordination
Perceptual motor match
Eye-hand coordination (symbol)
Perception of symbols in space
Recognition of symbols
Association of symbols
Short and long term memory for sequencing symbols
Auditory association
Spelling
Expressive language (written)
Sequencing of symbol-sounds
Auditory memory for symbol-sound association
Incidence of peri-natal or early childhood trauma
Cannot cross mid-line
Perseveration
Conceptual disorganization under stress
Negative family history of language disorders
Some family history of EEG abnormalities
Establishment of laterality and dominance
Soft signs
Over-reaction to error
Body image confusion
Catastrophic reaction

A MODEL CONTINUUM OF BEHAVIORS AND CHARACTERISTICS

GLOBAL

Minimal Brain Damage

The chart plots each characteristic (columns) against a continuum of degree/severity (rows). Markers (◇) indicate the placement of each characteristic on the continuum.

Characteristic	Seriously Impaired	High Degree of:	Impaired	Moderate Degree of:	Minimally Impaired	Some Degree of:	Developmental Immaturity Evidenced by, Difficulty in:	Below Average	Average	Above Average
General appearance									◇	
Familial history of language disorders				◇						
Inferential reasoning (abstract thought)		◇								
Balance (posture)				◇						
Large muscle coordination				◇						
Short and long term memory for events		◇								
Spatial reasoning		◇								
Expressive language (oral)				◇						
Quantitative language (mathematics)		◇								
Ocular control				◇						
Laterality and dominance not established										
Right-left orientation										
Sequencing of geometric forms				◇						
Figure-ground confusion				◇						
Immature speech patterns										
Low frustration threshold			◇							
Social perceptions				◇						
Body image reversals										
Hyperactivity			◇							
Rigidity			◇							
Emotional lability										
Verbal comprehension				◇						
Field dependency										
Anxiety (will test poorly)			◇							
Distractibility			◇							
Impulsivity			◇							
Reading		◇	◇							
Grammar		◇								

Perceptual motor match

Eye-hand coordination (symbols)

Perception of symbols in space

Recognition of symbols

Association of symbols

Short and long term memory for sequencing symbols

Auditory association

Spelling

Expressive language (written)

Sequencing of symbol-sounds

Auditory memory for symbol-sound association

Incidence of Peri-natal or early childhood trauma

Cannot cross mid-line

Perseveration

Conceptual disorganization under stress

Negative family history of language disorders

Some family history of EEG abnormalities

Establishment of laterality and dominance

Soft signs

Over-reaction to error

Body image confusion

Catastrophic reaction

Incidence of hard signs

Speech patterns

Laterality development

Sequencing of symbols

Explosive behavior

Perceptual constancy

Position in space

Short and long term memory for information

Eye-hand coordination for geometric forms

Auditory memory and association for words and sentences

Some professional evaluation of a child with a suspected learning disability is the optimum situation. However, some urban communities have decided that *full* evaluation has become a fiscal and personnel impossibility. The desire has been to discover and help *all* the children who are in need. The reality has been that there just simply is not enough personnel to handle adequately the necessary *clinical* evaluation procedures.

Therefore, the trend is for these communities to have the classroom teacher, rather than psychologists, use proscribed screening instruments. These screening instruments allow the teacher to evaluate a student's performance critically. This teacher evaluation is based primarily on the child's performance of given classroom behavioral task objectives.

The major differences between a clinical evaluation and classroom screening procedures are twofold: (1) evaluation gives ongoing guidelines for the most favorable development of the "whole" child protocol, and (2) evaluation obviously gives a more accurate prognosis for adulthood. There is no question that full evaluation offers a deep probing of any child's processing efficiencies/inefficiencies.

In many ways the recognition and evaluation of learning disabilities are some of the most complicated analyses of the possible handicaps that can afflict children. These evaluations require an evaluator to be sophisticated, judgmental, and sensitive.

For parents and teachers the really important aspect of testing is the resultant diagnosis and prescriptive profile. Of course, the parents, the examiner, and the involved medical personnel are interested in the etiology of the child's problems. But the parents and teachers, most especially teachers, are primarily interested in the deficit areas that the child displays. Etiology is the past. Deficits are the present and, as such, must be dealt with in the classroom and at home.

The results of an evaluation provide a protocol of the child in question. We discover his strengths, weaknesses, emotional stability, and the level of academic achievement he has managed to reach in spite of his dysfunction. With this knowledge can come a prescription for remediation; a *prescriptive profile* emerges from the long hours of work—help for the child because of *his specific* problems.

It is not possible to "cure" a learning disability. It is possible to offer full opportunity for achievement up to the child's potential.

Part Three

I plage allegins to the
flag of the Unut states
of amaca, and to the
Republick for wich it
stands one nation
under god undavisabul
and justist for all

4

Children who have learning disabilities need a number of "things" if they are to achieve. They need academic remediation. They need specific environmental standards and parameters. They need emotional support. And, often, they need adjunct pharmaceutical assistance. Further, they need all these factors in a systematic, programmed aggregate of effort.

The need to be able to read is a contemporary problem. As recently as fifty years ago people simply did not have to read with any great skill or sophistication to survive socially or financially. Since World War II the demands on, and for, education have escalated enormously. Science and technology introduced a whole new vocabulary, and at least a working knowledge of more sophisticated technical matters became a necessity for everyone. Curricula were accelerated and, to a large extent, education met the challenge. But we have paid a heavy price for our leap into the space age.

We talk in terms of millions of children having learning disabilities. This is accurate. However, these discussions imply that the incidence of these children is something new. This is inaccurate. They have always been here. But they did not always have to perform efficiently in a highly technological educational and cultural milieu.

To meet the academic needs of the nation as a whole, we tended to forget individual needs. Schools have become factories offering assembly-line education. For a child who does not fit the mold, who walks to a different drummer, who needs to be taught as an individual, assembly-line education means failure.

Children fail kindergarten, first or second grade because, though we know better now, we are still offering assembly-line education. We cannot seem to learn that we must teach the child, not the curriculum.

There are indications that changes are coming. More young people in college are taking specialized training in the field of learning disabilities. The youth of today seem to be able to identify with the child in trouble. Perhaps, this is because so many were disenchanted with their own education. Most certainly, it bodes well for the future.

■

Learning disabled children are not homogeneous. Regardless of any attempt to cluster the varying characteristics of learning disabilities, each child is different. Only three factors always touch each and every child:

They need evaluation and diagnosis.

They need prescriptive planning for their academic progress.

They need to be taught with specialized techniques: multisensory approach, small increments of data, association, repetition, a structured environment, all within the framework of individual cognitive styles. A clinical teacher is *always* aware of not just *what* a child learns but *how* a child learns.

A teacher is not interested in an etiological label. Educators must deal with the symptoms and dysfunctions as they appear in the classroom and how they affect the learning process. This must be the primary concern.

Techniques for teaching children who are learning disabled vary in their complexity, in the length of time necessary for remediation, and the projected prognosis for success. Just as learning disabilities present a continuum from mild to severe, so there is a continuum of teaching techniques. The more severe the individual child's problems, the more intense must be the application of teaching methods and programming for the child.

Most clinical methods follow logical, step-by-step progressions that help build associative and memory pathways within the child. As with evaluation, the earlier a child receives the special teaching attention he requires, the easier it is for teacher and child. The length of time necessary for such special teaching varies with the individual child and depends upon the type and degree of severity of his handicap. The techniques must be adapted to meet the specific nature of the *individual child's efficiencies and inefficiencies in functioning.*

To choose the right techniques for the right child, a teacher needs a prescriptive profile of the child. For the child who has even a minimal learning impairment, diagnostic planning becomes so vital as to be beyond description. One can readily understand the impact of a prescriptive profile on remediation when it is realized that the ability to interpret and reproduce symbols (alphabet), sequentially placed (words), in an information-producing order (sentences and paragraphs) is the most difficult acquired skill of mankind. This is the use of language. We must all be able to use the language if we are to communicate with our fellowmen. This use of language is often the reason why a learning disability is not recognized until a child enters the first grade. Until then, because he can talk and can react to our words (communicate), although language may still be immature, we do not realize that the child is impaired.

A six-year-old child who is going into the first grade is expected to perform at a certain level. If, however, he is only four years old neurologically, he cannot perform at the six-year-old level. His neurologically four-year-old brain and nervous system cannot process the visual, auditory, and haptic stimuli at a level that will allow him to achieve in the classroom.

What happens to the six-year-old first-grader if his auditory reception and/or his visual–motor age is only four? He is defeated before he starts. The simplest tasks requiring perception, easily learned by other children, are denied to him.

There are perceptual errors that can demonstrate what happens to the neurologically immature child when he goes from the concrete childhood experiences into the perceptually different experiences of the classroom.

The classic example of this is the b–d reversal and the p–q inversion. One of the first objects a child meets as an infant is a cup. A cup can be used as an analogy to the b–d–p–q classroom problem. Take an ordinary kitchen cup. Hold it in your hand as if to drink. Now, reverse the handle to the left; it is still a cup. Hold the cup upside down, handle first to the right, then to the left. Still a cup. In other words, the position in which the handle is placed doesn't matter—up, down, right, or left—the object is still a cup. Look again at the symbols b–d–p–q. All they really are is a circle with a straight line—geometric forms. The only difference between each is the position of the circle in relation to the line. But what a difference. The use and sound of the symbols are changed completely as we move the circle about to form b–d–p–q.

We expect children who have concrete knowledge of a cup, recognizable as such no matter what the direction of its handle, knowledge that they have known all of their lives, to enter a classroom and almost instantly be able to master a whole new concept that changing the position of the "handle" changes the identity of the unit. We have changed the rules of the game in the classroom, and changed them drastically, and we haven't informed the child that we have done so. Learning the new perceptual rules is a formidable task for a child *without* perceptual problems, impossible for a child *with* perceptual problems.

What else do we do to, or expect of, our first-graders perceptually? We not only expect them to master the language, but quantitative language skills as well. Mathematics is also a language, a difficult-to-master language. Here, again, is opportunity for failure. The new math is a complicated *conceptual* language as well as being quantitative. While old math was vertical and the basics usually memorized, a simple new math problem may consume a half page of written symbols and the reproduction of a series of horizontal sequences of symbols. With new math we further plague our students even when they enter junior high school. Traditional math is base 10, because we have 10 fingers. In junior high, the new math switches bases, to 7, for example. Easy enough perhaps for the student without impairment, but not for the child who has struggled for years just to master 10-based calculation.

■

At age 6, girls are usually earnest little things that strive to do their best work no matter how distracting their working environment may be. Few boys, with or without a learning problem, can match a 6-year-old girl's track record for neurological maturation. Male children are just naturally more responsive to distractions in their environment. Clutter attracts and distracts.

When considering the teaching of children with learning disabilities, the immediate classroom environment is of crucial importance. Because children with learning disorders are easily distracted, the area in which such children are taught must be free of unnecessary sound and of "things" on the walls and desks and even the teacher. The teacher should not have to *compete* for the child's attention. Noise, a smudge on his paper, pictures on the walls, a left-over lesson on the blackboard, teacher's bracelet that jingles, are all distractions. In a clinical school or tutorial room, these things are not permitted. Some educators argue that they enrich the environment, and to a degree this is true. There can and should be a happy medium between the totally nondistracting and the enriched environment. Whatever satisfactory middle ground is reached, everything must be kept orderly.

Noise also intrudes upon the learning process for children. In any classroom of 25 to 35 students more than enough noise is generated by just the children to make concentration difficult. Add to this traffic noise, noise from the class next door, the class upstairs, movements in the hallways, and the result can be an auditory bedlam for the handicapped child.

Seat placement is sometimes the small thing that, like the straw on the camel, breaks the child's learning back. Traditionally, teachers assign seats on the basis of physical size, alphabetically and/or by ability grouping. These practices may not be fair to the child who desperately needs to sit directly in front of the teacher at all times. For a child with impaired visual percepts, his position in relation to the blackboard is vital. It can be agony for a child who can barely use the alphabet to have to stretch constantly, overcome glare, and decipher chalk shadings from a distance. The child with an auditory perceptual impairment who is seated far from the teacher's desk will be even less able to discriminate the teacher's words or sort the nuances of these words.

Regardless of seating, there is the problem of instruction sorting—of hearing accurately the teacher's instructions. A teacher may be interrupted constantly, or interrupt herself, while giving the class instructions. "Now, class, take out your social studies book —Johnny, who gave you permission to sharpen your pencil?—turn to page one hundred—yes, Mary, you may be excused—page one hundred and three. Today, we will study about vol—Eugene, stop that racket!—volcanoes." This becomes a trial of fortitude, a true test of sorting ability for both the teacher and child. The teacher comes out on top, not the child.

If just four simple reforms—uncluttered classrooms, noise abatement, proper seat placement, and simplified instructions— were initiated in our classrooms, it would be a major step in the right direction for all children, not just learning disability children.

Assuming that the academic environment is under control, what then are these mysterious "clinical" teaching techniques? How are

they different than "regular" teaching? Why do they take longer?
What is so special about them? What is the "difference of degree"
and intensity? How does a teacher employ the fundamentals of
learning—reception (input), association (processing), and expression (output)—if a learning disability has disrupted these
learning chains?

Teachers use, either in tandem or in isolation, the four basic
channels or pathways of learning: V. A. K. T.—visual, auditory,
kinesthetic, tactile. The first two, visual and auditory are, of
course, the primary and classic classroom learning pathways.
Adding the haptic (kinesthetic–tactile) channel aids immeasurably
the learning process for disabled children. Haptic activity rein-
forces what the visual and aural channels are seeing and hearing.
For example, when a child uses his finger, a large primary crayon,
or chalk to trace a word, it helps him establish what his eye is
seeing—it is almost as if there is a physical "pull" that reaches
into the brain to help the child with the necessary cognitive
association.

A clinician cannot always use all four V. A. K. T. channels at
the same time. For some children it would be too overwhelming.
The teacher needs a prescriptive profile to know which learning
pathways to use and in what combinations for the individual child.

For most learning disability children, the use of V. A. K. T.,
singularly or together, is ineffective if the child cannot associate.

There are two forms of association: cognitive and mechanical.
We know that the former refers to automization, memory, and
processing.

The latter, mechanical, is a form of association that is often
overlooked as an aid to learning, even in some clinical schools,
and ignored in almost all workbooks on the market today. For
example, teaching a child the letter "a." A workbook will have a
line that looks like this:

| a | b | e | c | d | a | f | a |

The child is instructed to circle all of the "a's" in the line. *Circle the a!* Circling the "a" is not a learning activity. This is only telling the teacher that a child knows how to do a task. The circling or X'ing of a letter does not form an association for the child. If, however, a child *outlines* the "a's" in the row of letters, another dimension—an associative dimension—is added to the learning technique, and the workbook is not merely a task-testing instrument.

In addition, it is vital to use the *force* of association correctly. To circle or X a letter is to actually use other letters of the alphabet (other symbols), thus further confusing the whole issue for the child with impaired perceptions.

A clinical teaching technique that uses the mechanical to achieve cognitive association can be illustrated with a true classroom story. The story concerns a boy who, after painstaking work, finally learned to sound and blend the composite *parts* of the word "until" but as a *whole* the word remained meaningless to him. He could not "pull" the word from his memory when he tried to read it. Finally, he said to his teacher, "If I could just *see* an 'until,' I know I could remember it." The boy was searching for an associative clue and visual image as an aid to his memory for this slippery adverb. What was needed to complete the boy's mastery of the word was an associative teaching method, one that would utilize all learning channels (V. A. K. T.) plus association—V. A. *A.* K. T.

The boy was instructed to verbalize, *from within himself,* his idea of the word. What did "until" mean to him? For this youngster, "until the cows come home" was a vivid memory because he had once lived on a farm. This phrase then would be the basis for his "word picture." On a sturdy 9 × 12 sheet, the word "until" was precisely printed with a thick black crayon and with the paper backed by the rough side of his slate board to achieve a textured, Braille-like effect. The boy then carefully drew a picture—a few cows, a fence with a gate, the barn, with the cows going home— thus giving concrete visualization to his inner concept of the word "until." To complete his word picture, the mnemonic phrase "until the cows come home" was printed in the upper left corner of the page. Finally, the child traced the word with his fingertip a minimum of fifteen times, repeating the mnemonic phrase each time. He traced, he repeated, he looked at his own drawing, and learned "until" from his own associative clue. Gradually, he progressed from the complete word picture to smaller word cards, to a book. If he felt insecure as he progressed, he would pause to visualize his picture and use his mnemonic clue.

This achievement was not inconsequential for either teacher or child and was well worth the time invested in the single word. For many learning disabled children, the difficult-to-visualize words, usually the adverbs, remain stumbling blocks to reading comprehension for years. To achieve success a child must use all his major avenues of learning—plus association.

Once a child is able to read, he operates at three reading levels: independent (reads and comprehends easily), instructional (current classroom operating level), and frustration (child is still missing at least half of what is read). These levels are important, as a child should never be asked to function *outside* a classroom at anything but his independent level. Otherwise, the child is placed in a stressful situation. Parents should always be aware of their child's reading level.

An awareness of some of the symptoms that can indicate poor reading ability is important. In speaking, these include incorrect pronunciation of vowels or consonants, as rug for rag, fad for fat; perservation of words or sounds; lack of comprehension of what is being read; transposition of sounds—pat for tap. In reading, there may be complete omission of words or sentences; or, when going from one line to the next, an inability to recognize the same word when seen again; difficulty with "sound alike" words; reversals or inversions.

Some of these difficulties are fairly normal for any young child. If these problems still persist or show no sign of improving when the child has reached the last third of the first grade, or above, a long hard look at the child becomes necessary. Look then, not later. Do not wait for him to "grow up a little."

■

The question might logically be asked, "Why not wait a little longer?" The answer is in the following lists. A first-grader meets a staggering work load and if he does not successfully complete this work load efficiently by the end of the first grade he is already on his way to school failure. If you doubt this, read these lists carefully, always keeping in mind that the child who must accomplish this work needs competent visual and auditory percepts.

BASIC SKILLS A FIRST-GRADE CHILD MUST ACQUIRE FOR READING

THE ABILITY TO:

Recall a sequence of geometric forms
Detect likenesses and differences in abstract figures
Achieve perceptual constancy
Visually discriminate details in pictures
Perceive spatial relationships
Understand concept of directionality
Compare and contrast configuration of words
Recognize lower-case and capital letters
Complete pictures with missing details
Visually discriminate words of similar appearance
Sequence symbols
Understand differences in consonant blends
Recognize word patterns
Recognize digraphs and dipthongs
Understand common words as spoken
Reproduce pronounced three-syllable words
Perform rhythmic training drills
Recognize rhyming elements
Reproduce rhyming sounds
Recognize words to rhyme with pictures
Recognize and discriminate common sounds
Recognize and discriminate similar sounds
Give initial consonant sounds to pictures
Hear similarities in initial consonant sounds

Use common abbreviations such as Mr., Mrs.
Understand the concept of inflectional endings—s, ed, ing
Classify common objects
Understand the concepts of when, where, what, who
Tell time
Understand sequence of events
Anticipate holidays, etc.
Understand the concept of directing words—stop, go, etc.
Understand the concept of up, down, first, last, etc.
Interpret pictures
Follow a picture sequence
Draw conclusions
Interpret punctuation
Understand and use capital and small letters as an aid to learning
Use capital letters for names and beginning of sentences
Understand use of word "and" to connect two ideas
Understand weather concepts
Match color names to colors
Associate action with words, come, run, etc.
Understand difference between fact and fantasy
Understand meaning of first-grade vocabulary
Have a visualization of what is read
Follow one-step directions
Classify ideas
Understand sentence meaning
Have meaningful use of new words
Match first sounds of words
Hear first, last, and middle sounds in words
Hear vowel differences
Hear and reproduce all consonants
Hear and reproduce long vowels
Hear and reproduce short vowels
Hear and reproduce consonant blends
Use short and long vowel sounds
Use consonants in final position
Perform blending of vowels and final consonants
Perform blending of consonants in initial position
Use word patterns—vowel plus final consonant
Use silent final "e" rule
Use digraphs—sh, th, wh, ch, ng, ck
Use diphthongs—oo, o͝o, oi, oy, ou, ow, au, aw.
Use blends—mp, sp, pl, spl, nt, tr, bl, st,
              all "r" and "l"
Use final "y" and "y" as "i" and "e"
Use the two-vowel rule—oa

Add "s" to verb
Give word classifications—ight, etc.
Use vowels plus "r"—er, ir, ur, ar, or
Use ack, all, ay, oy endings
Use the three sounds of "ed" endings—ed, d, t
Use "all" and "old" words
Use rhyming phonograms
Understand the concept of singular and plural
Identify individual items included in a general term
Answer questions based on reading
Select a sentence to answer a question
Select a phrase to complete sentence
Follow two-step directions
Select quotations
Give antecedents of pronouns
Have awareness of sentence structure
Visualize the thought in a story
Answer inferential questions based on reading
Give appropriate abbreviations
Understand the concept of true and false
Understand opposite thoughts connected by "but"—compound sentence
Use context clue for meaning of new word
Understand and use compound words
Understand the concept of subject and predicate of sentence—"who" did
    something?; "what" did he do?
Understand the concept of use of possessives—mine, yours, etc.
Understand the concept of words that can be used as both noun and verb
Determine which sentence tells about some point in story—relevancy
Select title
Understand the concept of first, next, last
Comprehend what punctuation means to sentence structure—paragraph
    structure

INITIAL MATH SKILLS (5 to 7 years)

Mathematics initially involves subjective learning of basic math concepts, followed by their concrete application. There is a constant overlapping of the use of all learning channels—eye, ear, hand, motor (visual, auditory, haptic) plus association.

Readiness

Identify sets (0–5)
Tag and reproduce sets (0–5)
Match equivalent sets (10 and under)
Match one to one (equivalent sets) (10 and under)
Match nonequivalent sets (10 and under)

Identify shapes
Reproduce shapes

Concrete Identification of the Part-to-Whole Concepts

Introduction—number symbols 1–20
Natural order of numbers 1–20
Count 1–20 (orally)
Recognize numerals 1–20
Write numerals 1–20
Discover odd and even patterns
Solve oral problems using "one more"
Solve oral problems using "one less"
Follow directions in readiness vocabulary (few, less, more, most, fewest)
Identify ordinals—1st–5th
Identify penny, nickel, dime
Identify sets 6–10
Tag and reproduce sets 6–10
Recognize symbols "+" and "="
Reproduce symbols "+" and "=" (dictated)

Addition Skills and Reinforcement of Concepts, Level I

Add facts 0–5 horizontally and vertically
Introduction of partial counting 0–10
Introduction of zero (empty or null set)
Add 5–10 horizontally and vertically
Use terms "greater than" and "less than"
Solve oral addition problems 0–5
Count 10–20 orally
Recognize 10–20
Find missing addend 0–5 (horizontally and vertically)
Add one to numbers 0–5
Find missing addend 6–10 (horizontally and vertically)
Add 1 to numbers 6–9
Identify ordinals 6th–10th

Subtraction Skills and Reinforcement of Concepts, Level I

Introduction of subsets
Removal of a subset
Introduction of minus (−) sign or symbol
Subtract with numbers 0–5 (horizontally and vertically)
Subtract with numbers 6–10 (horizontally and vertically)
Subtract one from numbers 1–10
Subtract 2 from numbers 2–10
Find component parts of numbers 2–10
Subtract zero with remainder of zero

Subtract with doubles
Subtract with even and odd numbers
Compare money values, penny, nickel, dime
Add zero to numbers 1–10
Add like numbers (2, 3, 4, 5) (doubles)
Add 3 numbers in column form, 10 and under
Add 3 numbers horizontally (under 10)
Find the sum (addition) (10 and under)
Find the missing addend or component part (2–10)
Find remainder (subtraction) (0–10)
Find difference (subtraction) (0–10)

Beginning Abstracts: Reading, Writing, Grouping, Matching, Rote Memory

Introduction of symbols $<$ $>$
Use symbols to describe the order relations between pairs ($<$ $>$)
Match numeral to number word
Write number words to ten
Identify numbers 0–50
Recognize numbers 0–50
Write numbers 0–50
Add objects using tens and ones
Group and count objects by 10's—10–50
Group and count objects by 5's—5–50
Group and count objects by 2's—2–50
Count by 10's (orally)—10–50
Write numbers counting by 10's—10–50
Write numbers counting by 5's—5–50
Write numbers counting by 2's—2–50
Introduction of number lines 0–10
Match number line to addition number sentence 0–10
Add facts 11–19 (horizontally and vertically)
Find sum zero as an addend
Find missing addend 11–19 (horizontally and vertically)
Partial counting 11–19
Solve oral addition problems 11–19 (translate problem into number sentence)
Match number line to addition number sentence 11–19

Addition Skills and Reinforcement of Concepts, Level II

Add two-digit numbers—no carrying or regrouping
Match equation to number line 11–19
Match subtraction word problem to equation (11–19)
Identify numbers 51–100
Recognize numbers 51–100
Write numbers 51–100

Introduction of place value, 10's, 1's (0–50)
Rename 10's and 1's through 50
Write place value, 0–50
Identify even and odd numbers
Rename 1's to 10's
Add two-digit numbers, renaming in 10's place
Add by endings horizontally (renaming in 10's place)

Subtraction Skills and Reinforcement of Concepts, Level II

Subtract facts 11–19
Subtract zero (zero as subtrahend or addend)
Subtract one- and two-digit terms, no regrouping
Find missing terms in 1, 2, 3 digit subtraction problems, no regrouping
Subtract one- or two-digit equations, regrouping in minuend (sum) 10–19
Solve subtraction word problem to equation (with regrouping)
Write place value—1's and 10's—51–99

Daily Life Functions: Memory and Retrieval

Recognize and record ½ hours and o'clock
Reproduce time symbols—A.M., P.M.
Name days of week
Name months of the year
Introduction of money symbols—$, ¢
Addition of money with cents symbol to 10¢
Introduction of $ symbols—$1, $2, $3 (no addition)

Multiplication Readiness

Picture representation of multiplication sets
Multiplication as repeated addition (2 table to 10)
Introduction of multiplication symbol ($\times$)
Match picture to multiplication sentence
Introduction of multiplication expression containing 1
Introduction of 0 in multiplication
Introduction of multiplication expression containing 0
Write multiplication sentence to match picture
Write multiplication expressions 2 $\times$ 0, 1, 2, 3, 4, 5 (horizontally and vertically)

It has been stated repeatedly that children with learning disabilities must be taught on the basis of their prescriptive profile. The following information taken from a teacher's manual* offers guidelines for the intelligent use of a prescriptive profile. It was developed under a Federal grant by a project staff consisting of Eleanor Levine and Genevieve McG. Donlon, specialists in learning disabilities, Dr. Carol Fineman, a psychologist specializing in learning disabilities, and Dorothy Ozburn, Dade County Assistant Director for Exceptional Child Education, assisted by a number of eminent consultants.†

The manual entitled Prescriptive Profile Procedures for Children with Learning Disabilities (PPP) states, "As a teacher of children with learning disabilities your overall objective is to provide an educational program which will be individualized to meet the specific needs of each child. To meet this objective you must have adequate information about the Pupil: his strengths, weaknesses, educational background, motivations, behavior, etc. You also must have sufficient educational programs and tools to provide the appropriate learning Process for each child. The third requirement is you, the Prescriber, and your ability to match Pupil with Process and to provide the behavioral setting in which learning can take place." In other words, the teacher should review prescriptions for teaching and integrate them into an individualized prescriptive plan encompassing prerequisite skills, basic school subjects, and behavioral factors.

* ESEA Title VI-B Grant (No. P.L.91230). Public schools may contact ERIC; parents may contact State Department of Exceptional Child Education, Tallahassee, Florida.
† Dr. Howard Adelman and Jeane Fryer (topic: personalized instruction—interactional model); Dr. Warren Heiss (topic: reading disabilities); Pearl Hornstein, math specialist (topic: language of math); Anna Jackson, specialist, intellectual disabilities (topic: document review and preparation); Dr. Nicholas Long, Hillcrest Children's Center (topic: psychodynamic intervention techniques); Dr. Phillip Mann (topic: programming in the classroom, prescription writing); Frances K. McGlannan and the McGlannan School Staff (topic: methods and materials for remediation); Dr. Gerald Minskoff (topic: language disabilities); Robert Taddonio, exceptional child psychologist (topic: cross analysis of tests, Detroit Tests of Learning Aptitude).

tive

Prescriptive
Profile
Procedure

Involves

Pupil	Prerequisite Skills	Basic School Subject Proficiency	Behavioral Factors
Process	Psycho-educational Diagnosis	Structured Program	Motivating Forces
Prescriber	Individualized Prescriptions	Curriculum Prescriptions	Individual and Classroom Management Prescriptions

'PPP' COMMUNICATION MODEL

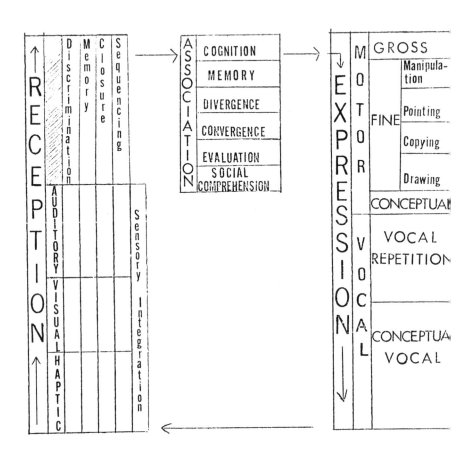

The conceptual framework for the prerequisite skills profile is the PPP Communication Model. This model was adapted from Dr. Samuel Kirk's Clinical Communication Model and is, essentially, an elaboration of the receptive (input), associative, and expressive (output) processes. Test scores relevant to each process and level are plotted according to a point system on the prerequisite skill worksheets. The student's basic receptive, associative, and expressive integrities are then profiled on the summary sheet. The teacher is also provided with information as to subtest task demands for in-depth prescription and correlation with task demands in the basic school subjects.

Prerequisite skills interpretation and prescription are based on interpreting triad* discrepancies. The manual states, "There is a significant discrepancy in a triad whenever there is a gap of *two or more* rating points between one subtest and the other two. The one subtest may be two or more points above or below the others."

"Triad discrepancies occur when the low subtest (subtests) requires task demands that are not required by the other tests and that are not adequately developed. In most situations, the teacher will find the discrepancies are due to one or two skill areas that show up as low points on the summary sheet. When this occurs, the teacher is not only more secure in pinpointing these low areas but also in pinpointing the child's strengths."

"In order to evaluate triad discrepancies, the areas containing them and the high and low subtests are diagrammed. This makes it easy to note the communality among the variant tests."

---

*The PPP *triad* refers to the three subtests that are grouped under the specific receptive, associative, and expressive cognitive processes.

Evaluation 10

RECEPTION

GLORIA GUPPY

Visual

Discrimination	Simp. Score	3	2	1	0	
Picture Comp. (WISC)						
Visual Recep. (ITPA)						
Picture Arr. (WISC)						Comp. Rat.
Totals						9

Memory	Simp. Score	3	2	1	0	
VASO (Detroit)						
Mem. for Des. (Detroit)						
Coding (WISC)						Comp. Rat.
Totals						9

Closure	Simp. Score	3	2	1	0	
Vis. Closure (ITPA)						
Block Design (WISC)						
Object Assem. (WISC)						Comp. Rat.
Totals						9

Sequencing	Simp. Score	3	2	1	0	
Vis. Seq. Mem. (ITPA)						
V A S L (Detroit)						
Picture Arr. (WISC)						Comp. Rat.
Totals						9

Auditory

Discrimination	Simp. Score	3	2	1	0	
Aud. Recep. (ITPA)						
Sound Blend (ITPA)						
Information (WISC)						Comp. Rat.
Totals						

Memory	Simp. Score	3	2	1	0	
Digit Span (WISC)						
A A S U W (Detroit)						
Arithmetic (WISC)						Comp. Rat.
Totals						

Closure	Simp. Score	3	2	1	0	
Aud. Closure (ITPA)						
Gram. Clos. (ITPA)						
Aud. Assoc. (ITPA)						Comp. Rat.
Totals						

Sequencing	Simp. Score	3	2	1	0	
Oral Direct (Detroit)						
A A S R S (Detroit)						
Aud. Seq. Mem. (ITPA)						Comp. Rat.
Totals						9

Haptic

Tactile	Simp. Score	3	2	1	0	
Verbal Exp. (ITPA)						
Sequin A						
Sequin B						Comp. Rat.
Totals						9

Kinesthetic	Simp. Score	3	2	1	0	
Motor Sp. (Detroit)						
Oral Comm. (Detroit)						
Orient. (Detroit)						Comp. Rat.
Totals						9

SENSORY INTEGRATION

	Simp. Score	3	2	1	0	
Pic. Arr. (WISC)						
Oral Dir. (Detroit)						
Gram. Clos. (ITPA)						Comp. Rat.
Totals						9

Reception (input) is that cognitive process that offers recognition and/or understanding of what is taken in through the senses. The major sensory channels are: auditory—sense of hearing, visual—sense of sight, and haptic, which includes the sense of movement (kinesthetic) and the sense of touch (tactile).

Visual and Auditory Discrimination reception is the ability to indicate whether two stimuli (auditory, visual, haptic) are the same or different.

Visual and Auditory Memory reception is the ability to recall within seconds stimuli presented auditorially, visually, or haptically.

Visual and Auditory Closure reception is the ability to identify stimuli (auditory, visual, haptic) from incomplete or distorted information.

Visual and Auditory Sequencing reception is the ability to reproduce and/or recognize stimuli presented sequentially.

Tactile reception is the ability to recognize and/or understand what is received through sense of touch.

Kinesthetic reception is the ability to recognize and/or understand what is received through sense of movement.

Sensory Integration reception is the ability to process multiple stimuli that are being transmitted through different modalities.

ASSOCIATION

COGNITION	Simple Score	3	2	1	0	
Vocabulary (WISC)						
Visual Assoc. (ITPA)						
Object Assem. (WISC)						Comp. Rat.
Totals	//////					/9

MEMORY	Simple Score	3	2	1	0	
Information (WISC)						
Arithmetic (WISC)						
Coding (WISC)						Comp. Rat.
Totals	//////					/9

DIVERGENCE	Simple Score	3	2	1	0	
Verbal Ex. (ITPA)						
Picture Construction (Torrance)						
Aud. Assoc. (ITPA)						Comp. Rat.
Totals	//////					/9

CONVERGENCE	Simple Score	3	2	1	0	
Similarities (WISC)						
Visual Asso. (ITPA)						
Block Design (WISC)						Comp. Rat.
Totals	//////					/9

EVALUATION	Simple Score	3	2	1	0	
Pic. Arrang. (WISC)						
Verbal Exp. (ITPA)						
Block Design (WISC)						Comp. Rat.
Totals	//////					/9

SOCIAL COMP.	Simple Score	3	2	1	0	
Comprehension (WISC)						
Social Adj. A (Detroit)						
Pic. Absurd (Detroit)						Comp. Rat.
Totals	//////					/9

Association is that cognitive process that offers deduction of relationships from what is, or has been, heard, seen, or felt.

Associative *Cognition* is awareness: the immediate discovery, rediscovery, or recognition of information in various forms. Comprehension or understanding.

Associative *Memory* is the retention or storage, with some degree of availability, of information in the same form in which it was admitted to storage and in connection with the same cues with which it was learned. (Often referred to as associative memory.)

Associative *Divergence* is the generation of information where the emphasis is upon variety and quantity of input from the same source. It leads away from the specific to a creative form of production.

Associative *Convergence* is those skills that emphasize the accurate assimilation of facts, ideas, relationships, contrasts, or similarities. Drawing necessary conclusions.

Associative *Evaluation* is the process of comparing a product of information with known and logical criteria, reaching a decision concerning criterion satisfaction.

Associative *Social Comprehension* is the utilization of practical judgment and common sense based on experiential background.

EXPRESSION

Motor

GROSS MOTOR	Simple Score	3	2	1	0		COPYING	Simp. Score	3	2	1	0	
Oral Comm. (Detroit)							Coding (WISC)						
Manual Express (ITPA)							"PPP" Copying Test						
Orientation (Detroit)						Comp. Rat.	Memory for Design (Detroit)						Comp Rat.
Totals	/////					9	Totals	/////					9

MANIPULATION	Simple Score	3	2	1	0		DRAWING	Simple Score	3	2	1	0	
Block Design (WISC)							Motor Speed (Detroit)						
Object Assem. (WISC)							Picture Construc. (Torrance)						
Visual Seq. Mem. (ITPA)						Comp. Rat.	Oral Directions (Detroit)						Comp Rat.
Totals	/////					9	Totals	/////					9

POINTING	Simp. Score	3	2	1	0		CONCEPTUAL MOTOR	Simple Score	3	2	1	0	
Visual Recep. (ITPA)							Manual Express (ITPA)						
Visual Clos. (ITPA)							Oral Directions (Detroit)						
Visual Assoc. (ITPA)						Comp. Rat.	Oral Comm. (Detroit)						Comp. Rat.
Totals	/////					9	Totals	/////					9

Vocal

VOCAL REPETITION	Simple Score	3	2	1	0		CONCEPTUAL VOCAL	Simple Score	3	2	1	0	
AASRS (Detroit)							Comprehension (WISC)						
Sound Blending (ITPA)							Vocabulary (WISC)						
Auditory Clos. (ITPA)						Comp. Rat.	Verbal Express (ITPA)						Comp. Rat.
Totals	/////					9	Totals	/////					9

Expression (output) is that cognitive process that offers the use of skills necessary to express ideas verbally (vocal) or by gesture or movement (motor).

Gross Motor expression is the skill involving natural movements, balance, and rhythm.

Manipulation expression is the ability to work with the hands to move, adjust, or place objects.

Pointing expression is the simple skill to indicate a choice by touching or gesturing.

Copying expression is the ability to utilize a writing instrument in reproducing visual stimuli.

Drawing expression is the ability to utilize a writing instrument in creating a visual pattern without a sample to be copied. Encompasses both lines and pictures.

Conceptual Motor expression is the ability to express ideas motorically (with movement).

Vocal Repetition expression is the ability to mimic, pronounce, blend, and articulate.

Conceptual Vocal expression is the ability to express ideas vocally. Includes labeling, describing, defining.

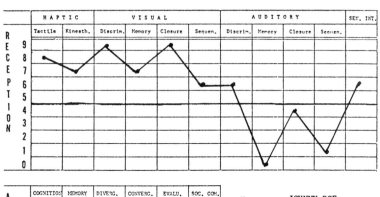

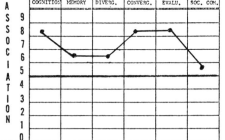

Name _____ JOHNNY DOE _____

B.D. _9/16/64_ Sex _M_

Date _____ Sept. 1972 _____

Teacher **Miss M. Poppins**

School _____

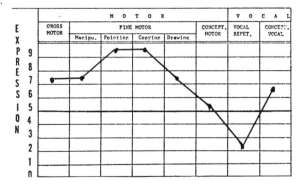

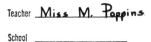

PPP

Prerequisite Skills
Summary Sheet

Writing

Writing, a highly complex process, is a visual symbol system for ex-
pressing thoughts, feelings, and ideas which represents experience.
Disorders of written language may be due to perceptual and/or cognitive
deficits. The learner requires the visual and auditory stimulus processing
ability necessary for spoken and written language. He must have developed
the visual-motor integration necessary for forming and structuring letters.
Finally, the learner must have acquired the cognitive functions needed to
select and organize his thoughts into meaningful sentences.

There are so many causative factors which might interfere with writing,
that this area presents a major problem in assessment. Comprehensive
knowledge of the child's basic pre-requisite integrities, in the language
communication model of the PPP, combined with his functioning in Reading
is of paramount importance in ascertaining factors contributing to this
disorder. A systematic examination of all these factors must be made by
either formal or informal means.

Diagnosing Writing Difficulties

The Durrell Analyses of Reading Difficulty (Handwriting Subtest) was
selected as a means of diagnosing handwriting ability since it was already
being used as the diagnostic reading instrument. In this subtest, the
words are written from memory and letters are copied at a Grade I level.
At the Grade II level, a paragraph is copied and timed. Norms and a check
list of difficulties in handwriting are provided. The teacher is to
determine the speed of writing, letter formation, position of hand, pencil,
paper and body, and the height, spacing and slant of the letter. She is
also to note the hand being used for writing. See Johnny's Durrell
Handwriting Test, page 106 .

PPP Writing Test was developed to enable teachers to pinpoint the level
of writing functioning a child has attained based solely on his near-point
copying ability. The test progresses developmentally from shapes, to partial
letters, to lower and upper manuscript letters, to lower and upper cursive
letters, to single and multiple numerals, to single two-letter words up to
single six-letter words (manuscript then cursive) to a manuscript sentence
and finally, a cursive sentence.

(1) Administration. This test can be administered individually or to
an entire class. The child and/or teacher are to fill in the information
at the top of the test. The child is then directed to place his finger
on Row 1, the first row of figures to be copied. He is instructed to
copy the figures into the empty space provided beneath the figures exactly
as he sees them. Teacher says pointing: "This one here, this one here,"
and so on to the end of the row. The same procedure is used for Row II,
III, IV, V and VI. There is no time limit for this test.

Johnny Doe

Durrell Analysis of Reading Difficulty

Visual Memory of Words, Spelling, and Handwriting

INSTRUCTIONS. For these tests ask the child to write certain words according to the directions in the Manual.

Visual Memory of Words — Intermediate	*Phonic Spelling of Words*	*Spelling Test*
1. _____	1. _____	✓1. run
2. _____	2. _____	2. wuk
3. _____	3. _____	3. bak
4. _____	4. _____	✓4. look
5. _____	5. _____	5. col
6. _____	6. _____	6. ar
7. _____	7. _____	7. dan
8. _____	8. _____	8. her
9. _____	9. _____	9. tim
10. _____	10. _____	10. nid
11. _____	11. _____	11. pap
12. _____	12. _____	12. bok
13. _____	13. _____	13. tern
14. _____	14. _____	14. m
15. _____	15. _____	15. mrk
SCORE _____ GRADE _____	SCORE _____ GRADE _____	16. p _
		17. _
		18. _

Norms for Visual Memory and Phonic Spelling of Words

GRADE	VISUAL MEMORY	PHONIC SPELLING
4	5	7
5	7	9
6	9	11

Norms for Spelling Test

GRADE	LIST 1	2
2	8	—
3	12	6
4	16	9
5	—	12
6	—	15

19. _
20. _

SCORE **2**   GRADE *low first*

CHECK LIST OF DIFFICULTIES

VISUAL MEMORY
____ Omits letters; syllables
____ Adds letters; syllables
____ Marked insecurity

PHONIC SPELLING
____ Omits sounds; syllables
____ Adds sounds; syllables
____ Incorrect sounds used
____ Marked insecurity

CHECK LIST OF DIFFICULTIES IN SPELLING

____ Omits sounds; syllables
____ Adds sounds; syllables
____ Incorrect sounds
____ Slow handwriting

Norms for Handwriting

GRADE	2	3	4	5	6
LETTERS PER MINUTE	25	35	45	55	65

CHECK LIST OF DIFFICULTIES IN HANDWRITING

____ Speed too slow
____ Poor letter formation
____ Poor position: hand, pencil, paper, body
____ Irregular: height, spacing, slant

HAND USED   ✓ Right   ____ Left

Young children who have not been taught cursive writing are still required to complete the cursive portions of the test to the best of their ability. This serves the teacher as an indication of the child's readiness to begin cursive instruction.

(2) <u>Scoring</u>. In order to establish appropriate cut-off points, the PPP Writing Test was standardized on one hundred and fifty elementary school children, ages 6-12, including 45 children with specific learning disabilities. It should be kept in mind that this instrument is intended as a sample of the child's best writing performance rather than of his typical production. The child's age <u>must</u> be taken into account in scoring due to the development of eye-hand coordination as the child matures. Above the age of 9, the child is expected to be able to adhere to the exactness of the sample figure.

One point is credited for each figure or group of figures in a given square that is an adequate replica of the sample, taking the child's age into consideration. Five points is given for a correct replication of a total sentence. One point is taken off for each inaccurate letter up to five errors, in a complete sentence.

A total of ten points may be earned for each Section, I-VI. A total score of 60 points is the maximum that can be earned. Fifty points or above is considered adequate performance. Rather than the score itself, the most important information for the teacher is the specifics of the child's writing production which can help her decide on the appropriate writing instruction for the child.

Johnny Doe's Writing Data

Looking at Johnny's Durrell Handwriting test, page 106, Miss Poppins noticed that his preferred style of writing was manuscript. The letters were well formed and spaced. He used his right hand at a speed considered normal for his grade level. Since Johnny was only eight years old, he was not required to have exact replicas.

In order to derive more information about Johnny's developmental level of writing, Miss Poppins administered the "PPP" Writing Test, page 108. Johnny's score of 57 indicated adequate performance on near point writing tasks.

Profiling on the PPP Writing Check List. Since formal standardized tests do not assess all possible factors contributing to disorders in writing, the teacher should evaluate performance on specific tasks and note them on the check list. An example of the PPP Writing Check List follows, page 111. Profiling writing skills in this manner will delineate the child's strengths and weaknesses in this area.

"PPP" WRITING TEST

Name _Johnny Jake_ Date _9/15/72_ Age _8_ Total Score _57_

I. Score _9_

△	○	□	◇	⊬→		∠	⊃	⋀	∨	⊢
△	O	□	◇	⊬		⊢	7	⋀	∨	⊙

II. Score _10_

P	S	f	a	h		D	F	J	W	G
P	S	f	a	h		D	F	J	W	G

III. Score _10_

ℓ	f	g	m	p		W	D	E	n	K
ℓ	f	g	m	p		W	D	E	n	K

IV. Score _9_

9	6	5	3	7		24	38	74	506	936
9	6	5	3	7		24	38	74	506	936

V. Score _10_

at	dog	stop	chirp	animal
at	dog	stop	chirp	animal

go	tub	came	parts	become
go	tub	came	parts	becom

VI. Score _9_

Spot was a black and white dog.
Spot was a black and white dog.

Tim saw the big brown horse.
Tim saw the big brown horse.

A Diagnostic Handwriting Chart is also useful for further diagnosis. The Pressey Chart for Diagnosis of Illegibilities in Handwriting published by the Charles E. Merrill Company was drawn up as the result of research which revealed the characteristic types of illegibilities and malformations made by pupils in their writing. Some of the errors listed on the chart are as follows:

Words broken	a like o	c like e
Too angular	a like ci	c like i
Words crowded	b like bi	c like a
Letters crowded	b like k	d like I
a like u	b like f	d like a
e closed	n like u	s like o
e too high	n like v	t like l
e like c	n like s	t cross above
f like b	o like a	t no cross
of like oj	o like r	t cross right
g like y	o closed	t cross left
h like li	o like u	u like oi
h like p	r like i	ur like w
h like b	r like s	v like n
h like l	r too small	v like r
i like e	r half n	w like u
i - no dot	' r like u	w like ur
k like h	r like e	D not closed
l closed	s indistinct	I like cl
l too short	s like r	T like F
m like w	s like i	w like m

Johnny Doe's Profile

Miss Poppins filled out Johnny's "PPP" Writing Checklist, page 111. She then had before her a profile of his strengths and weaknesses in that area. It clearly showed that the only discrepancies in writing skills were those that depended on the reading task. As his skill in reading progresses these writing tasks would improve automatically.

Since Johnny was able to copy a sentence in cursive, Miss Poppins realized that Johnny just needed practice enough to make cursive writing automatic. She decided to make use of his high abilities in the expressive fine-motor areas when remediating his low auditory memory and auditory sequencing.

Prescriptive Planning for Writing

As stipulated previously, the teacher must be aware of the task demands. The general task demands of writing are:

1. Desire to communicate

2. Decide on writing as the method of communication

3. Decide the general content of the message

4. Determine the sequence of the message content

5. Recall the necessary auditory-language symbols

6. Recall the graphic-language symbols for the auditory-language symbols

7. Focus visual attention

8. Recall the necessary sequence of the graphic-motor acts

9. Have adequate eye-hand coordination

10. Have necessary pencil skills.

11. Make motor (writing) response.

In order to determine the point of breakdown in the writing process, a specific developmental hierarchy of writing tasks must also be identified. An example follows:

1. Manipulation of writing instrument

2. Random scribbling

3. Imitation of strokes

"PPP" WRITING CHECKLIST

Name **Johnny Doe**   Date _____

Grade **2**   Age **8**   Teacher **M. Poppins**

	A	B	C	D	E	F	G	H	I	J	K	L	M	N	O	P	Q	R	S	T	U	V	W	X	Y	Z
Man. U.C.																										
Man. L.C.																										
Cur. U.C.											✓															
Cur. L.C.																✓		✓				✓				

	Poor	Minimal	Satisfactory	Very Good
1. Copying geometric figures				✓
2. Copying letters manuscript				✓
3. Copying letters cursive				✓
4. Copying numerals				✓
5. Copying words manuscript				✓
6. Copying words cursive				✓
7. Copying sentences manuscript				✓
8. Copying sentences cursive				✓
9. Copying - near point				✓
10. Copying - far point				✓
11. Gross motor coordination				✓
12. Fine motor coordination				✓
13. Tracing				✓
14. Left-right			✓	
15. Directionality			✓	
16. Laterality			✓	
17. Basic language ability			✓	
18. Reading ability	✓			
19. Oral comprehension	✓			
20. Spelling	✓			
21. Completion task			✓	
22. Creative writing	✓			
23. Speed of writing			✓	
24. Legibility				✓
25. Neatness				✓

111

4. Initiation of strokes

5. Tracing of letters

6. Copying of letters

7. Completion tasks employing recall

8. Writing from dictation

9. Creative writing

In writing, as in all other areas of the curriculum, the teacher must analyze the relationship between task demands, in terms of what is required of the child, and learner innate integrities, in terms of basic pre-requisite strengths and deficits. Then based on these relationships, prescribe a program relevant to individual needs.

The remediation program might include training in revisualization, reauditorization, symbol-sound association and/or letter formation.

When the cause of a writing disorder is a language dysfunction, the teacher must remediate the language areas, not the formation of letters. If the problem is the inability to relate spoken language, then remediation must be in terms of developing skills in reading. A writing disorder, which is caused by a dysfunction of the motor components of writing, must be remediated by training in the production of well-formed letters and improvement in the quality and speed of handwriting.

Therefore, after a thorough differential diagnosis, the teacher must design remedial procedures which correspond with each child's individual needs.

Writing Disorders

There are three diverse problem areas in writing disorders of concern to teachers. An awareness of each of these areas is necessary for adequate diagnosis and remediation.

A Dysfunction of the Language System. Auditory-vocal language ability precedes reading. Facility with reading precedes writing. If a child has difficulty comprehending oral or read language, he will probably have a writing disorder. He may not be able to encode his thoughts in written symbols but may adequately perform by tracing or copying. Those with oral deficits tend to write the way they speak, without correct grammatical structure.

A Dysfunction of the Auditory or Visual Perceptual System. Severe auditory discrimination problems will be reflected in writing errors, as words will be misspelled and syllables omitted. Severe visual perception problems will affect writing because of discrimination, sequencing and memory problems.

A Dysfunction of the Motor Components of Writing. A disorder resulting from a disturbance in visual-motor integration will be reflected in an inability to associate mental images with the motor system for writing.

Writing Methods

Look-Trace-Copy Method or Visual to Motor Method. This method, or a modification thereof, is employed by all the basic handwriting series of books being used in elementary schools. The instructional sequence follows this general order:

1. Introduction of strokes used in the formation of letters

2. Training in correct posture while writing

3. Placement of paper in relation to the hand

4. Copying the alphabet

5. Letter size - large in the first grade and gradually reduced throughout the elementary grades

6. Manuscript to cursive

7. Practice and review throughout

Visual to Auditory to Visual-Motor Method. Approaches to this method is in this order:

1. A clear visual pattern is presented

2. A detailed auditory vocal description of the movement is given

3. The teacher performs the action as the child watches

4. The child imitates the action

Kinesthetic to Visual-Motor Method. The sequence of this method is in the following order:

1. Child closes eyes (Elimination of the visual aspect).

2. The teacher guides the child's fingers and hands until the tactile-kinesthetic experience established a muscular memory of the movements necessary to writing.

3. Child opens eyes and watches movement of his hand.

Kinesthetic to Auditory to Visual-motor Method: This method procedes in this manner:

1. Child closes eyes

2. The teacher guides the child's fingers and hand in the desired movements pattern until the tactile-kinesthetic experience establish a muscular memory of the movements necessary to writing.

3. The teacher verbalizes the movement pattern as the child, with his eyes closed, performs under guidance.

4. Child opens eyes and watches the movement of his hand.

Johnny Doe's Writing Prescription

Miss Poppins established Johnny's writing abilities as being quite adequat for his age and grade level. Using his high visual areas, she decided to strengthen his cursive writing by introducing new letters employing the Look-Trace-Copy Method.

Spelling

Spelling is an important part of the total language arts program consisting of listening, speaking, reading, writing and spelling. Ability
to perform in other aspects of the language arts may not be an indicator
of adequate abilities in written spelling, since spelling requires the
translation of speech sounds into their visual symbol equivalent.

The vast majority of poor readers are seriously deficient in spelling
since it requires simultaneous ability to revisualize and to reauditorize
letters. That is, a "speller" requires perfect recall where a "reader"
is given a stimulus word for recognition.

Acceptable spelling requires accurate integration of visual, auditory,
and kinesthetic abilities.

Diagnosing Spelling Difficulties

Levels are determined and formal information about the spelling ability
of children are ascertained by use of either individual or group formal
spelling tests.

Diagnosing with the Durrell Analysis of Reading Difficulty. The Durrell
contains a spelling test consisting of two lists of twenty words each.
List 1 is for grades 2 and 3. List 2 is for Grade 4 and above. The spelling
test yields a grade equivalent. A check list of spelling difficulties is
included.

Profiling on the PPP Spelling Error Analysis Chart.   Teachers
can learn a great deal about spelling difficulties by careful use of standardized achievement tests and nonstandardized instruments.

An analysis of errors should be made by asking these questions;

1. Does the child learn any part of the word to the exclusion of other
   parts? Beginning letters versus ending sounds?

2. Can the child fuse the sound parts of words together into whole words?

3. Does the child reverse letters?

4. Can the child remember board work a few minutes after it is erased?

5. Does the child learn words when he hears the sequence rather than sees
   it?

6. Does the child omit sounds?

7. Can the child write the correct symbol for single sounds when they
   are dictated to him orally?

8. Can the child identify sounds?

PPP Spelling Error Analysis Chart

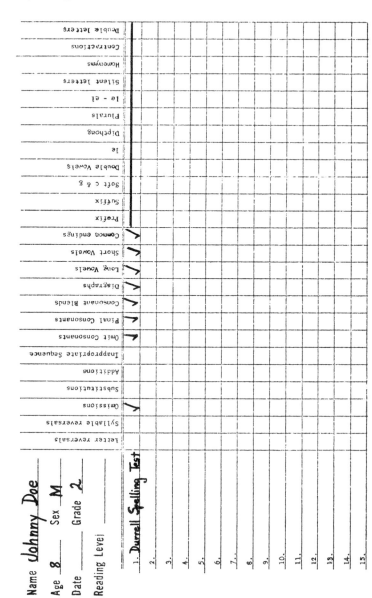

Name **Johnny Doe**
Age **8** Sex **M**
Date Grade **2**
Reading Level

Columns: Double letters · Contractions · Homonyms · Silent letters · ie - ei · Plurals · Dipthong · ie · Double Vowels · Soft c & g · Suffix · Prefix · Common endings · Short Vowels · Long Vowels · Diagraphs · Consonant Blends · Final Consonants · Omit Consonants · Inappropriate Sequence · Additions · Substitutions · Omissions · Syllable reversals · Letter reversals

1. Durrell Spelling Test
2.
3.
4.
5.
6.
7.
8.
9.
10.
11.
12.
13.
14.
15.

An analysis of how a child spells rather than at what level, enables the examiner to make a diagnosis and give a prognostic evaluation and guidelines for remedial teaching. First, an assessment of a typical spelling pattern should be made. The child is asked to write (or spell orally) eight or more words from his known or sight vocabulary. Then he must spell the same number of words from an "unknown" vocabulary. Analysis of the known words spelled reveals the child's ability to revisualize, while analysis of the unknown words spelled reveals his ability to spell phonetically or reauditorize.

In any given spelling test, the teacher is to note the quantity and types of errors each child displays on the "PPP" Spelling Error Analysis Chart, page 116.   Adequate performance is left blank.

Johnny Doe's Spelling Data and Profile

Miss Poppins gave Johnny the Durrell Level I Spelling Test since he was a second grader. The twenty words were a combination of words from his known and unknown vocabulary and would be used as a diagnosis of Johnny's phonetic ability.

Johnny spelled only two words absolutely correct out of the total list, page 106,   which showed he was functioning at a low first grade level in spelling.

Miss Poppins then made a check by the types of errors Johnny displayed on the PPP Spelling Error Analysis Chart, page 116 . She drew a line through the errors not covered in this test which came higher on the developmental sequence of spelling skills. Blank spaces on the chart indicated adequate performance.

Prescriptive Planning for Spelling

One must keep in mind that some children may not perceive and retain the memory of words as configurations, the sound in the correct relationship to make up the auditory gestalt of the word, or the sequential movement pattern of letters. Sounds are usually not associated with symbols.

Since spelling is an area in which clues to learning disorders may be found, the skills which a child must possess in order to succeed in spelling must be delineated. An example of an analysis of a spelling task follows:

Instructional Objective: Given an unknown word unit, the child must write the word in ten seconds.

1. Focus auditory attention
2. Hear and discriminate letter sounds
3. Note sequential order
4. Associate sounds with letter forms
5. Recall the exceptions to rules for sounds
6. Recall the correct letter formation and letter connections
7. Recall the exact letter sequence in association with its correct sound and feel
8. Make a motoric (writing) response

Errors in spelling are indicators or clues to learning disorders in reception, association or expression. Following are examples of difficulties relating to each area of the PPP.

Receptive Difficulties

Visual Perception Difficulties

a. Inability to distinguish between lines and spaces
b. Difficulty recognizing or reproducing letters and words
c. Trouble focusing on chalkboard
d. Difficulty reproducing from chalkboard to paper

Auditory Perception Difficulties

a. Does not hear the sound
b. Inability to reproduce a sound once heard
c. Unable to distinguish between tones

Body Movement Problems

a. Cannot walk or skip with both sides of body
b. Reversals of arm movement
c. Reversals of imitative and interpretive movements
d. Directionality problems
e. Difficulty in inhibiting movements

Associative Difficulties

Memory Impairment

a. Words out of sequence
b. Parts of words out of sequence
c. Words, letters, values and symbols all mixed up
d. Difficulty following more than one direction
e. Unable to put together what he sees and hears simultaneously
f. Cannot coordinate body response with visual and auditory stimuli

Expressive Difficulties

Vocal

    a. Difficulty saying words
    b. Difficulty spelling letters in words

Motor

    a. Difficulty writing words
    b. Difficulty writing letters

Spelling Methods

Each child must be helped to learn in his own unique way, utilizing the sensory modalities through which that child learns most effectively. Versatile approaches must be used to develop and reinforce the underlying perceptual and academic skills necessary for competent spelling.

Visual. The child with strong visual development, as assessed on the PPP summary sheet, will probably learn to spell with greater ease by using the visual approach or look-and-spell method.

The child says the letters as he looks at them. Color cues are used to teach the difference between lines and spaces and to make important foreground figures stand out against the background.

Auditory. This approach to spelling is the auditory or hear-and-spell method. The teacher says the word, spells it orally and says the word again. The child repeats in the same order. The use of steady rhythmic patterns and spelling by syllables is begun early. The length of sequences grows as the child masters the ability. A tape recorder is very beneficial for recording individual word lists.

Kinesthetic. The kinesthetic technique of tracing and copying letters, or "finger-writing in the air" is used in combination with the other methods for teaching words in most spelling programs. This enables the child to firmly establish the language pattern in a properly formed, properly oriented, and sequential manner.

Integrative. This teaching technique includes the multisensory approach such as Grace Fernald developed to help children study words as whole words and in syllables. The child is asked to see, hear and feel as the teacher relates each new concept. Consequently, the child's stronger modality is used to bridge the gap of the weaker, while learning is increased by constantly reinforcing, expanding, and relating previous experiences.

Johnny Doe's Spelling Prescription

Johnny is a child who has a limited sight vocabulary, reads by whole-word Gestalts, and is unable to identify the component letters of the word. He lacks phonetic concepts, has few word-attack skills and is unable to sound out or blend the letters or the syllables of a word. The only words he can spell correctly are those in his sight vocabulary that he can visualize, since he does not have the ability to reauditorize. Miss Poppins made an assessment of Johnny's pre-requisite skills area of the PPP. It showed him to be high in the visual area and deficient in the auditory area. An analysis of Johnny's reading skills in the Basic School Subject section of the PPP verified his inadequate phonic ability.

Miss Poppins knew Johnny needed a specialized approach, using his areas of strength to teach him basic spelling skills. She decided to use the visual, look-and-spell, method combined with the kinesthetic technique of tracing and copying letters in sequence, to develop phonetic concepts.

Name Johnny Doe
Date
Age 8   Sex M

PPP PRESCRIPTIVE PLANNING PAGE

PREREQUISITE SKILLS

		Strengths	Deficits	PRESCRIPTION
H A P T I C	T	*		Use haptic strengths, particularly tactile(e.g. tracing techniques) in teaching. Incorporate visual cues to develop auditory memory and sequencing skills. Use M.W.M. program. Don't over-simplify concepts. He is a good thinker and needs intellectual stimulation.
	K		✓	
	D	*		
	M		✓	
	C	*		
V I S U A L	S		✓	
	D		✓	
	M		*	
	C	*		
	S		*	
	I		✓	
A U D I T O R Y	C	*		
	M		✓	
	D		✓	
	C	*		
	E	*		
	S		✓	
	C			
M O T O R	Gross		✓	Vocal repetition is a problem only due to auditory receptive deficits. Use all expressive channels. Develop vocalization through games, written cues etc.
	F M	✓		
	I P	*		
	N C	*		
	E D	✓		
V O C A L	Conc		✓	
	V R		*	
	C V	✓		

BASIC SCHOOL SUBJECTS

		PRESCRIPTION
R E A D I N G	Begin instruction with Initial consonants (c,d,h,r,w) Good comprehension and word usage.	Use color-coded phonics system. Use synthesizing exercises - Tracing - use visual cues. Merrill Linguistic Readers, Continental Press Materials, Experience stories.
A R I T H M E T I C	Introduce Regrouping of addition facts over ten.	Use visual and Imagery Method. - Use Cuisenaire rods to develop understanding of what is happening to the numbers added. Use abacus.
W R I T I N G	Develop skill in cursive writing. Upper-case K Lower-case (p-s-w)	Provide tracing activities to emphasize haptic size and motor strength
S P E L L.	Have an individual weekly word list. Omissions Poor phonetics	Use sight vocabulary and word families for spelling list. Emphasize revisualization strength

BEHAVIOR

		PRESCRIPTION
A	8 talks to neighbors.* in seat. visitors, substitutes, verbal, finished early, difficult assignment	Move away from Bill. Watch length and difficulty of assignment
B	7 Out of seat* long, difficult assignments, auditory	Watch length of assignments Remediate auditory.
C	4 Distracting noises. Listening activities.	Avoid pure listening tasks. Build listening skills slowly. Ignore noises.
D	0 Not aggressive. Good peer relationships.	Have him help peers with his strong areas. Good at sports etc.
E	1 Tries to do work well	Encourage and support good work.
F	9 Daydreams (Listening tasks) Self-blame* (when criticized)	Use self-appraisal Inventory. Develop self-concept. Praise. Avoid listening tasks.
G	19 - * Needs much* teacher attention. Gives up * easily. Watch auditory, verbal and reading	General academic and remedial programming.

RECEPTION DEFICIT PRESCRIPTION

	TACTILE	KINESTHETIC	VIS. DISCRIM	VIS. MEM.	VIS. CLOS.	VIS SEQUEN	AUD. DISCRIM	AUD. MEM.	AUD. CLOS.	AUD. SEQUEN	SEN. INTEG.
Symptom of Behavior	1. Difficulty with activities involving touch	1. Difficulty with activities involving rhythm	1. Does not enjoy picture books 2. Can't describe pictures 3. Can't label pictures	1. Can't spell 2. Reverses letters	1. Does not recognize partial pictures 2. Can't pick an object out of a picture that is too detailed	1. Cannot Spell 2. Does not read words in order	1. Does not understand what he hears 2. Does not follow verbal directions 3. Can't identify sounds	1. Can't remember multiple directions 2. Difficulty learning lessons heard	1. Can't understand foreign accents or records with static 2. Noisy backgrounds distract 3. Can't blend separate sounds with words	1. Difficulty repeating a sequence of symbols just heard	1. Difficulty with stimuli introduced through more than one sense 2. Can't watch movies or television
Training Deficit Area	1. Sandpaper 2. Templates 3. Tracing	1. Kephart exercises 2. Charades 3. Physical Education	1. Labeling 2. Categorizing 3. Matching objects 4. Identify colors, letters, numbers, and geometric forms	1. Retell a flannel board story 2. Put several items on a table — remove — let child name them 3. Draw picture of what is seen on an outing 4. Draw map of room at home	1. Identify incomplete silhouettes 2. Find hidden forms in a picture 3. Pick out a figure from the ground	1. Copy sequence of beads 2. Dot-to-dot 3. Follow a maze	1. Train listening skills 2. "Simon Says" games 3. Write from dictation	1. Teach nursery rhymes line by line 2. Give simple directions and work up to multiple 3. Follow directions of song on record player	1. Exercises with missing letter of rhyming word 2. Introduce sound blending with objects in the room 3. Choral reading	1. Number sequencing songs and games as "Ten Little Indians"	1. Use textured flashcards (Visual & Tactile) 2. Cut pictures to match words (Visual-Motor) 3. Language Master (Auditory-Visual)
Teaching Techniques Using Strengths	Use strong auditory or visual channel	Use strong auditory or visual channel	1. Use phonic method of reading 2. Give additional clues 3. Use records and tape recorders 4. Listening station 5. Trace on transparencies on over-head projector	1. Use additional cues 2. Use tracing activities 3. Use audio-visual aids	1. Provide auditory cues 2. Use color and texture clues 3. Start with distinct figures and slowly omit figures	1. Let him repeat sequence of a visual stimuli auditorially 2. Use tracing activities	1. Use short phrases 2. Give visual clues 3. Whole-word approaches in reading 4. Kinesthetic method in learning spelling words 5. Experience charts	1. Use visual cues 2. Write while memorizing 3. Give simple one-concept directions 4. Use visual aids	1. Provide visual cues 2. Speak clearly and distinctly 3. Get the child's individual attention	1. Provide visual cues 2. Use haptic activities	1. Use strong modality and slowly introduce one new modality at a time

ASSOCIATION DEFICIT PRESCRIPTION

	COGNITION	MEMORY	DIVERGENCE	CONVERGENCE	EVALUATION	SOCIAL COMP.
Symptom of Behavior	1. Does not relate what he sees and hears in a meaningful way 2. Does not understand directions 3. Word calls when reading but no concept formation.	1. Does not retain and connect cues previously learned.	1. Is not creative in his thinking	1. Has difficulty drawing conclusions	1. Does not reach logical decisions	1. Displays no practical judgement 2. Little common sense shown
Training Deficit Area	1. Use familiar analogies 2. Relate pictures of common objects to each other 3. Predict outcome of stories 4. Identify logical relationships	1. Classification 2. Relationships 3. Sequencing training	1. Predict outcome of stories 2. Cause and effect 3. Make inferences 4. Draw conclusions 5. Distortions	1. Predict outcome of stories 2. Problem solving experiences 3. Cause and effect 4. Logical relationships 5. Comparisons 6. Drawing conclusions	1. Pantomime 2. Cause and effect 3. Problem solving 5. Comparison 6. Incongruities	1. Charades 2. Cause and effect 3. Problem solving 4. Facts and opinions 5. Incongruities
Teaching Techniques Using Strengths	1. Ask one-concept questions 2. Elicit short answers 3. Accept concrete answers 4. Provide visual or auditory cues as needed 5. Permit tracing of correct responses	1. Provide visual or auditory cues 2. Provide haptic experiences to strengthen memory 3. Use mnemonic devices to stimulate memory	1. Use auditory and visual clues to open-ended questions	1. Provide simple stories with logical conclusions 2. Progressively get harder 3. Use visual, auditory, haptic cues	1. Provide many experiences for reaching decisions 2. Provide cues and use mnemonic devices where needed	1. Use audio-visual materials with open-ended conclusions.

EXPRESSION DEFICIT PRESCRIPTION

| | MOTOR | | | | | | VOCAL | |
	GROSS MOTOR	MANIPULAT	POINTING	COPYING	DRAWING	CONCEP. MOT	VOCAL REPET.	CONCEP. VOC.
Symptom of Behavior	Has difficulty with sports and playground activities	Has difficulty with games, blocks, beads and puzzles	Cannot express himself with a simple motor activity	Cannot copy letters and numbers either near-point or from the black board	Cannot express ideas in pictures	Cannot express ideas using gestures	Has difficulty repeating simple words, phrases, sentences	Has difficulty expressing ideas vocally
Training Deficit Area	1. Balance Beam 2. Label feet (left-right) 3. Simple games 4. Walking a string 5. Exercises	1. Hand puppets 2. Jigsaw puzzles 3. Stringing beads 4. Modeling clay	1. "Show me" game 2. Flashlight pursuit	1. Follow the leader with letters in the air 2. Tracing 3. Sand-paper 4. Felt letters 5. Templates 6. Simon Says	1. Teacher draws object and child finishes it	1. Charades 2. Finger games 3. Act out songs 4. Pantomine 5. Simon Says 6. Dramatics	1. Choral reading activities 2. Use Language Masters to repeat sounds, words, phrases and sentences	1. Picture reading 2. Describe objects 3. Show and tell 4. Tell stories 5. Riddles and drama
Teaching Techniques Using Strengths	1. Do not insist on performance in front of the group 2. Verbalize directions	1. Start with simple manipulative materials and progressively get harder 2. Provide visual and auditory directions 3. Allow child to verbalize his efforts	1. Allow child to express his ideas verbally as well as manually	1. Provide many experiences for developing skill 2. Verbalize directions 3. Use templates, color, and texture to provide cues	1. Allow child to relate verbally what he has drawn 2. Provide visual and auditory outlines for developing drawing skills	1. Let child express ideas verbally as well as manually	1. Give moral support 2. Give verbal cues 3. Provide opportunity and time for response 4. Provide visual cues and mnemonic devices	1. Give clues 2. Provide mnemonic devices 3. Allow the use of notes 4. Allow child to act out while talking 5. Use tape recorder

Pupil, **P**rocess, **P**rescriber: the Prescriptive Profile Procedures are designed to aid, and test, the teacher in her efforts to offer prescriptive teaching to her students and the learner chain: reception (input), association (processing), and expression (output).

No discussion of learning errors would be complete without a discussion of what a child is traditionally *not* allowed to do. J. F. and S. R. Jastak give us an excellent overview of far too often what, a school child "dare not do."

The literature on reading instruction contains various prescriptions as to what children should not be encouraged to do in learning to read. Sometimes such prescriptions are in the form of indirect allusions that children are slowed down when they use certain ways of learning. Among the taboos are pointing with the finger, moving lips, oral reading, reading without comprehension, spelling aloud before reading, reading without inflection, phonic reading, breaking words up into syllables, etc. These interdictions are taught with complete confidence in their validity without evidence that they are bad habits except that they "slow children down." Furthermore, they are applied as absolute rules to persons of any age and at any point of the learning stage. We have heard of supervisors and reading specialists visiting classrooms for the sole purpose of checking whether any of the children move their lips or point with their fingers while reading. Teachers whose children move their lips are condemned as inferior and are given poor professional ratings. This strange behavior on the part of supervisors and reading experts causes more retardation in reading than any moving of the lips or pointing with the finger has ever done. It can be demonstrated that some children who point with their fingers read faster and more accurately than when they do not point. The fallacy of "being slowed down" stems from the observations that good readers do not point with their fingers but poor readers do. It is known, however, to students of statistics that correlation is not causation. The poor reader, finding that he loses his way or that his performance is not what it should be, hits upon the device of using his finger to help himself. Pointing with the finger becomes an important temporary aid in overcoming the coordination difficulties that exist in poor readers. Pointing with the finger is not a cause but an effect of reading disability. It is helpful in the early stages of learning to read and is spontaneously abandoned as the skill of reading gains in efficiency.

If the inversion of cause and effect were carried to its logical extreme, one might be justified in concluding that only those children would learn to read fast whose fingers are cut off, whose lips are taped, and whose vocal cords are paralyzed.

Everyone who has a child who is having difficulty in learning to read must agree with the Jastaks—anything that helps a child to learn should be used.

There is no need to belabor the attitudes and competencies of our teachers and school systems. Some are good, far too many are bad, and the bad are that way for a variety of reasons with which only society as a whole can deal. Here, we must be much more specific.

A teacher who lacks sympathy or understanding can devastate a child. To say, "I know you can do the work, but just won't" reflects a lack of sensitivity that is appalling. Yet these very words have been said to millions of children over the years.

The principal who says, "I can't send him to the guidance counselor, we're overloaded already, but we'll try to work him in before the end of the year," is cheating the child. He is literally stealing the child's education from him just as surely as is the school board member who says, "There is no such thing as a learning disability. See, there's nothing in the budget for that item." Such a person is ignorant of the field in which he is acting with authority and should be so labeled publicly.

The aging politician who says, "Why are we talking about special legislation for learning disabilities? We just appropriated money for retarded kids" is failing in his public trust and should, and can, be tossed out of office. Unfortunately one cannot toss out the parent who ignores his child's problems, who does not fight whomever and whatever is necessary to get his child the help he needs.

The use of the word "fight" above was deliberate. Parents must do the ground work themselves. Parents must study the field to understand their child's problems, seek evaluation that is sincere and sophisticated, and then make one of three possible academic choices for their child.

These choices are: dependence upon the public school system, clinical schooling, or independent tutoring. Each choice requires knowledgeable judgment from the parents.

PUBLIC SCHOOLS. It is not easy to generalize about public schools because so many changes are taking place within the various systems that what is applicable today may not be tomorrow. However, as it stands, there are three choices. First, there is the school that has virtually nothing to offer the learning disabled child. In this instance, the child must have independent help.

Next there is the school that has self-contained learning disability classrooms. These are classes where the children are isolated from their peer groups, categorized, and are learning in an environment suitable to their needs. Partly because of the recognition of the social problems that arise when a child is isolated from his peer group, these classrooms are being rapidly legislated out of the academic scene.

Finally, there is the school where all children share classrooms together and the learning disabled students are released on an individual basis to a resource room where they are given special help. This approach of classroom plus resource room is the wave of the future.

CLINICAL SCHOOL. This should offer a whole school for the whole child in a *clinical* environment. This is not the traditional private or independent school such as many children now attend. This is a clinical school and as such has a specially trained staff. The primary factor here for parents is cost. The price range is dependent upon geographical area, number of facilities in a specific area (competition), and services offered. As with evaluation, a parent must be cautious and searching. Some people who are totally unqualified open clinical schools because a great deal of money can be made. Some facilities do not offer tutoring as an integral part of their program and therefore the child winds up still just sitting in a classroom. Seek out the school which belongs to a private school association, which sets reliable standards.

The parent must investigate the credentials of the staff. Have they had clinical training in reading? What does the facility look like? Are the walls just thrown up with no thought to noise abatement? Is the school clean, uncluttered? How large are the largest classes? How do they group their students? Are there emotionally disturbed children in the school and, if so, do they have classes of their own? Is there close communication between the parents, interested medical support personnel, and the school administration? *How long has the school been in existence?* Finally, who refers students? The public school, doctors, psychologists, other parents?

A parent must learn first, then look, then listen, and finally, decide.

Tutorial. This is an independent, adjunct action which is usually coupled with public schooling. There are individual private tutors, tutoring services, and facilities at university or college clinics. The cost is again dependent upon geographical location and can range from $8 to $20 per session.

A university or college clinic often has students who are studying at the graduate level as tutors. These individuals are supervised by the clinic director.

Parents should check credentials of private tutors. It is also wise to discuss the abilities of the individual with someone who has had experience with the service.

One to three, even five, tutoring hours per week is going to be sufficient for only a small number of the most minimally handicapped children. Those with more serious handicaps must have a full clinical program.

The time of day that your child is to be tutored also has a direct bearing on productivity. A young child, after a full day in school, will be unable to learn at his optimum capacity in the late afternoon. However, an older child may, depending upon his needs, do quite well in an afternoon session.

Some private schools offer what they call tutoring services. The parent must be cautious in this situation. Ask questions. Is the child's tutor to be a regular classroom teacher who will "tutor a bit" in the afternoon or is she a fully qualified clinician whose only duties are clinical tutoring for the private facility? *Do not accept anything less than the latter.* Private school tutoring services are usually very expensive and can be used as a selling point for enrollment. (In the past, tutoring meant extra help in a specific subject and did not mean clinical tutoring, which requires highly specialized training.)

Since the possibility is quite strong that many parents will eventually have to seek private clinical schooling for their child, whether this be tutorial or full-time, here are several useful pointers that other parents have discovered over the years.

(1) Private clinical schooling is a business, just like the supermarket. You, or rather your child, gets exactly what you pay for. There are never any bargains in clinical schooling.

(2) Investigate *every* facility in your area before placing your child. It is rare, but there have been instances of fee-splitting in the field.

(3) If you don't understand the credentials that you are shown, copy them and take them to someone who will explain them to you. Your local university will usually be glad to help.

(4) Check the community reputation of the facility or tutor.

(5) If a school is clean, if the maintenance is good, then usually the school is good. Somehow it seems that if the school cares enough about the grounds and buildings to keep them clean year round, not just painted once a year, then they will care enough about your child to teach him well.

(6) Find out what professional memberships the facility/tutor holds.

(7) Find out whether the curriculum is fully clinical. Are geography, mathematics, social studies—not just reading—taught on the basis of clinical teaching techniques and needs?

(8) Finally, learn the clinical language. If you do, you will not be overwhelmed by a whole new set of words. If you don't understand, ask for an explanation and persevere until you do understand.

Clinical education can be expensive but most satisfying. It is not recommended for those fortunate enough to live within the district of a public school system that offers adequate help to the learning disabled child. If this is your situation, consider yourself fortunate.

5

The whole area of minimal learning disabilities is emotion-packed. The mother pleads with her pediatrician, "There's something wrong—I know it—find it for me." The teacher knows what the mother means but is bound by administrative procedures that may delay the evaluative process for so long that the child may be academically lost before he receives help. The father may think aloud, "He just isn't trying." And the child is guilt-ridden; he doesn't know why he can't learn; why he can't live up to the expectations of his parents and teachers.*

Dr. L. P. Shirley summarizes the child's situation in the following manner:

> The child finds himself in a dilemma which he cannot understand and from which he can find no satisfactory avenues of escape. He finds himself the victim of concern, anxiety, and resentment, and perhaps begins to feel alarmingly different from his classmates. He loses self-confidence and self-esteem. He may feel rejected, looked down upon and disliked. In defense, he may break out with aggressive, hostile behavior. Or, he may become dominated by chronic anxiety, acquiring a variety of nervous habits, withdrawing from social activities, resorting to physical

* It is recommended that all parents who have a child with a global disability read *The Other Child,* by Lewis, Strauss, and Lehtinen. New York: Grune and Stratton, Publishers, 1960.

complaints, or indulging excessively in day-dreaming. He may eventually succumb to defeatism, losing interest in school work, paying little attention to class activities, and refusing to try. The longer he remains unable to progress in reading, the more deep-seated becomes his emotional disturbance and also his aversion to trying.

Today, the child's silent scream of pain, the parent's plea, and the educator's concern can be met with a positive plan of action. If it were possible to single out one discipline as having come the farthest the fastest in meeting the challenge of recognizing the needs of these children, it would have to be pediatric medicine. This is not meant to underrate the efforts of other involved specialties, for they, too, have accelerated their forward thrust. But a decade ago, pediatricians were rarely concerned, or even aware of, learning disabilities as a serious handicap. Today, this is not so. Parents now often find the pediatrician a comforting source of guidance as they wend their way through the complexities of evaluation, education, environmental controls, and home management.

■

Life should be defined in terms of growth, not just maintenance. It is important to realize that most parents have trouble viewing their young children as the adults they will become. We tend to think of our children as extensions of ourselves rather than other humans with individual identities. Recognizing individual identity is vitally important when helping a child with a learning disability. The home environment and management must not *assault* the child. The goal should be a peaceful coexistence of the child's problems and his family unit. The future must always be kept in mind. The academic remediation process may seem incredibly slow, but it will pay off for the future. The management problems at home may, at times, seem overwhelming or even futile, but they, too, will pay off in the future. Remember, the basic principle is a life-style that will enhance the child's present in a manner that will serve his future well.

Management and environmental control are not happy words. They imply almost a prisonlike situation, but this need not be the case. Some learning disabled children live with an "inner storm" that they are unable to control. They must be taught control. If parents train themselves to observe, they will soon be able to see how their child reacts to a given situation, to learn what routines the child cherishes, and to help him to stay within his needed boundaries. A child's life can be so guided that the routines of living help him gain better understanding of his problems.

A busy mother of a young child who is a "holy terror" may think many of the child's behavior manifestations bothersome. The child can seemingly trip on an eyelash; he is always losing his belongings; he forgets from one minute to the next; he has little self-control. Perhaps when he was a baby he was a screamer or a short-sleep child. Maybe he has "ants in his pants" or his leg never stops jiggling when he sits.

These are the children who literally run from one activity to another. Their attention span is short; they blurt their reactions and their words. Rarely is a project that is started finished. They can lash out in response to even an everyday instruction or question. Some can have a catastrophic reaction to the simplest event in their lives. A behavior chain controls them because they have impaired percepts and concepts—the parts of their environment do not come together for them so that they see the whole. They miss the forest for the trees.

Many parent–child clashes could be avoided if parents realized this single aspect of their child's problem: he cannot always see and understand the whole of a situation because he cannot integrate the parts.

A child who has impaired *auditory* perceptions is often in deeper trouble at home than the one with visual perception problems. He is constantly asking, "What did you say?" He may mimic your words. If the parents do not understand that he is trying to sort sounds with his mimicry or questions, it may seem that he is being deliberately "smart alecky" or dumb.

Usually, it is the very minor incidents in life which set the child off. The major ones, by the very fact that they are major, are more easily understood by him and are thus easier for him to cope with. The child will move along smoothly and then some minor incident will induce a reaction that is out of all proportion to the incident because the child is inadequately *empowered* for coping with the ever-widening range and variety of life situations.

Sometimes there is a pyramid situation. A question is asked of the child, his answer is not appropriate, the questioner chides him for being silly, not trying. The child does not understand the questioner's attitude and feels wrongfully maligned. He tried to answer the question to the best of his ability, so he becomes infuriated at being wrongfully accused and reacts with a torrent of anger.

A child with a neurologically influenced learning disability loses friends, becomes shut off from his peer group, and invites punitive measures on himself because of his impulsivity and inner anger. Depending upon his age, his behavior is sometimes variously described by those who do not understand as anti-social, strange, nutty, childish, bratty, spoiled rotten, sociopathic, or stupid.

These are ugly adjectives that tread deeply into the very souls of a child and his parents. It is possible, however, to reverse some, possibly most, of this behavior. Although learning disabilities, per se, cannot be "cured," a child can learn inner control. Before this can be accomplished, the parents must *consciously* acquire *their own* inner control.

■

There are guidelines that offer help to parents in the necessary environmental controls and family relationships.

ROUTINE. This is vital to these children. Any disruption of their cherished patterns of living can be a great burden for them. A calm, orderly life is what they desire the most, and certainly this is one of the easiest contributions adults can make to their welfare. If, for example, a mother feels the urge to move furniture around, she should wait until the child is home and can help. This will aid him in re-establishing a new routine in his mind in respect to furniture replacement, which is, in reality, home object orientation. This is especially vital where the child's own room and personal belongings are concerned. Above all, he should not have surprises or drastic changes sprung on him out of the blue. A little forethought in any given situation will help immeasurably. Even though it may seem as if these children thrive on activity and change, they do not. They need a reliable routine to use as a base of security and a steppingstone throughout their daily lives.

A CONSISTENT APPROACH. Such an approach to all dealings with the child will, in the long run, be more of an aid to the adults concerned than to the child. These children are very inclined toward "scatter" and must have their wishes, needs, and routines cared for in a consistent day-in-and-day-out manner. To give in to pleading requests, or to changing the rules from day to day, will only complicate the problem, deepen the "scatter," and turn a minor problem into a major one. Do not let grandparents or a babysitter change the rules; it only disrupts the child's patterns and you will bear the brunt of this disruption for days after, as you will have to pull him together again. Parents must especially watch their own fatigue level when trying to maintain consistency. It is very easy to give in when you are tired, a momentary weakness that you will rue later.

CAREFUL GIVING OF ONE-STEP INSTRUCTIONS. This is mandatory. We constantly force children, all children, to sort out our instructions from a flood of words. We love our children, but when we want them to do something, we often get our love, personalities, and prejudices involved. "Come wash for dinner" is much more easily understood than "Darling, dinner is almost ready, please come in and wash. Make sure you get your hands clean, use the blue towel—we're having your favorite dinner, steak and corn on the cob. Honey, did you hear me?" Meanwhile, the child is standing at the door, trying to sort what it is you want *exactly*. He had responded to the call "Darling," he knew you wanted something, but he is lost in the riptide of your words. So keep it simple and to the point. If he is to wash for dinner, tell him so, period. If you are telling him you love him, hug him, kiss him, tell him so, period. Don't confuse the issues; love is love, food is food, and in his mind the two have nothing to do with each other.

GIVING TASKS WHERE THE CHILD CAN "SHINE." This is important to all children, but it is especially important to these children. They have trouble achieving academically and socially. Parents must strive, therefore, to replace this constant failure with solid achievements that bring a sense of belonging and usefulness. This does not mean that you should not expect them to achieve either academically or socially, and you should let them know that you expect success from these areas. Providing motivation and short-term goals that can be handled and achieved is one of the best ways to help these children train themselves toward success.

DON'T GIVE CHOICE COMMANDS. This must especially be avoided in the nonpleasure areas. A child may be allowed to pick out the coloring book he wants, but he should not be given a choice as to whether he will take a bath now or later. In the realm of life functions and daily tasks, consistency is necessary.

WATCH YOUR VOICE LEVEL AND TONE. These children should not be yelled at, nor should they be spoken to in a monotone or in a "put upon" tone of voice. Proper modulation and emphasis can give the child clues to what you want from him, thus helping him to sort out the words and the desired performance that you expect. Remember, he badly needs all the help he can get and you can give him. Besides, these children are very clever at picking up attitudes from the adults in their environment. Your voice, more than any other thing, can relay your attitudes and feelings about him. It is a dead giveaway to your relationship with him and how you feel about him. You can literally destroy his ego with your voice.

DON'T CONVEY YOUR ANXIETY TO YOUR CHILD. This admonition is closely related to that concerning voice control. At the same time, don't try to ignore his disability, either within yourself, or to him. He knows that something is wrong, and he needs to know, too, that you are concerned. Excess tension will not help; warm understanding and frank discussion of the problem, at a level appropriate to the child's age, will. To let him go through life knowing something is wrong, but not knowing what that something is, is cruel. Remember, he is not incapable of understanding. In fact, it is through understanding that he will be able to gain inner self-control. To deny him this opportunity is wrong. Conversely, communication with those outside of the family unit is also important. This requires self-control, delicacy, and judgment on your part. Some parents feel it necessary to tell all their neighbors, relatives, friends, and fellow workers that their child is "not really stupid, or silly, or spoiled, or whatever but that he just suffers from a learning handicap." They hold the phrase in front of them like a flag that will protect them and their child from all wrongdoing. The explanation does not give protection and, unfortunately, we still have a long way to go in our culture for a full and unconcerned acceptance of anything that varies from the norm. To advertise indiscriminately that a child is "different" can only add to his burden, as well as that of the whole family unit. Both adults and children can be incredibly cruel, even when they don't intend to be. You may put your child on the spot for every neighborhood incident; it is easy for other parents to blame the child who is known to be "different" for everything that happens instead of looking to their own children for responsibility for a neighborhood or school mishap. Your child may suffer from hypokenesis (slowed activity) and thus basically be disinterested in the world around him, but it is he who will be blamed if a cat gets his tail set afire, not the kid down the street who is so rotten spoiled that even sales clerks hate to see him coming. So be careful, but at the same time, the family should not attempt to hide the fact that the child has a problem. It is a delicate matter, requiring a judicious blend of frankness and discretion so that all concerned will be helped.

DON'T LET THE CHILD AND HIS PROBLEMS RULE THE HOME. This is the easiest trap of all to fall into. You want to help your child; you know he is worth helping, that the future for him is not totally grim and unrewarding. Therefore, it is only natural that you expend a great deal of personal and family energy on him. But your other children, regardless of their age and how well they understand the problem, need equal attention. And there is nothing that will turn a father against a child faster than to have mother totally preoccupied with a single child. The dangers are equally great for the one-child family. Again, there are father needs to be considered. Also, if the single child is spoiled, he will never be able to function as an adult.

The question of mother–father relationship is very important to your child. A divorce, or parents who quarrel all of the time, can be so ego-destroying for these children that no amount of help can repair the damage. Any child is hard pressed to understand why his parents don't get along. The child who is neurologically impaired will usually assume that he is the cause of his parents' problems and will react accordingly, a reaction which may cause disaster in later years. No marriage is perfect, so there will be quarrels, but try very hard to have them away from the child's viewing or hearing.

If divorce becomes absolutely necessary, think of the child. Prepare him with the adult reasons couched in child's language, *a little bit at a time*. Let him know *for certain* that it is not his fault, even to the point of lying to him. For the younger child, the story can be that father has moved to another city for business. For the older child, the explanation can be that father doesn't love mother anymore because she dyed her hair red and she doesn't love him because he bought a new car or for some cause that is appropriate to his age. If you must lie, use a lie that can be slowly corrected as the years go by, one that will not harm the image of either partner (no matter how bitter your quarrel with each other may be). Make it one that the child can live with, without guilt, under the new circumstances.

The question of father's visits must be decided upon, in this case not by the courts but by the parents after seeing how the child reacts to the father's visits. If it upsets the child for days afterward, they should be discontinued. If the child looks forward to them and they don't overexcite him, then they should be continued on a *regular and consistent basis*. Once the pattern is established, the responsibility for maintaining it cannot be denied. If the pattern has to be changed, do it slowly, with conversation and explanations. Above all, you must both think of the child's present welfare and the all-important future emotional strength—it is your duty to your child.

■

When the child first goes to school, whether kindergarten or first grade, the teacher knows very soon that she has a problem child in her class. This is the child who spills all the finger paints, climbs to the top of the tree, has six minor tussles with other children in one play period, is the first out of the door at the end of the day by dint of pushing and shoving, or is sweet as honey in the morning but a potential terror in the afternoon.

Or she knows he's there because he is painfully afraid, can't seem to remember class routine from one day to the next, has difficulty changing activities, or has trouble with organized games.

Usually, in her conference with the parents, the teacher tries to spare their feelings with phrases such as: "Derek is so interested in discovering the world, but he needs some organization to his searchings." "Tom's social and tidiness habits need a little maturing." "Jim has trouble keeping up with the class—he's still young for his age." "Billie-boy is so cute, he still likes to cuddle. Of course, I can't let him. I don't really have the time and the other children make fun of him."

If, after a child has reached the age of 6 years, 9 months, and the teacher still says that he is "a little immature for his age" or uses any of the other euphemistic phrases so common to the language of education, remember that such phrases are often used to buffer the parent—and the teacher—from the reality of the situation. They should be warnings to the parent to try to hear what the teacher is *really* saying. Get to the bottom of the dialogue.

This doesn't mean that the parent should berate the teacher for being too harsh or for attempting to hide something. Instead, the parent should cooperate. Ask for specifics. Look at your child's work papers. Discuss his daily activities to find out exactly *how* he disrupts or does not join in classroom activities. The probability is that your child is simply brattish due to your spoiling, or he may be truly emotionally immature for his age (which can be helped and alone is no great problem), or he may be in real trouble. Whatever is the case, full cooperation between parent and teacher is needed.

There are many case histories of children who could have done so much more, truly achieved their potential, if only their parents had asked for help at an early age. If, rather than ignoring the signs, they had accepted the limitations of their child, aided the teachers, and avoided either rejecting him or babying him into neurosis, much could have been achieved.

Children are like trees. When young they can be bent, they can bear a lot, and like a young willow snap back and continue to grow. But the older they get, the more difficult it becomes for them to change. If a child's environment has been hostile to him, he will develop a deepening emotional overlay.

Drs. L. J. Hanvik and H. B. Hanson state: "The physical aspects of milder brain injuries in children have a good chance of being 'healed over' through forces of growth and development but resulting psychological scars could be severe and permanent if not properly understood and treated."

For the parent whose child is diagnosed as suffering from a reading and/or learning disability complicated by neurological involvement, the first step should be complete acceptance of the child and his handicap. Before the child can learn to accept himself and achieve the inner controls necessary to overcome his problem, his parents must acquire their own set of inner controls. The educators can help the child to learn and function, but it is the parents who have to make him whole, happy, and secure in the knowledge that he is loved.

These children can be so easily discouraged and are given to great internal sadness about their limitations. From the younger years, on up into teen-age life, until the protective shell forms, they will literally and figuratively "cry a lot."

These hurt children are found everywhere. There are no protective boundaries of race or color, socio-economic status, or national origin, ethnic or cultural backgrounds. Throughout man's entire history we have had, in all degrees and types, brain-injured individuals. Fortunately, over the years, we have gained knowledge of the problem, especially about these very limited types of dysfunction that have been discussed here. We know now that the hyperactivity of these children is the result of the problem, not the problem itself; that the emotional overlay comes from the years of failure but that this also is a result and only becomes the problem when it is so firmly entrenched that we cannot break through it to help the child start achieving.

Today, a firm diagnosis of minimal brain dysfunction or damage is not the end of the world for either the parents or, more importantly, the child. With appropriate educational facilities and techniques, and proper parental attitudes, the child will progress, slowly to be sure, to productive adulthood. In this process, the main burden falls on the parents rather than the child or his teachers. It is their ability to overcome their feelings of dismay; to ignore for the time being their sense of expectancy for achievement from the child, that will make the greatest difference. Above all, parents should remember the admonition, *don't rush, time is in your child's favor.*

All of us tend to try to "stretch our children"—because of the intellectual capacity of these children, they can be stretched—indeed, they should be for their own sake. But the process of stretching must be with reins on the child, the teacher, and most of all the parents, else all may spin out of control.

6

What do dogs, pigeons, M&M candies, and love have to do with each other—and with children's learning disabilities?

Pavlov, a Russian neurophysiologist, working with dogs and lights, developed the theory of stimulus response. He found that rats could be made to suffer nervous breakdowns when presented with an insoluble problem. Using a circle and an ellipse of light as a form of stimuli conditioning, Pavlov discovered that the rats became disorganized in their behavior pattern, sometimes even to the point of convulsion or rigid comatose states, when the stimuli differentiation was reduced to the point where they could not judge what response was expected of them. This technique is abbreviated as SR.

B. F. Skinner, a behavioral psychologist, working with pigeons, added another dimension to SR: Operant Conditioning. Conditioning is a part of all learning. We automatically condition our children, for instance, to go to school. By the time a child is of age to enter school, there is no question in his mind that he should go.

Whereas Pavlov's dogs did *not* have to do anything with their

Grateful acknowledgment is given to Dr. Barry Kaplan and Genevieve Donlon for their invaluable advice with regard to this chapter.

stimuli but they still reacted, Skinner's pigeons *had* to do something. Skinner had added another step by asking for reaction to action. The dogs received food whenever the light was on; the pigeons had to push a button after the light came on to obtain food.

Behavior means different things to different people in different situations. Usually, when parents or teachers discuss behavior, they mean conduct. And this conduct is more often thought of as social conduct. Johnny does not pick his nose in public. Jane does not sharpen her pencil in class without teacher's permission.

Conduct is everyday deportment. We all practice this simplified form of behavior modification in almost all of our dealings with children and each other. Behavior that is maladaptive, whatever the cause, is not conduct.

Behavior is action–reaction. A learning disabled child acts in a way that is contrary to what his environment expects of him, and we have action. The teacher reacts to the child's inappropriate behavior, and the child in turn reacts to the teacher's reaction. It can be, and often is, a vicious, unbreakable circle for both teacher and child. The same holds true for home behavior. No matter the degree of maladaptive behavior, the child is not learning and he cannot learn until external environmental forces help him discover internal controls for his behavior patterns. In this context, elimination of maladaptive behavior and acquisition of acceptable behavior goals become a necessity in the academic environment.

Behavior modification terminology uses a key word, reinforcer. A child does what we want, we reinforce his good action, but we must be very careful. A child's needs are often complex and perhaps his idea of a "good" reinforcer is one that we would never knowingly offer him.

As an example, a child suddenly stands up in the classroom. The teacher says in a firm tone of voice, "Sit down, Johnny!" The whole class turns to watch Johnny sit down, but he doesn't. Teacher repeats her command. Johnny does not respond. Finally, the teacher threatens expulsion from the room, and Johnny then sits. The boy has received the desired reinforcer, the teacher's attention, *and* the attention of the class. He is happy.

A negative reinforcer, but one that would have been of real value to the teacher, would have been to ignore Johnny's actions. Thus, she would have defeated his purpose and he would not be likely to re-enact the episode. After all, why bother, if the teacher doesn't notice and respond?

When a teacher consciously does not recognize this type of behavior, she is practicing behavior modification. Eventually she will extinguish Johnny's inappropriate classroom antics.

When behavior modification techniques first came into use, it was felt that a concrete (physical) reinforcer was needed. M&M candies were used quite frequently; it is now known that many forms of reinforcer material are available to a teacher and parent: verbal approval, points, playtime, physical rewards—the list is endless.

The key of what to use is based on knowing the child. The reinforcer, either positive or negative, must have *meaning* to the child involved. If it is not meaningful, it will not elicit response and naturally will not be effective.

None of the three behavior management strategies—behavior modification, sensori-neurological, or psychodynamic—is successful without one basic cornerstone, an awareness of the level at which the child is functioning. The decision as to which strategy is necessary to help an individual child can only be made by a professional. It is not a decision a lay person can make.

The second most important factor is based on knowing the above, then devising a systemized approach to behavior goals. Once these goals have been established, consistency is absolutely vital.

Let us view each of the three techniques separately.

BEHAVIOR MODIFICATION. This technique may be performed by parents and teachers with a modicum of training. It works best with the child who exhibits impulsivity and hyper- or hypoactivity. The emotional overlay has not yet become too thick to be penetrated and the primary goal is modification of the behavior patterns toward gaining inner controls so that educational goals may be achieved. No matter how fine the clinical teaching methods used, a child cannot learn if his inner behavior controls are so impaired that he is in a constant state of disruption or ennui.

In using this technique, one sets tasks (behavior goals) for the child at a level that he can handle and reinforcers are decided upon. The child is made fully aware of what is expected of him. *Each end every time* he performs adequately, he is rewarded, and *each and every time* he fails, reward is withheld. The original goals are set short-term, and they are lengthened or made more sophisticated only when the child is able to cope with the next step. This timing is extremely important, because the child *must succeed,* or the effect is damaging. In fact, success is the whole point of behavior modification—success for the child in coping with environmental influences.

SENSORI-NEUROLOGICAL APPROACH. As the title indicates, this approach to behavior management is based on the child's sensori-neurological *functioning* level. As in language skills, though a child may be age 6 chronologically, it does not necessarily follow that *neurologically* he is at an age 6 maturational level.

The key to this program is to delineate carefully the child's operating level and start with the training at that point. If a child cannot walk, you do not expect him to run. Therefore, you cannot expect 7-year-old behavior from a child who is only 4, sensori-neurologically speaking. The techniques must be scaled to those appropriate for a 4-year-old. This usually means returning to the tactile–kinesthetic (haptic) stage of development. A 7-year-old who is sensori-neurologically age 4 is still touching to aid the acquisition of percepts, his eye–hand coordination is poorly organized, and he can yell with total abandon and without guilt. Just as a clinician brings the child slowly up through the various sensori-motor skill stages, so must the professional help the child work his way up through his emotional and behavioral levels and maturational lag.

This technique is particularly appropriate for the neurologically impaired child. He will benefit the most from this approach.

Only specially trained teachers and parents may use this technique and only after thorough psychometric analysis has been performed. The psychologist, working with medical personnel and the educator, must guide the child's entire program, with each participant keeping careful progress reports.

Finally, there is the Freudian-based PSYCHODYNAMIC APPROACH. *No one* may use this technique without proper training and rigid controls. It is not for amateurs.

The children who need this form of treatment are those who present arrested emotional development. Here, we have a question of psychic origin which seriously deters not only academic learning but all the child's interpersonal relationships with his family, peer group, teachers, and culture.

The psychodynamic technique is founded on Freud's view of the *id, ego,* and *superego.* Psychoanalytic theory believes that these are the three factors that underly all mental activity. The *id* is the basis of our instinctual life, or, put another way, our diencephalic drives, libido, and aggression. Libido is associated with the sex drive or energies we are born with and must cope with all our lives. This sex energy has nothing to do with our physical capacity for sex and thus may be thought of in terms of our unconscious activity as presented in the form of fantasy, dreams, disinhibitions, or wishes.

Since none of us is allowed the freedom of total wish fulfillment, our *ego* helps control us and our actions. The ego tells us what we can and cannot do according to what it has learned about our environment. We see this most spectacularly when we study different cultures. Bare-breasted native women, cannibalism, or ritual dancing, for example, all fall under the category of environmentally influenced ego learning and resultant control.

The *superego* is that portion of the ego by which we measure and thus control ourselves. The bare-breasted aborigine conforms to her peer group standards, and she is content. Most superego information is gleaned from society's standards of "you won't," "you shouldn't," "that's wrong to do." The superego seems to be a negative moralizer that controls our social mores through a sense of what we are not supposed to do.

Our superego evolves through stages; it grows and changes as we grow and change. A young child gathers his data from his family, a teen-ager from his peer group. Adults seem to blend the gleaned knowledge to formulate a life-style that allows them to function in an adult world.

The development of the id, ego, and superego goes through distinct stages, just as our sensori-motor system. If any one of these stages is incomplete or disrupted, arrested emotional development results.

The child is at odds with both his environment and his interpersonal relations. It would be an absurd understatement to say that this in turn hampers the educational process. It does not just hamper; it can totally halt learning.

Before a teacher can teach a child who is so badly encumbered, the child must first be able to have warm, trustful feelings not only toward his teacher but toward his entire world.

The psychodynamic technique is one of permissiveness coupled with judicial doses of awareness of the manipulative powers of children. It is especially exhausting for both the therapist and the participant. But it is the solution to some of the problems of some of our children in helping them to learn and to adapt to their environment and to grow into productive adults.

■

The parent must understand that there are few children who suffer a learning disability who do not need some form of behavior modification. It should also be understood, and accepted, that this is not a starting point for achieving a "perfectly behaved child." There is no such thing. Who among us is ready to judge what is "perfect behavior"? Standards of conduct are constantly changing, being modified by society, and that is not our concern here. The kind of behavior that concerns us is aimed directly at the learning process, both at home and in the classroom; inner chaos which throws its symptoms externally into the environment needs behavior modification.

Most parents and teachers should learn about behavior modification. Such knowledge will not only help your child; it may also help your marriage, job, and yourself. Behavior modification in this view is a self-teacher.

Two books are especially recommended. *Living With Children,* by Gerald R. Patterson and M. Elizabeth Gullion (Champaign, Ill., Research Press Co., 1971) is a programmed approach to behavior modification. *I'm OK—You're OK,* by Thomas A. Harris, M.D. (New York: Avon Books, paperback), concerns Transactional Analysis and can be invaluable to parents who are learning to cope with their own inner controls as well as those of their child's.

The following teacher's worksheets reproduced from the PPP manual show clearly how a teacher must take into consideration, and work with, a child's behavior and classroom symptomology.

Then there is a charming list of sixty-five ways that a parent or teacher can say to a child, "Good for You," which was compiled by *Grade Teacher* magazine. Why such a list? Because the *primary goal* of all behavior modification, no matter the technique used, is support. You support the child until he learns to support himself. Remember this, it is vital to his future! It does not take great insight to realize that this word "support" translates to mean "love."

USE OF PPP BEHAVIOR RATING SCALE

"PPP"

Classroom Behavior Rating Scale

Student Name_____ No._____ Date_____ Age_____
Please rate the student on the following items. Circle the statement that
best describes the student. Make your judgment after three weeks' observation time. *MAKE ONLY ONE CIRCLE PER ITEM.*

1. OUT OF SEAT BEHAVIOR (Peers)

   What behavioral effect does the above named student have on other
   class members?

Out of seat behavior serious bother to others	Out of seat behavior distracting to others	Often out of seat but not disturbing	Seldom out of seat without asking	Out of seat only after asking

2. OUT OF SEAT BEHAVIOR (Teacher)

   What behavioral effect does the above-named student have on your
   efficiency as a teacher?

Out of seat behavior serious bother to you	Out of seat behavior requires much attention	Often out of seat but not much problem	Seldom out of seat without permission	Out of seat only with permission

3. TALKING OUT BEHAVIOR

   How often does the student exhibit inappropriate verbal behavior?

Constantly talks out without permission	Often talks out without permission	Occasionally talks out without permission	Rarely talks out without permission	Never talks without permission

4. GROUP PARTICIPATION

   How often does this student make positive contributions to class-re-
   lated discussions?

Never takes part in discussions	Rarely takes part in discussions	Occasionally takes part in discussions	Usually takes part in group discussions	Always takes part in group discussions

5. AGGRESSIVENESS

How much "acting out" behavior does he exhibit?

Behavior seriously harmful to others	Behavior must be watched closely	Occasionally a behavior problem	Seldom a behavior problem	Never a behavior problem

6. PEER RELATIONSHIPS

How is he accepted socially by other class members?

Avoided by all other students	Avoided by most, liked by few	Accepted by most students	Liked by most, avoided by a few	Liked by all students

7. GENERAL ATTITUDE TOWARD PEERS

What is this student's attitude toward other class members?

Never tries to make friends	Rarely makes friends	Occasionally makes friends	Usually makes friends	Always makes friends with other students

8. DISTRACTIBILITY

Is he able to continue working, although minor distractions occur?

Loses concentration at slightest distraction	Finds it very difficult to maintain concentration	Can concentrate for short periods	Becomes so absorbed, oblivious to surroundings	Good concentration

9. INITIATION OF ASSIGNMENTS

Is the student able to initiate assignments?

Never initiates assignments	Needs excessive prodding to initiate assignments	Needs occasional prodding before initiating assignments	Usually initiates tasks independently	Always initiates assignments independently

10. COMPLETION OF ASSIGNMENTS

Is the student able to follow through on independent assignments?

Never completes task	Rarely completes task with excessive prodding	Occasionally completes task with prodding	Usually completes task independently	Always completes task independently

11. IMPULSIVITY

How painstaking and exact is this student in his work?

Haphazard, hopelessly careless work	Usually inexact, slipshod, may turn out precise work on occasion	Can do a good job if pushed but often careless and inexact	Usually painstaking, occasional lapses, poor work	Very exact, careful and painstaking in all work

12. GENERAL ATTITUDE TOWARD SCHOOL

What is this student's attitude toward school work?

Openly resentful, no interest in school	Vague feeling of resentment, interest hard to arouse	Inattentive and indifferent	Interested in most work, occasionally bored	Enthusiastic, eager each day

13. EMOTIONAL CONTROL

How does this student respond emotionally?

Reacts violently when no provocation exists	Usually uncontrolled emotions, may attempt to hide when slightly provoked	May attempt control, but just as often will display feelings	Usually controls emotional outbursts	Highly controlled, accepts society limits in expressing emotions and chooses alternative behavior

14. DISINHIBITED—IMPULSIVITY

How often does this student respond without forethought?

Always performs (actions and words) without forethought. Responds without considering consequences	Sometimes	Occasionally	Rarely	Never

15. PERSEVERATION

How often does this student continue a task inappropriately?

Always a task (action, words or topic) far beyond appropriateness of activity	Sometimes	Occasionally	Rarely	Never

16. FRUSTRATION

How does this child cope with frustrating situations?

Low tolerance for frustration	Withdraws from situation when immediate success is not achieved	Withdraws from situation after second unsuccessful attempt	Makes several attempts at activity before giving up	Copes well with extended frustrating situation

17. PERFORMANCE IN COMPETITIVE SITUATIONS

How does competition affect this child's performance?

Behavior always deteriorates in competitive situations (withdraws or becomes bully)	Behavior deteriorates in some competitive situations	Performs in competitive situations only with teacher or peer prodding	Performs adequately in competitive situations	Incentive derived from competition

18. PASSIVENESS

Does this child participate in group activities?

Daydreams, withdrawn	Shy, timid	Difficult to participate in group activities	Participates in most activities	Participates actively in all group activities

19. MOTIVATION (Reinforcement)

What is the most successful reinforcement for this child?

Immediate gratification needed (candy)	Delayed gratification of a substance nature (points earned for specific item)	Simple scholastic reward (star-gummed labels)	Social reward (smile, pat on back)	Inner satisfaction in a job well done. Long-term goals, high interest level in all activities

65 Ways to Say "Good for You"

Everyone knows that a little praise goes a long way in any classroom. But "a little praise" really needs to be something more than the same few phrases repeated over and over. Students need more than the traditional "good," "very good" and "fine" if encouragement is in the cards. Here are some additional possibilities: *

That's *really* nice.   That's great.
Thank you very much.   I like the way you're working.
Wow!   Keep up the good work.

* From *Grade Teacher* magazine, September, 1972; page 47.

Everyone's working so hard.

That's quite an improvement.

Much better.

It's a pleasure to teach you when you work like this.

Good job.

What neat work.

You really out did yourself today.

This kind of work pleases me very much.

Congratulations. You only missed _____.

That's right! Good.

Terrific.

I bet your Mom and Dad would be proud to see the job you did on this.

Beautiful.

Very interesting.

Now you've figured it out.

Clifford has it.

Now you've got the hang of it.

Super.

That's a good point.

That certainly is one way of looking at it.

Sherrie is really going to town.

You've got it now.

Far out.

I liked the way Bill (the class) has settled down.

Excellent work.

I appreciate your help.

Very good, why don't you show the class.

Thank you for (sitting down, being quiet, getting right to work, etc.)

Marvelous.

Groovy.

Right on.

For sure.

Sharp.

That looks like it's going to be a great report.

I like the way Tom is working. My goodness, how impressive!

You're on the right track now.

That's "A" work.

John is in line.

Mary is waiting quietly.

Dickie got right down to work.

Ann is paying attention.

It looks like you put a lot of work into this.

That's clever.

Very creative.

Good thinking.

That's an interesting way of looking at it.

That's the right answer.

Exactly right.

Superior work.

That's a very good observation.

That's an interesting point of view.

Thank you for raising your hand, Charles, What is it?

Nice going.

You make it look easy.

That's coming along nicely.

7

"... these drugs may ameliorate listening ability, over-excitability, forgetfulness, and peer relationships as much as 'over-activity.' As such, psychopharmaceuticals are not chemical straitjackets and may be compared with eyeglasses or other necessary prosthetic devices which enable more normal functioning." This statement by Hunter H. Comly, M.D., summarizes what this chapter is all about.

If your child were a diabetic, would you deny him the use of insulin? The use of chemotherapy for the learning process should be thought of in the same way.

When we think of children and schooling, it is the burden of American parents to believe that their children should, indeed must, meet certain standards. These have been set forth as a sort of pie-in-the-sky goals. It is a touchy subject.

The opposite of normal, in the English language, is abnormal. Given a slight or moderate deviation in a child's physiological composition, learning ability, emotional stability, nutrition, or maturation, and he is automatically labeled abnormal. The technical sense of the term may be correct, but the destructive label with

Grateful acknowledgment is given to Richard Bendinger, B.S. Phy., for his help with the chemical nomenclature.

which the child must live for the rest of his life is wrong. It is the "foreverness" of a label that is the crux of the problem faced by physicians and educators as they attempt to aid, correct, or replace a physiological "fault" in a child.

No parent wants his child tagged abnormal. And no child *should* be tagged in this way because of a problem that dictates the need for chemotherapy.

The use of central nervous system (CNS) chemotherapy is *not* drug abuse, nor should it even be considered as "drug usage" in the common sense of that term.

As with insulin and thyroid therapy, specific medical examinations must be given before prescription. And, as with any medication, a successful therapy program can be extremely complex, especially for the person who proves to be the exception to the rule.

The physician is in charge.

The teacher and to a degree the parent will see the results of the therapy in the classroom and in the home. The aim of chemotherapy is to bring a child with a diagnosed problem up to a normal functioning level. *Chemotherapy supports the child physiologically.*

Traditionally, only the manipulation of environment and teaching techniques have been emphasized when discussing efficient or inefficient learning in children. Strauss and Werner helped to shift the emphasis from the *external* environment and teaching to the *internal*—the learner. This whole child concept, *physiologically speaking,* parallels Piaget's species theories and must eventually be accepted by the nation's schools. It is no longer possible, in view of the massive research data available, to deny the role of the central nervous system and its functioning in regard to the acquisition of learning.

The CNS is dependent upon certain subtle chemical balances and electrical impulses. These electrical impulses must "jump" the synaptic cleft. Sometimes, this "jump" is erratic or short-circuited; sometimes, the brain is indiscriminately flooded. High or low productivity levels, too rapid or too slow secretion of any of the multitude of affecting chemicals may cause an interruption or breakdown in the CNS functions and ultimately the learning process. Chemotherapeutics aid a controlled synaptic "jump" and chemical balances so that a child is able to function at full or at least increased power. A child sitting in a classroom with a CNS dysfunction is not learning normally because he *cannot*. It is not a case of will not; it is cannot.

■

The chemotherapeutic agents used to assist the learning disabled child fall into three broad categories: CNS stimulants, anticonvulsant agents, and, to a lesser degree and usage, medications from the tranquilizer family which are used alone or in combination with one of the first two.

CNS STIMULANTS. Clinical literature on the use of psychostimulant agents has accumulated over thirty years of research. The first report of positive results achieved through the use of amphetamines as an aid to learning appeared in the professional literature in 1937. As so often happens with a new idea, the report was reviewed critically, which effectively inhibited further immediate research. Then, in 1958, Drs. Zimmerman and Burgemeister reported good results with the use of methylphenidate. Throughout the fifties and early sixties many studies were produced. Unfortunately, far too many of these early research projects were poorly controlled, used contaminated samples (i.e., the children were not correctly diagnosed and grouped), and could not be used with any scientific validation.

But the research efforts were not static. Other, more careful, scientists set themselves to the task of finding out the when, how, and why of chemotherapy for certain learning processes.

The resultant research on dextroamphetamine (Dexedrine) and methylphenidate (Ritalin) clearly demonstrated that the use of such supportive chemotherapy is valid for the field of learning disabilities.

The November 1971 issue of the *Journal of Learning Disabilities* under the guest editorship of Dr. Eric Denhoff, a pediatric neurologist, was devoted to the subject of psychostimulant drugs. For the first time, the major researches and data regarding CNS stimulants were reviewed in a professional journal.

One article in this issue, that by Dr. Gerald Solomons, cited the major studies that had been performed and summarized the significant data presented during the preceding thirty years:

Laufer et al. (1957) reported that a significant number of hyperkinetic children have low photo-Metrazol thresholds and that amphetamine raises the threshold to normal in these children. A low photo-Metrazol threshold is thought to be indicative of dysfunction at the diencephalic level and, as it is reported by Marazzi and Hart (1953), that amphetamine inhibits synaptic transmission, the site of action of amphetamine may be related to the brainstem reticular-activating system. By raising the level of synaptic resistance at the diencephalic level, the normal function of the diencephalon is restored and prevents a flooding of the cortex by a stream of impulses.

The mechanism of action of amphetamine in decreasing hyperkinetic behavior is not yet understood. Logically the hyperkinetic behavior should increase with amphetamine and be reduced by barbiturates. However, Eisenberg (1966) points out that barbiturates are contraindicated because of the frequency of paradoxical excitement.

Connors and Rothschild (1968) state that the drug action in the hyperkinetic child is not a pharmacologically true paradoxical effect, but rather a direct stimulating effect of the amphetamines which causes an increase in general alertness and excitation along with an increase in the ability to focus attention. Responses to interfering stimuli are then decreased. . . .

Knobel (1962) perceives the problem as one of cortical maturation, or rather, the lack of it. This "expresses itself in a typically subcortical behavior characterized by lack of control, poor reality-testing capacity and a handicapping of the physical capacities."

Millichap and Fowler (1967) analyzed the drugs used for hyperactivity according to effectiveness and toxicity. They found methylphenidate to be the drug of choice and amphetamine sulfate the second most successful drug.

The use of psychostimulant agents is not a treatment that is prescribed lightly. As Dr. Keith Connors says, "We are not doping the children into submissive activity. Studies of free-field activity, using actometer measurements and time-stop photography, show that the stimulant drugs actually *increase* total amount of activity. It is definitely the *quality* of activity, not the total *amount* of energy expended, which is changed by these drugs." Dr. Connors is telling us it is quality, not quantity, that makes the difference.

How does this qualitative physiological change in activity and response translate into better learning in the classroom?

The lessening of hyperactivity (or, in the case of hypoactivity, the increased response) allows the child to concentrate on the task at hand. An internal change has an external manifestation. This explanation does not, however, do justice to the very complex and subtle changes produced by supportive chemotherapy in most children. For instance, a parent may see and report "no change" to the doctor. But the parent is not usually in a position to note the subtle effect that the psychostimulant has had on her child in the learning milieu. Indeed, even the child's teacher may need to sharpen her powers of observation to note the fine differences which, discreet as they are, add up to success for the child at the end of the school year.

Perhaps the most important aspect of the enhanced learning performance is the capacity of the child to make careful decisions in a smooth and uninterrupted manner.

For some children, however, the change in their learning status will be dramatic. It is as if—and this is the major point—the whole child is "hung together."

For those parents who may feel some concern about the future of the child who needs such agents for the learning process, Dr. Denhoff offers assurance:

> It has been found clinically that most children outgrow this disorder [hyperkinesis] by their late adolescence or early adulthood. It is, therefore, a major problem mainly during the early school years. This is a particularly unfortunate time for these traits to prevail since they severely limit the ability of children to attend to and profit from the learning experience provided in conventional school situations. . . . If

these drugs can help certain children focus their attention and concentration, and thus profit more from the many hours spent in the school, then they serve a useful function for these children at this particular time in their academic and psychosocial development.

Dr. George Lytton, writing about the effect of methylphenidate (Ritalin) has on immature nervous systems, says, "This effect seems to be one of chemically induced maturation, almost as though one changed an immature, inefficiently functioning nervous system to a mature, efficiently functioning nervous system with goal directed activities."

And, finally, let us put to rest the one burning question that all parents have, "What about addiction?"

Dr. O. M. Reinmuth, professor of neurology, states in no-nonsense terms, "The children practically never report any awareness of feeling differently, and this absence of a pleasurable response combined with the open and nonsecretive manner of receiving the drug are adequate as reasons to remove any fear of addiction or habituation."

■

The second group of chemotherapeutic agents which may be used for learning disabled children fall into a completely different category. Commonly known as anti-convulsant drugs, they differ physiologically and are prescribed for different reasons. The need for these agents is indicated by an irregular electroencephalogram (EEG). The most widely used medication currently is diphenylhydantoin (Dilantin). Presently, there are a number of other new and refined medications under development for use in this form of therapy.

The term "anti-convulsant" can be misleading, *as this form of chemotherapy has proven to be of value when no actual convulsions or gran mal seizures are present.*

To understand this form of medication and its effectiveness, it is necessary to be familiar with the diagnostic tool known as the electroencephalogram (EEG).

Everyone is familiar with the electrocardiogram (EKG), which is obtained by placing electrodes on strategic points of the body to monitor cardiac function. To obtain an EEG reading, electrodes are placed on the scalp to monitor the electrical impulses which are developed in the cortex by activity of the brain. Admittedly, this procedure does not result in a graph that shows the brain activity as sensitively as we would like. But the irregularities which are demonstrated can be of great importance, particularly when read by a professional who is highly experienced in the interpretation of childhood EEGs.

Of course, if the electrical activity in the brain is sufficiently irregular to produce obvious physical reactions (e.g., severe fainting episodes or the bizarre behavior of psychomotor epilepsy) prompt medical support should immediately be sought, but this is not our concern here.

Our concern in the learning disabilities field is for those children who demonstrate on an EEG a borderline irregular brainwave *which is not medically significant,* but can be significant for the learning process.

Here, we are faced with some difficulties. Since the EEG is not conclusive as a diagnostic test to determine the presence or scope of a learning problem, the tendency has been in professional circles to question its value.

However, controlled research conducted by Dr. Murray Jarvik at New York University may hold a clue to the importance of borderline irregularities. Jarvik's work showed that the effect of the *mildest* electro-subconvulsive shock on the memory trace can be to interrupt its consolidation, thus, an "amnestic" or memory-erasing effect was induced. This amnestic effect was greatest when the mild shock was administered *immediately* after learning new material.

Applying Jarvik's findings to the child in the classroom who is experiencing irregular, subconvulsive electrical activity of the brain repeatedly during the school day, a pattern emerges. Careful classroom observation has noted severe memory defects occurring in children, even those with above average intelligence, who have EEGs which demonstrate irregular "spikings," even when these "spikings" are not considered to be, as previously stated, medically significant. These children seem to have their memory traces literally "erased," sometimes within minutes after learning new material.

Dr. David Krech stated in a speech to public school administrators:

The physical basis of any memory, whatever else it may be, involves either the production of new proteins, the release of differentiated molecules of ribonucleic acids (RNA's) or the induction of higher enzymatic activity levels in the brain. In a word, for every separate memory in the mind we will eventually find a differentiated chemical in the brain— "chemical memory pellets," as it were. . . . Immediately after every experience, a relatively short-lived reverberatory process is set up within the brain. This process continues for a time after the stimulus disappears and permits us to remember events which occurred moments or minutes ago. But this reverberatory process fairly quickly decays and disappears—and as it does, so does the related memory. [*We would be overwhelmed if we remembered everything in our lives!*]

However, under certain conditions, the short-term reverberatory process, before it disappears completely from the scene, triggers off a second and quite different series of events in the brain. This second series of events involves the release of new RNA's or the production of new proteins and other macromolecules.

If a memory should be retained, such as an academic fact, the physiological functioning of the body prepares itself for this act, and thus we have the *memory trace* laid down in the cortex. These chemical changes are relatively long-lasting and serve as the physical basis of our long-term memories.

The acquisition of memory is a constant sorting process. What is important to remember? A teacher standing in a classroom presumes that her students are able "to sort" from the lesson; our environment tells us what we should remember by getting our attention: "This is an item to remember." In this manner, the trace process is begun. But this trace is fragile and will decay and disappear if it is not (a) reinforced properly or, (b) if there is physiological interference, e.g., subconvulsive electrical brain activity. Naturally, the degree of effect of such subconvulsive activity is dependent upon its scope, location, and intensity.

From memory trace, we progress to memory consolidation. Memory reinforcement is, physiologically speaking, a sequential event and an ongoing process. The item is taught; it must be reinforced within three minutes; and for those children who seemingly lack this ability to achieve consolidation, it must be then reinforced within several hours and possibly again in several days. In other words, *reinforcement* assists the consolidation-of-memory process.

If, during this time span of hours or days, the borderline subconvulsive brain activity erases the memory trace, it cannot become consolidated.

When a teacher instructs a child with this irregular EEG pattern (regardless of whether he is on chemotherapy) she must constantly be aware of how memory works and how it must be reinforced, and above all, how easy it is to lose.

Often, the children who suffer this dysfunction are the ones who are described as "He knew it on Friday, but Monday morning he acted like he had never heard the word before in his whole life."

There are other manifestations of an irregular EEG pattern. Explosive or bizarre behavior may be a prime indicator that an irregular EEG is present. And, again, the irregularity may not be medically significant, but the behavior is readily apparent to a parent or teacher. A more subtle indicator, one that is not so readily noticed, is very brief episodes of staring.

Memory dysfunction, bizarre or explosive behavior have been "eased" by the use of Dilantin. Unfortunately, side effects and allergenic reactions to this medication have proven to be a problem. Hopefully, one of the medications currently being developed and tested will eliminate these hazards.

An interesting aspect of this question of medically insignificant EEGs is that some children have demonstrated irregular brainwave activity as a result of a low glucose level. The spiking brainwaves actually flattened after glucose was administered during the electroencephalographic procedure. The implications here for proper glucose-tolerance testing and diet analysis are self-evident.

Electroencephalograms are administered while the subject is awake and/or asleep. Often this sleep is drug-induced; however, for a suspected borderline case, a natural-sleep EEG is often preferable. This can be difficult to obtain, and it is hard on the parent and the child (usually the child has to be kept awake most of the night), but if this is the recommendation of the neurologist, follow his instructions; they are important.

The third group of chemotherapeutic agents that may be used as supportive therapy for learning disability children are the tranquilizers (ataractics). They are used to a far lesser degree than are the CNS stimulants.

Tranquilizers have proved to be of value, either alone or in combination with CNS stimulants, when the emotional overlay is especially heavy. For older students, those who have a "low boiling point" or low frustration tolerance and are inclined to hostile "acting out" behavior, Librium, Thorazine, and Valium are most frequently prescribed, sometimes in combination with Ritalin and Dexedrine. Close monitoring and objective observations from the teacher and parent are necessary for accurate, nonbiased reporting to the neurologist or pediatrician.

We have considered thus far the most commonly used forms of chemotherapy for learning disabled children. However, there are other chemotherapeutic techniques which should be discussed to give a complete picture of the field.

Thyroid therapy, which ranks among the first medical therapies initiated to improve learning in retarded children, is important to a limited number of learning disability children. Current intensive investigation is aimed at discovering new uses and forms of treatment.

Triiodothyronine has proved effective in increasing alertness, social response, and language development in schizophrenic pre-schoolers who were evaluated as not low in thyroid but who profited from increased thyroid activity.

Phenobarbital is cautiously used, even as an anti-convulsant for hyperactive children, due to its frequent paradoxical reaction.

Deaner (deanol acetamidobenzoate) was being prescribed more than a decade ago. However, results were disappointing. Currently, renewed interest is being shown among some professionals who are conducting experiments with the use of this drug in combination with orthomolecular therapy.

Linus Pauling, Nobel Prize winner in biochemistry, first focused attention on what he called *orthomolecular therapy*. This tech-nique is commonly but incorrectly called megavitamin therapy.

In the beginning, Dr. Pauling and Dr. Abram Hoffer of Canada worked with children suffering from certain forms of mental ill-ness. Their work has since been extended to include children with learning disabilities.

Orthomolecular therapy may be defined as "the provision of optimum molecular composition of the brain, and especially the optimum concentration of substances normally present in the human body." While more research is needed, there is evidence that certain cases may be helped by massive doses of selected vita-mins. With orthomolecular therapy:

. . . three to six months is the usual time in which significant changes are seen. The child begins to understand and obey commands, exhibiting a willingness to cooperate with his parents and teachers. . . . Statistics show that those children whose treatment begins early in life—ages two or three to seven or eight—respond faster and fre-quently better than those further advanced in age. In those cases in which positive results have been obtained, treatment included niacina-mide or niacin, ascorbic acid, pyridoxine and calcium pantothenate used in massive doses. Many parents and physicians have reported significant changes when only pyridoxine was used in massive doses.

This statement was made by Dr. Allan Cott, writing on the treatment of learning disabilities in the *Schizophrenia Journal.*

■

The language and the concepts of chemotherapy are not simple. If you have any serious questions regarding the information these pages contain you should ask your pediatrician or neurologist to explain it in greater detail. The use of chemotherapy is never to be taken lightly nor is it to be considered without full and complete control by a qualified *medical doctor.*

Some of the therapy strategies listed in the latter part of this discussion are unacceptable to many practitioners and if a doctor you trust says no, then content yourself until further evidence either proves or disproves his views. In the long run, it would be better for your child not to have any form of chemotherapy than for him to be under treatment by an incompetent person. It cannot be stressed too strongly that only a medical doctor is qualified to decide on chemotherapy. Any medication can be dangerous and it takes a high degree of skill and in-depth knowledge to supervise these forms of treatment.

This chapter is in no way to be considered a recommendation *for* or *against* any of these agents, but rather it is meant only to be informative in the event that your child, upon medical advice, should need such treatment.

8

The consequences of the many components of abilities/disabilities discussed in this book—development, processing, evaluation, education, management, behavior modification, and chemotherapy—must eventually fuse inside the walls of a school. *Children plus learning disabilities equals special needs* is an equation faced constantly by parents, teachers, school administrators, and local, state, and federal governments. For some of those involved, governments, for example, the subject is dissociated from parental anguish, teacher concern, and child helplessness. For others, though they are vitally concerned, there is a daily attrition of the emotions and sometimes even resolve. This erosion can come to parents when a particular school or locale is not responding to their child's problems; it can come to a teacher who must every morning face thirty, forty, and sometimes even sixty students, all of whom need her help. Parents can seek help and find a void; teachers can attempt help and be overwhelmed by the totality of their responsibilities.

Because of the certain knowledge that there are schools in urban communities in deep trouble and that there are schools in suburban communities where there is no provision for a learning disabled child, it is with a certain hesitancy that a discussion and description of a private clinical school is begun. The argument may be given that of course private schools are better than public because they operate within the framework of a closed circle, enroll only those students they want, and are not bound by rules and regulations of governing agencies. Above all, they are sought out and paid a fee, a fee which automatically stipulates accountability. Technically, these parameters are valid. But, at the practical level, the view is much different. In fact, it is these very components that stimulate private clinical education. The well-rounded clinical school of today can offer: a highly trained faculty with a working knowledge of each child's evaluation, coordinated prescriptive teaching in the classroom, continuing diagnosis for their students, clinical teaching techniques, one-to-one tutoring (or at least a one-to-one reading program for each child), parent counseling, interdisciplinary cooperation (often acting as coordinating agency), therapeutic physical education, and a supportive emotional milieu for the children and their parents.

Private clinical education has, over the past two decades, contributed far more than its share to the identification and remediation of learning disabilities. Additionally, many such schools are involved in research programs, act in an advisory capacity to federal and state authorities, and give unstintingly to the local community of their services and programs.

■

To offer the reader a case study of a private clinical school is a difficult task, especially when the goal of the case study is to show only the *clinical* aspects.

By focusing on the *clinical* much of the human element is lost. Also, one must avoid the trap of making the school chosen sound like a paragon of virtue, that it sprang into being full blown almost overnight, or that the children and staff march through their days in a lock-step regimen that ends in glorious success for all concerned.

To relate a clinical case study of a clinical school it is necessary to discuss from a technical standpoint the systems, philosophy, organization, curricula, and children. It is virtually impossible to portray in any detail the years of struggle to develop programs that are now an *assumed* part of the curricula, the quality and dedication of the staff, the just plain hard work of ten-hour days, the phone calls to the director at night or on weekends by an anguished parent with a child in distress, or to tell the funny and not so funny stories of what has happened in over a decade of involvement. The rules of a case study disallow such human-interest details.

Even though only one school* has been chosen for this case study, equally fine facilities are to be found in many sections of the country.†

■

The school which is the subject for case study was founded in 1964 and moved to its present location in 1970. The student population averages 135–140 students each year, ages 6 through 14. There is a teaching faculty of 30–35, a professional supervisory staff of 4 and 10 in support personnel. Semesters follow the traditional academic year, the school is funded solely by tuition, and there are no boarding facilities.

Enrollment and evaluation referrals come from local and out-of-state physicians, psychologists, public and private schools, and parents.

The evaluation department tests approximately 70 new children per year; about 20 percent of those tested will be enrolled in the school. The other 80 percent are referred to the appropriate academic milieu for the child in question. The function of the evaluation department is continuing diagnosis of the enrolled population.

The school routinely makes multidiscipline, off-campus referrals

* The McGlannan School, a Language Arts Center, Miami, Florida.
† See *Directory of Facilities for the Learning-Disabled & Handicapped* by Careth Ellingson & James Cass, New York: Harper & Row, 1972.

for adjunct testing in neurology, pediatrics, neuro-otolaryngology, endocrinology, ophthalmology, and for psychological or psychiatric support.

There is a strong parent communication program which is initiated when a new parent first calls the school. The basic reasoning behind this is that a "lone" child is not evaluated or enrolled. The child is an integral part of a family unit. It is vital, therefore, not only to the child but to the family, that the unit as a whole, become fully aware of his problems. This, in turn, results in an ideological shift that emphasizes interpersonal cooperation between the family, child, and various disciplines that will be involved with the child.

The parent information process begins with the evaluation conference. Here, both parents are given an explanation of their child's problems. His *deficits and strengths* are fully discussed and graphed for the parents, needed medical referrals are given, and the recommended academic referral is offered. This initial conference averages two hours.

If, at this time, it is felt that the school will serve the child's needs, the parents are invited to participate in the next step, an orientation evening.

This evening meeting requires nearly three hours and is designed for small groups of parents who are considering enrolling their child in the school. During the course of this meeting the parents receive an overview of learning disabilities and gain insight into the school's philosophy and academic approaches. The orientation is completed with a showing of the same slides that are used in teacher-training workshops. The parents are also made fully aware of the need for full cooperation between parents, school, and outside support services.

If a child is not recommended for enrollment, or if the parents do not choose to enroll, they are informed that a full evaluation report will be made available to any other qualified facility they may choose, and that they are welcome to return for further information regarding learning disabilities.

Before a child enters the classroom as a full-fledged student, the school and his parents will have spent well over 36 hours on preparation and processing procedures. When a child is ready to leave the processing takes 18–20 hours.

In mid-fall, small groups of parents are again invited to attend an evening meeting to review with the staff their child's work and progress and to have a conference with his reading clinic tutor. This entire meeting is devoted solely to academic matters.

During the year, at least one, sometimes two, other individual parent conferences are held. These are clinical in nature, integrating the data from staff resumés, medical and behavior support services, and reporting the progress being made toward the child's goals.

Interim conferences are held on an "as needed basis," often by telephone. The telephone conference is a two-way street. The parents are encouraged to pick up the phone when they see a need to communicate. In this manner, a developing situation is given immediate attention and decision.

■

One of the primary objectives of any school for learning disabled children is to change the child's academic environment in such a manner that the child is surrounded by fewer hazards, whether in the physical plant, the level of vocabulary the child meets, or the emotional atmosphere. When the school was built, Dr. Byron Bloomfield of the Environmental Design Center of the University of Wisconsin was consulted. Many of the theoretical principles of Dale Harmon, currently being proven at the university, were incorporated into the school's design. Some of the design features that affect the academic environment should be mentioned.

VISION. Windowsills are at horizon height so that even small children are able to maintain a sense of visual integration and internal orientation, and these windows are at the rear of the classrooms to hinder visual distractibility.

A double lighting system is used so that there are no shadows in the classrooms. The lights are those designed by Dr. John Ott, who pioneered the research on "natural light." This natural light is the closest in the spectrum to sunlight.

The children's desks may be slanted the proper 15° for optimum vision.

Walls are painted pale green because the retina of the eye has the greatest receptivity to this color; it is the most restful for the eye to receive since it offers the greatest luminosity (5500 to 5600 angstroms).

AUDITORY. Many learning disabled children are more distracted by sound than by visual stimuli. The ceilings are constructed at an angle, with dropped beams, to break the sound bounce. Special insulating material is used throughout the complex. "White sound" is allowed into the classroom to cover distracting noise.

CLASSROOMS AND EQUIPMENT. While almost any school, public or private, has within reasonable limits basically the same equipment, or access to the same equipment, careful preplanning can make the difference between just a room with "equipment" in which children are taught and a room in which the two are molded not only into a functional but also a cheerful environment.

All blackboards are adjustable up or down and slanting ones are available for those children who are still at the proprioceptual level.

Each pair of classrooms has a combination viewing and curriculum storage room. One-way mirrored camouflaged windows allow supervisory personnel and professional visitors to see, hear, and observe classroom activity.

The intercom has a double-tone system; there are no loud bells. Learning disability children have a definite internal need to be warned of a coming event so that they may prepare themselves. Also, loud obtrusive sound gives them almost a sense of pain, as it jars their systems uncomfortably. The intercom emits a warning tone two minutes before classes are to change and then a second tone is sounded for the actual class change. One hears the tones but does not feel intruded upon or jerked to attention.

Since the students have "structure needs" and a strong sense of property rights, it is necessary that their materials, books, pencils, and papers, be organized for each separate subject for every student. This is a basic principle of Montessori. The "tote tray" system is used to carry out these multi-purpose goals. Even the youngest children change classes and the tote trays allow a sense of ownership as well as helping to keep desks and classrooms neat and uncluttered (stimuli free).

The overall classroom is kept as clutter-free as possible. Everything is in a drawer or cabinet space and nothing is brought into view unless it directly concerns the activities of the moment. Yet, and this is surprising, the rooms do not feel sterile; they look like an ordinary classroom.

This meshing of room, standard equipment, and clinical needs has been done so well that one has to force the conscious awareness that these are clinical teaching rooms in a school for learning disabilities.

SOCIAL ENVIRONMENT. It is believed that, if children are offered an environment that is conducive to a sense of value, they will respond with a personal sense of worth, not only internally but externally as well.

The main corridor of the school is a redwood beamed gallery with screened skylights. Traffic flow is controlled by planter bins. These bins soften the school's atmosphere and serve as a living source of material for minibotany lectures.

The buses begin picking up the first children at 7:15 A.M. Miami has great distances to be traveled and some children must ride the bus for over an hour. A long bus trip can be trying to any child. For a learning disabled child, it can be the keystone to a disastrous day. The children who attend the school work very hard and, although it may sound like pampering, some buses on the longer routes carry only 18–20 students instead of the standard 36. Heat, traffic, noise, sometimes no breakfast (the school checks every morning for this so that no child starts the day hungry), all can gang up on a child's senses to the point where he can feel disorganized or his "sorting" mechanism becomes faulty. This is one of the reasons every effort is made to keep the grounds and buildings of the school like an oasis of quiet. Heavy shrubbery and large oak trees surround the buildings to help obliterate the traffic noise. To scarify the land around any school is to lose a natural source of environmental control for that building. Trees and shrubs are nature-given, fascinating to children, and buffers against cold, hard concrete and brick.

Bus 3 brings five of the children who will gather in Homeroom D. Homeroom groups are designated by the letters A through H. A child's homeroom placement is based on his prescriptive profile, which includes psychometric, scholastic, and social factors.

A member of the administrative staff meets all incoming buses to receive the drivers' reports and any messages that may have been sent in by parents. Additionally, a specially trained faculty member meets the buses to observe each child and take "emotional temperatures."

All is fine today on Bus 3, with one exception. Craig is judged to be "on the fine line." He is very upset and seems ready to explode. Craig is following a behavior modification program designed for him by one of the school's consulting psychologists, Dr. K. However, for the past two weeks, staff anecdotal reports have indicated that an unknown factor is undermining the modification program and placing the boy under emotional stress.

Concerned by the morning report and aware of the staff resumés of the past two weeks, the director of the school instructs the teachers to be alert and sustain Craig through what will probably be a difficult day for him. The support routines are set in motion, and a "full staffing" is tentatively arranged for 3:00 P.M. The administrative personnel have been watching the situation closely because it is felt that Craig's inner turmoil is stemming from events in the home, especially over the weekends.

Class D in Homeroom 3 consists of 4 girls and 12 boys, averaging 9 to 10 years of age. These 16 children, even though they will disperse on the basis of their individualized schedules, will meet as a group for homeroom, lunch, film lectures, and physical education.

As the teacher greets the arriving students, each is encouraged to tell the class "something that's on his mind." Homeroom activities can run the gamut from a calendar and time-line discussion to an intense chess match for the older students.

At 8:30 A.M. the first buzzer sounds. The second will come in two minutes and Class D, along with the rest of the school, will start their day.

Where do 136 kids go? What, exactly, do they do all day in this special environment that has been designed for them?

The students are grouped, regrouped, and then subgrouped again. Every child follows his own program, at his own level, for an overall total of ten school subjects and as many sub-subject skills.

The school day is divided into three major teaching time blocks of 75 minutes each for reading, mathematics, and language arts, with two shorter time blocks for physical education and science/ social studies.

In September, using a color-coded system, even the youngest children learn their schedules in about three days.

For Group D, the first period is in the reading clinic where they will be joined by the students from Group C.

Both emotionally and technically, the reading clinic is the heart of the child's program. The "reading clinic" sounds like one large room, but it is not. Actually, it's an entire department, with three interlocking divisions: small group classes for word and structural analysis and comprehension skills development, and one-to-one tutoring.

Word and Structural Analysis is a study of the rules that govern the formation of words in our language—the alphabet, the sounds of the alphabet, how these sounds are affected by the sequencing of letters, blends, syllabication, roots, prefixes and suffixes—the *total mechanical code* of vocabulary. Eighty-five percent of our language is regular (patterned and standardized) and is based on this *code*. For example, by learning only one rule, the identification of open and closed syllables, a child can unlock the pronunciation of hundreds of words for his vocabulary use.

Comprehension skills development is the opposite of structural analysis. The subjective aspect of reading is stressed—who, what, where, when, why, and how. The multiple meanings of everyday words are explained. For examples, the word "light" has sixteen common interpretations, or, nearly 90 percent of three-letter words with the consonant, short vowel, consonant (CVC) pattern are used both as nouns and verbs. Once a child discovers that words can, and often do, have multiple interpretations and gradations of meaning, it clarifies his "conceptualization" of language.

These two clinic group classes are task-oriented and present the bulk of the routine information needed to learn to read.

Each child will take from these group classes on word and structural analysis and comprehension what his ability will allow. What he cannot, and what will therefore impede his reading progress, will be taught to him daily by his one-to-one clinician.

The tutor is oriented to the *child* as an organism who must process through learning pathways whether this processing is efficient or inefficient. This absolutely necessary "to the child" orientation requires a tutor to have finely honed insight and knowledge of her students. She must take an individual with a fluctuating range of modality strengths and weaknesses and make day-to-day judgments constantly correlating to the educational requisites. This is a task that pyramids from a cornerstone of timing.

Timing, for most people, would merely mean how long should a method be used or how long will it take for a child to accomplish a given task. For clinical education, timing means much more. It is a subtle, constantly changing influence upon tutor and child alike.

Timing involves when to initiate a multisensory approach, a task, a given technique, an assault on a deficit pathway, a retreat

HISTORY:

Birthweight: ....7 lbs. 8 oz.
Vision: ....Normal
Hearing: ....Normal
Walked: ....at 11 months
First Words: ....at 14 months
Serious Illnesses: ....None

This is Susie . . .
She's seven,
charming and intelligent.
She loves white kittens,
jellybeans and music.
She hates boys,
frogs and studying.

**SHE IS LEARNING
TO READ . . . .**

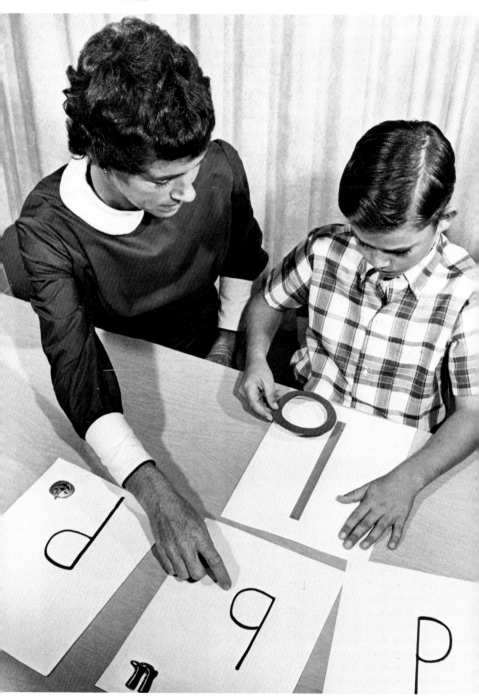

Photographs of the McGlannan School courtesy of *Saturday Review* and the school.
Photographers: Bob East, Jon Cone, and Allan Gould.

to a strength; when to use repetition, reinforcement; when to shift or change a task approach; when to eliminate a learning channel; when to stimulate flagging interest; when to stretch a child, and when to relax to prevent an overload.

It is the reading clinician who determines a student's instructional vocabulary level. This in turn automatically sets the child's placement on the *core vocabulary*. This core vocabulary is a highly structured listing of linguistically oriented and patterned words which has been designed to assure a uniform vocabulary flow throughout the school.

This core vocabulary placement allows the child's proper instructional level to be maintained for the child in all classroom subjects throughout the day. A child cannot learn mathematics, social studies, or science if he cannot read the words that are presented to him in the textbooks. With the core vocabulary system the teachers of these subjects know exactly the instructional vocabulary level of each student. The school has rewritten math application problems, beginning social studies, and grammar using and paralleling the core vocabulary.

To coordinate a student, core vocabulary levels, subject matter, word patterns, texts, supplementary texts, interests, and task objectives requires organized delivery and retrieval systems.

A simple example of delivery would be that the student library is color-coded to vocabulary levels. For retrieval the school has a flow chart which contains a scope and sequence analysis of the linguistic and semilinguistic series that are available on campus. This is far more complex than it sounds. There are a great many reading texts or series on the commercial market and, additionally, the school has a beginning reading series of its own. The problem, solved by the flow chart, is to know exactly where and when the emphasis on a specific word pattern may be found *as it differs in each and every series*. Without this knowledge a clinician cannot quickly assign to a student—one who has just learned "ike," for example—the correct book and the correct page in that book which will help reinforce this word pattern. With the flow chart this information is literally always at the clinician's fingertips.

■

Let's meet four of the children from Class D, Karen, Craig, Jeff, and Robbie, who are on their way to the reading clinic.

Karen is a dark-haired, violet-eyed charmer, the youngest child and only girl in a large family. Craig is our young man who came off the bus this morning feeling rebellious. He's skinny, sandy-haired, and his eyes sometimes have a faraway brooding look.

Karen and Craig go first to the same reading class in comprehension skills development. They have both scored low in Similarities on the WISC-R, demonstrating some impairment at the conceptual level and also evidencing a memory dysfunction. Karen is the more severely handicapped of the two children; their comprehension development programs will move more slowly than that of either Jeff or Robbie.

Jeff, with olive skin and dark eyes, has an absolutely magnificent smile which he is rapidly learning to use as a social tool. He will begin his clinic time block with a class in word and structural analysis. His perceptual problems keep him from learning successfully with the whole-word approach and he must depend upon a knowledge of the rules and structure of language for his reading progress.

Robbie, a natural leader, has that unusual color combination of auburn hair with a multitude of freckles; in fact, one could quite honestly say one large freckle. Robbie's first clinic time is with his clinician for one-to-one tutoring. The tutor will maintain a careful balance between remediating Robbie's deficit areas and maintaining scholastic progress by utilizing his "strengths."

This balance is vital because it can be very demoralizing to a child to have his deficit areas overprobed. Every child needs to achieve some daily success so that his ego can survive the natural sense of failure that comes with disability. It is often here, in the clinic, while working on a one-to-one reading basis that a child will achieve his first success. It is sometimes terribly difficult for an adult to realize how much a small success can mean to a child. Think for a moment what it is like to be a bright 9-year-old and never to have achieved the basic form of academic success, reading from a printed page, understanding what all those squiggly lines mean.

Some children come to the school with no ego strength at all. As their ego strength grows and becomes firmer through success, the clinician is able to accelerate the process of building deficit areas into more normal functioning channels.

Let's look over Robbie's shoulder as he works. Already he has achieved a fine command of regular words but still requires a multisensory, associative (V. A. *A*. K. T.) approach to irregular words. Today, he is concentrating on the irregular vocabulary from Level 8, the top of Grade 3. Later in the afternoon, the current series of words on which Robbie is working will be utilized in his language-arts class.

Students spend an hour and a quarter in this first time block of the day. By the time they leave, each will have rotated through all three departments of the reading clinic.

At 10:00 A.M., classes change, and the corridors are streaming with children.

Karen and Jeff walk together and, as they pass the trophy case, they pause to feast their eyes on the reading awards. Karen giggles at Jeff's posturing before the window. Last year, his friend Jimmy won the 3,000-page award. This year, Jeff is striving to make this goal. The awards are given for pages independently read in library books and every student participates in the program. The clinicians carefully count pages and ask "double checking" questions. The students know that they have earned their awards and treasure their individual trophies.

Half of the school's student body, including Class D, are scheduled for mathematics during this time block. With so many math classes in session simultaneously, a youngster may progress as rapidly as he is able. As soon as a student has reached the top of his class, he is moved up to the next math group. However, the initial group placement in September presents a variety of problems.

Because the school's population is enrolled with assorted gaps in math achievement, correct class placement must be carefully considered. Who has gaps where? What is the core vocabulary level? What are the social implications? A big-for-his-age 10-year-old who is lagging in math skills does not want to go to class with a tiny 7-year-old. Also, math, for this school's population, is usually a stronger subject than reading. It then becomes not just another subject but an exciting opportunity to move the student forward, an aid to his ego development through success. Since each student has his own cognitive learning styles, degree of handicap—and missing information—it is obvious that this opportunity for achievement can never be fully developed if a child is not properly placed, gaps and all.

Two mornings of testing and task analysis help to solve the problem. Results are translated into the math "systems" approach for task achievement. This, plus the fluidity of block timing, makes possible the precise scheduling which is needed.

Borrowing from the business world and computer technology, the school has taken the elements of math and broken them down into subcomponents, small increments of the information to be learned. These increments are then charted, not only for each unit of math but also for each individual child in the class. The students also fill in their personal progress charts, a technique that offers an immediate reward. With these charts, the student and teacher can see the gaps, see the progress, and, most of all, see the future. For example, Karen's class level is middle math block,[1] as shown in the sample class chart.

Mathematics is quantitative language and as such involves conceptual ability, memory, and efficient visual percepts. Many children with a reading problem can be functioning up to level in

Middle Block 1
Period 2

Items 1 thru 17
Addition

Items 18 thru 29
Subtraction

Names (columns, left to right): Cliff, Kenny, Kiyo, Karen, Mel, Chris, Paula, Elly, Michelle, Billy, Frances

1. Identifies and uses symbols and words for plus. addend. sum. equals. add

2. Completes addition matrix

3. Writes symbols **<**, **>**, or **=**, between 2 addition expressions to make a true statement

4. Adds 3 and 4 digit addends to find sums to 18

5. Adds 3, 4, or 5 addends using vertical form for sums to 18

6. Finds sums using 2 or 3 digit addends without regrouping

7. Translates word problems into addition equations

8. Finds sums of 1 or 2 digit addends with regrouping using horizontal or vertical expressions

9. Finds sums of 2 or 3 digit addends with regrouping using vertical notation

10. Translates story problems to an addition equation using sums **<** 100

11. Finds the missing number in an addition equation for placeholder

12. Finds sums with 2 or more addends of no more than 6 digits

13. Estimates sum by rounding off 2 digit addends

14. Rounds addends with 3 and 4 digits to find estimate of sums

15. Identifies examples of commutative. associative. and zero properties of addition

16. Applies addition property of equality to equations (a = b: 3 + a = 3 + b)

17. Lists all addends as ordered pairs for a given number

18. Understands function of zero in subtraction sums to 18

19. Identifies missing differences by thinking of missing addend

20. Determines that subtraction is not associative

21. Solves two subtraction equations related to partitioning of a set.

22. Matches word problems to equation with sums to 18

23. Writes equations for word problems with sums to 18

24. Recognizes place value and required facts for two-place numbers

25. Writes two-digit problems in vertical notation form

26. Identifies and uses terms: minus. equal. difference. minuend. subtrahend

27. Selects equations for word problems sums to 18

arithmetic *computation* skills but cannot *read* story problems. The ability to "read math" is important. Without it, these children are often unable to *apply* their math skills.

At the school the younger children use a program devised for them that utilizes written materials and products that were printed and made to order; for the older children, the problems are rewritten. Each math program, regardless of level, is based on associative teaching techniques, using manipulative and concrete materials.

Craig is not in class; the assistant director has quietly slipped him out of math to give him time to "talk things over" with her. It is hoped that by allowing the boy to express his feelings verbally, he will be calmed and then be able to restructure himself. His turmoil and resultant *scatter* have hampered his three reading clinic classes. But he is unable to communicate his worries to the assistant director, so an afternoon conference call is set up with Dr. K. A request is sent to the pertinent staff members that a report will be required on Craig this afternoon, and his file is pulled in readiness for the now confirmed afternoon "staffing."

It is now lunchtime. The lunchroom staff is directed by the nurse, for it is she who must also dispense the lunchtime medications to those children who are on chemotherapy regimens. She is also in charge of the mid-morning and afternoon protein snack programs for those children who are on special diets due to glucose intolerance.

At 11:45 A.M.—the most innovative program of the curriculum—another block-timed period, Language Arts, begins. The clinical teaching techniques that are usually reserved for a one-to-one tutorial situation are being successfully transferred to the group classrooms. It is dramatic to watch fourteen sighted children learning with eyes closed as they trace and retrace their "raised" Braille-like spelling words.

Spelling, handwriting, grammar, written and oral expression all comprise language arts. Abilities in these skills vary widely and very often remain problems for a learning disabilities child long after he is reading at grade level. To illustrate, let us consider a brief overview of four Class D students: Karen, Craig, Jeff, and Robbie.

Jeff is typical of a genetic type of specific reading disability complicated by the "plus" factor. His conceptual abilities are high; however, his perception for symbols is impaired. Jeff did poorly in Coding on the WISC-R, with a scaled score of only 5. He is currently approaching a 2^2 reading level. Jeff's spelling, in oral recitation, is at the 2^1 level, which is not far behind his reading. In other words, he appears to be very nearly balanced, but this balance is an illusion, for Jeff's problems lie in another area. When he tries to add a second modality, writing, to the spelling task, he cannot spell because he cannot sequence the symbols motorically on his paper.

This particular aspect of Jeff's disability had, for two years before he entered the school, thoroughly perplexed and even angered his parents. Jeff would come home from school and recite his daily spelling lesson beautifully, then present his mother with a zero paper. Now his parents understand the problem and offer great encouragement to their son as he works very hard to acquire this skill. Unfortunately, and his parents are aware of this, there is doubt that Jeff will ever become even moderately proficient in written spelling. He will probably be a phonetic speller all his life.

Robbie is in his last year at the school. His 128 IQ falls in the superior range; he may be considered as a prime example of specific dyslexia, the kind that is usually overlooked. Fortunately, Robbie's parents were exceptionally aware because his father is an associate professor of reading at a local university. At an early age, it was recognized that there was a high degree of difference between Robbie's performance and his potential. To prevent the onset of an emotional overlay, his parents began early remediation and a careful support program at home. At this point in his academic life, grammar is Robbie's stumbling block. His reading is up to level and his spelling and handwriting are progressing nicely. But, oh, how he can garble his grammar! His sentences become illogical and his story reports are out of sequence.

Since grammar is a major problem for most learning disabled children, and the available programs did not do the necessary remedial job, the school designed its own. Here, again, small increments are used as an approach to transpositional grammar along with associative techniques utilizing the base line of the core vocabulary. Robbie's language arts program will concentrate on written expression emphasizing grammar, so that next year he will be up to par at his new school.

Karen, a shy, quiet little girl, must struggle in most areas because of her conceptual impairments. Her medical protocol *technically* confirms minimal brain damage. She suffered a fall at age 7 months, 1 week that resulted in a skull fracture. Her handwriting and spelling are more than adequate. Her papers, from a penmanship standpoint, look as if she had attended "Miss Primm's School for Young Ladies" all her life. Her spelling is rarely wrong. But, and this is a big but, she has impaired processing abilities and associative memory; she has great trouble with originality and very little ability to sequence her thoughts and thus gain clear oral and written expression. Her language arts teacher is helping Karen classify her percepts into more clearly expressed concepts. Karen loves to take home a Language Master (an audio-visual aid) on weekends. With it, she uses the school's original associative vocabulary program. For her, this reinforcing program is fun.

Craig is a neurological dysfunction case complicated by an irregular and spiking EEG pattern. As we have seen, he is subject to inner storms and is emotionally labile. Although he is having a bad day, he can be all sunshine and light as long as his environment is stable. Since a totally static environment is impossible to achieve, Craig and his parents have a long way to go until this lability and his emotional outbursts are brought under control.

Craig has difficulty with all the language arts, not from the standpoint of performance alone, but also because of his high degree of distractibility and disinterest. He will sit and morosely poke holes in his work paper. Or, perhaps, he will write only two lines and then begin to scribble perseveratively. Often, he takes the view that grammar is just plain funny, making inappropriate comments in the middle of a lesson. He is just plain bored by the whole process of language arts. The challenge here is to find the key to motivation for this child.

Actually, language arts is basically boring to any learning disabled child. It requires considerable drill and repetition, and it would be foolish to assert that drill work is exciting for anybody. But where there's a will and a need, there is usually a way. The language arts program has been integrated with one of the favorite subjects for almost all children—science.

Language arts is expressive (output). When one combines the technical aspects of learning the language arts skills with a subject that automatically lends itself easily to expressive projects—science—it is possible to give children the learning excitement so necessary to overcome boredom.

Science or social studies, for Class D, is taken at 1:00 P.M., the last time block of the day.

The students absorb their facts in science and social studies from movies, film strips, and lectures. The range of commercial audio/visual materials is truly impressive. Every conceivable subject, at all levels of interest, is available for purchase. The audio/visual-based learning format enables the child with a reading problem to keep pace with his peer group in general information.

The information acquired by the children in the audio/visual classes is used as input for the language arts composition assignments. Thus, if spiders are the science topic, the children will have spiders for their language arts oral and written expression unit. A dual purpose is served. A variety of vivid material, at controlled levels, for use by the language arts teachers is available.

To achieve the required reinforcement in social studies, the students give plays, have debates, hold mock elections, and publish a historical newspaper.

One of the most interesting aspects of the social studies program is that the textbooks are in the reading clinic with the tutors. When a student is ready, it is the clinician who will help the child learn to cope with study skills, outlining in chapters, and reading in the content area. This concept of moving the social studies "reading" to the clinic has shattered the major learning barrier to the subject.

■

If asked, most children will tell you that their two favorite subjects in school are lunch and playtime.

Physical education for the learning disabled child should not be, even for the youngest, merely playtime. Rather, it should be an opportunity to develop areas that a teacher cannot successfully touch upon in the classroom.

As members of Class D go from the school buildings to the physical education field, they must first complete an obstacle course. Here, they balance on, jump over, swing through, and climb. This gives daily and systematic development to the proprioceptive system. Children with learning disabilities can hit a ball, but, then, they may run the bases the wrong way. They can catch a football well enough but may not remember or properly sequence the instructions from the huddle. Jeff's program calls for him to join two other boys in an extra ten minutes of work on the balance beam using advanced exercises. They will join the rest of the class when it is time for the games to start. All games have rules and instructions and these are used as the major focus of the physical education program.

The children really play hard because it's fun. Here, too, trophies are awarded at the end of the year for sportsmanship, attitude development, proficiency, and progress. Athletics are important to boys socially. At home, they are often the best on the block, which means a lot to them.

After physical education, Group D returns to Homeroom 3 to wait for the bus rollcall. When all the students have gone, a lonesome sort of quiet settles over the buildings as the staff starts its "other" day.

■

The afternoon staff schedule varies according to the day of week. There may be progress meetings for math or language arts teachers, analysis of behavior modification programs, administrative staff meetings, schedule changes, and, of course, always the inevitable paperwork.

Today is weekly progress report day, but the teachers set this work aside until they have prepared their reports on Craig for the "staffing." While these are being completed, the assistant director will call Dr. K., the psychologist.

The conversation with Dr. K. is a no-nonsense talk between two busy professionals. Dr. K. decides that Craig will be the subject of this week's professional visitation to the school. Since the school functions as the coordinating agency between the disciplines involved in Craig's overall program, a call will be placed to his pediatrician. This is standard procedure when any child requires a *full* staffing.

Staffing a student can sound ominous to a parent but it is a positive process whereby the dynamics of training, talent, and concern come together to help a child.

Craig's master folder has been pulled from the confidential files. It is about four inches thick. His past and present evaluations and test scores are in it; the correspondence from the various outside referrals have been integrated; and now the folder is brought completely up to date with the addition of this week's reports from the faculty. Craig's folder is like an unfinished novel: it has a beginning, a plot with problems, but the end is not yet written.

The clinical supervisors meet for nearly an hour, reading, making notations, and verbal comparisons with each other. Although each carries around a mental evaluation of every child, they cannot trust to memory here. The entire folder is reviewed in detail. Literally, Craig's life is laid out on the table in front of them and the room in which they sit becomes almost a courtroom. Few parents realize the extent to which educators and guidance counselors are daily involved with, and influencing, our children's futures, affecting their very ability to earn a livelihood, to be absorbed into the social and cultural mainstream of the nation, and eventually to function at a positive interpersonal level with their own children.

The decisions that evaluators and educators make can build a child's future or destroy it. Destruction can come from a hastily made, seemingly minor decision at the daily level. It is for this reason that the people sitting in the quiet room, viewing Craig's folder, watch themselves carefully. They are aware that "staffing" is a judgmental mosaic based on medical advice, support service review, and faculty recommendations. This information is the bone and sinew of Craig.

Next Week

A few days later at the completion of the conference with Dr. K., the necessary decisions regarding Craig's program were made. His pediatrician had concluded that since Craig's situation was not medically based; no change was to be made in medication. The basis of Craig's unhappiness and resultant breakdown of behavior was rooted in the current home situation and, if not alleviated, Craig might go into a serious emotional crisis. Since the home is directly involved, it would be necessary to offer specific recommendations to his parents. The parents were called for a conference to be held as soon as they were both available, but before the next weekend.

When the assistant director began her conference with Craig's parents, she sensed an uneasiness in the room. From experience, she knew that whatever was disturbing the parents had to be dispelled and the reasons for the ill ease uncovered before Craig's problems could be met. During the frank discussion it was learned that Craig's maternal grandparents had arrived for a long visit a month ago. Their visit was the crux of Craig's unexpected upset. His grandmother, an outspoken woman, did not really understand his unpredictable behavior or academic handicaps. She believed that her daughter pampered the boy. She constantly harped at Craig about little things, comparing him unfavorably to his younger sister.

Craig's mother had been living under great stress because of her own mother's negative attitudes and sharp criticisms. This, in turn, enraged Craig's father. The whole atmosphere of the house, especially on weekends with father home, was charged with tension. Craig's mother and father had been having screaming fights with each other and with his grandparents. In fact, even divorce had been threatened. Craig felt as if he were to blame. All the emotions flowing through the adults were coming to rest on his shoulders.

Additionally, his mother, because of her own distraction and stress, had forgotten to give Craig his earned behavior reward on the past two weekends. The order and structure that she had so carefully maintained since learning about Craig's problems and needs had been totally disrupted. The boy had developed a deep feeling of guilt. This, in turn, was leading to a disintegration of ego strength and an almost visceral surge of panic.

The immediate solution to the home problem was to bring the grandparents to the school and have a blunt information session. With a sense of relief, the parents agreed to this plan, feeling certain that once the grandparents really understood Craig's problem they would change their attitude.

The conference was concluded with an in-depth discussion of the restructuring of Craig's behavior modification program. His mother was told that Dr. K. wanted Craig's next appointment moved up by one week. The parents were also reassured that Craig's teachers under the guidance of the clinic director would put extra effort into success tasks. This would help stabilize the boy's emotional status until the home situation improved.

■

We have now seen a day in the life of a private clinical school. If it seemed like hard work, perhaps even tedious, it often is. But the rewards are inherent in the profession. Besides, for this school and many others, this daily life is only the tip of the iceberg. The children come here for help, but swirling around, silent and unseen by them, is another life—the life of research and service. This *single* school is involved in: cooperative medical research involving volunteer student and family populations; dermatoglyphic studies, autoimmune investigations, cooperative cyclical A. M. P. studies, glucose tolerance observations, computerized family studies, and investigation into the effects of barometric pressure on visual memory; supervision of on-campus field experience and internship programs at both undergraduate and graduate levels; cooperation with graduate students and doctoral candidates who use the data bank for thesis research; professional visits from here and abroad which range anywhere from a half day to two weeks; workshops, lectures, and membership on various federal, state, and local advisory committees.

The spin-off from this form of extra effort is having a positive influence on education for *all* children. Research and services are flowing from public and private facilities throughout the world.

The innovations, programs, and theoretical ideologies of learning disabilities produced by the professionals in the field are proving that every child has a need for a more individualized approach to learning. In our computerized, classified, too busy culture of the seventies, nothing could be more valuable to the future of education. Eventually society will realize that it is neither precise nor accurate to speak *negatively* of children with learning disabilities. Rather, speak *positively* of children's learning *abili*ties/*dis*abilities.

Part Four

9. Screening Instruments
   and Checklists

The prevention of learning disabilities lies in medicine, the diagnosis in the realm of psychology, while the "cure" is the responsibility of educators.

The Shadow Children

9

The questions most frequently asked by parents are at what age to test and how do you discover if a child needs evaluation. The following screening instruments and checklists are designed to help answer these questions.

The first is a portion of a Preschool and Kindergarten Performance Profile, published as a teacher's screening inventory by Educational Performance Associates of Ridgefield, New Jersey. The second is the visual retention section of a preliminary screening instrument for first- and second-graders.

The reader may use one or the other of these, depending upon the child's grade level, in conjunction with the behaviors checklist. This checklist is also viable for use for an older child.

The method of analysis is given before each instrument. This information, coupled with the knowledge gained from this book, should give you a fairly stable indication of your child's situation.

The screenings are not to be administered repetitiously.

If a child who is older than the age levels indicated for the instruments does especially poorly in performance, then this child should be evaluated forthwith.

If, after completion of these screenings, in your judgment, you wish to seek evaluation, obtain only professional help. If you are at a loss as to where to begin this search, then refer to the brief listing of organizations and/or reference sources to be found in the last pages of this book.

The following preschool and kindergarten performance profile is based on direct observation of the child. There is no formal scoring format. Because the goal of this instrument is "readiness," the scale is sliding, one through the final number. A 5-year-old with nursery experience would rate among the higher numbers; the younger, less experienced child would naturally rate lower.

Find the optimum your child can perform.

SOCIAL

• **Topic 1—Interpersonal Relations**

I. RELATING TO CHILDREN

1. Shows interest in others only when prompted
2. Is aware of and shows interest in others
3. Tries to establish a relationship with one or two peers
4. Establishes definite relationship with one or two peers
5. Has a give-and-take relationship with the peer group
6. Has a give-and-take relationship with groups other than peers

II. RECEIVING HELP

1. Accepts help only when imposed
2. Accepts help when encouraged
3. Recognizes need for and accepts help
4. Recognizes need for help and requests assistance
5. Selects appropriate sources for help
6. Encourages peers to obtain appropriate sources for help

• **Topic 2—Emotional Behavior**

I. FRUSTRATION

1. Is frustrated whenever immediate success is not achieved
2. Withdraws from situation when immediate success is not achieved
3. Withdraws from situation after second unsuccessful attempt
4. Makes several attempts at activity before giving up
5. Organizes materials to minimize chance of failure
6. Is able to rationalize and accept failure

- **Topic 3—Safety**

I. HAZARD AWARENESS

1. Needs continuous cautioning
2. Needs frequent cautioning
3. Is aware of hazards but needs occasional reminders
4. Avoids all hazards which have been indicated
5. Avoids all obvious hazards
6. Is responsible for own safety and is concerned about others

II. GROUP ACTIVITIES

1. Depends upon direct and constant one-to-one supervision
2. Participates in acceptable manner only when given frequent reminders
3. Participates in a desirable manner, needing only occasional reminders
4. Participates in a desirable manner in a supervised group
5. Participates consistently in a desirable manner
6. Guides others to participate positively

INTELLECTUAL

- **Topic 4—Communication**

I. INTELLIGIBLE SPEECH

1. Can be understood when listener knows what is being discussed
2. Can be understood only when gestures and words are combined
3. Can be understood, but often displays frequent sound omissions
4. Can be understood by peers in restricted discussion
5. Can be understood by peers in unrestricted discussion
6. Can be understood easily by children and adults

II. LISTENING FOR DIRECTIONS

1. Follows simple directions by imitation only
2. Follows simple directions only after repetition
3. Follows simple directions on first request
4. Carries out 2-step directions
5. Carries out a series of 3 sequential directions
6. Can carry out directions involving a time lapse

● **Topic 5—Basic Concepts**

I. CONCEPTS OF SIZE AND SHAPES

1. Differentiates between two grossly different objects only by handling them (physical screening)
2. Differentiates between two grossly different objects by visual screening
3. Selects the smallest and largest objects from a group of five
4. Selects the smallest and largest objects from a group of ten
5. Arranges five items from smallest to largest
6. Arranges ten similar items in low-to-high progression

II. ABSTRACTION (CONCEPTS AND COMPARISONS)

1. Is mostly limited to concrete thinking
2. Uses a few abstract terms (slow, fast, warm, cool, yesterday, tomorrow) but needs some explanation
3. Uses abstract terms appropriately and needs little correction
4. Can make simple comparisons (hot as fire, cold as ice)
5. Generalizes and uses basic comparisons appropriately
6. Shows some evidence of divergent thinking, e.g., names other uses for a brick besides a building

INTELLECTUAL

● **Topic 6—Perceptual Development**

I. VISUAL PERCEPTION AND DISCRIMINATION

1. Can pair like objects
2. Can pair similar objects when found in a dissimilar group
3. Can pair like geometric symbols
4. Can pair similar symbols when found in a dissimilar group
5. Identifies differences in language symbols, shapes, and patterns
6. Identifies fine differences in language symbols, shapes, and patterns

II. AUDITORY DISCRIMINATION WITHOUT VISUAL CUES

1. Discriminates between grossly different sounds, but requires frequent repetitions
2. Discriminates between grossly different sounds
3. Discriminates among the voices of several peers
4. Discriminates between differing sounds
5. Discriminates between similar sounding words
6. Discriminates among various musical instruments by sounds produced

PHYSICAL

● **Topic 7—Self Help**

I. SHOE MANAGEMENT

1. Places shoes on feet, but frequently wrong feet
2. Places shoes on feet properly
3. Places shoes but cannot tie bow
4. Ties bow with verbal directions
5. Laces and ties bows with success
6. Laces and ties bows for others

● **Topic 8—Gross Motor Skills**

I. CATCHING A BALL

1. Attempts to catch ball, but shows obvious fear
2. Positions hands, but frequently misses ball
3. Can catch only a gently thrown ball
4. Can catch a ball thrown from a distance of 20 feet
5. Gauges direction of ball, moves toward it, and catches it
6. Catches skillfully while running

● **Topic 9—Fine Visual Motor Skills**

I. CLAY, DOUGH, PLASTICENE

1. Handles materials only with assistance
2. Handles materials, experiments with finger movements
3. Uses hands, fingers, or body pressures to randomly produce shapes
4. Reproduces simple shapes
5. Produces a variety of shapes
6. Coordinates hands and tools to produce various shapes

II. CUTTING WITH SCISSORS

1. Operates scissors with two hands
2. Cuts using one hand in random snipping
3. Cuts and moves scissors forward in cutting a strip
4. Cuts paper, approximately follows line
5. Cuts, stops, and changes direction
6. Plans and cuts in relation to design

III. BUILDING WITH SMALL BLOCKS

1. Handles, carries, and piles blocks in irregular manner
2. Accomplishes line construction and simple design

3. Builds in three dimensions
4. Builds recognizable structures
5. Builds carefully with eye for symmetry and artistic design
6. Builds intricate representational structures

IV. COLORING

1. Holds crayons, but is able to use only with assistance
2. Scribbles on paper
3. Colors in approximate area containing design
4. Shows ability to stay within design
5. Colors with a motion that conforms to the design
6. Colors accurately a variety of outlined shapes

V. COPYING

1. Traces simple forms
2. Completes simple forms when outlines are provided, i.e., dots, dashes
3. Copies simple forms from samples in close view on desk
4. Copies simple forms from samples on blackboard (distal vision)
5. Copies basic geometric forms: square, triangle, or circle
6. Copies both letters and numbers from blackboard or desk

The following instrument was designed for use by doctors, teachers, and parents. The instructions are simple, the evaluation is even simpler.

Children who are in the last half of the first grade or in second grade are eligible.

An 80 percent rate of correct completion (10 designs) by the middle of the second grade is considered adequate performance. Be guided by this: a lower rate of performance is expected of a first-grader (especially one without kindergarten experience); a higher rate is expected of a third-grader.

PRELIMINARY SCREENING
(Visual Retention Section)

DIRECTIONS FOR ADMINISTERING

Materials:

1. Numbered set of 12 designs (recopy designs to enlarged size)
2. Crayon or pencil and 12 half sheets of paper (letter size)

Procedure:

1. Small groups—preferably 6*

2. Have students judiciously spaced—so they are unable to see each other's performance—but able to have a clear view of the stimulus cards.

3. This is a screening test of visual retention, therefore a distracting activity has been introduced. To implement this distraction, the examiner is to stand at the side of the room.

4. The students are instructed to put pencils down on table or desk, turn bodies (not just heads) to the side to view the design.

5. The design exposure is approximately 10 seconds—after which students turn back to their tables, pick up pencils and draw the design.

6. Allow approximately 15 seconds for simple design performance (1 or 2 symbols), approximately 20 seconds to reproduce the more complex design series (3 or more symbols).

7. After each design is drawn on the allotted sheet, the completed designs are collected by the examiner. The test is terminated as soon as a student reaches an obvious frustration level.

* Adapt for individual administration.

top

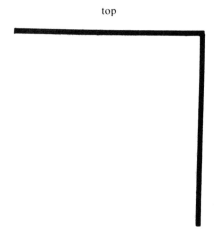

top

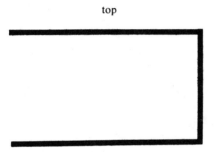

top

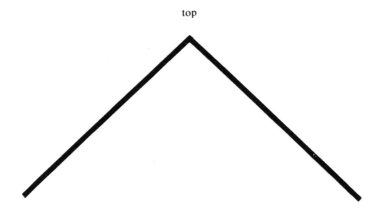

top

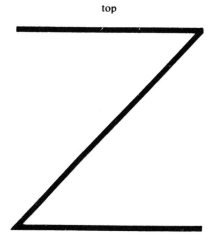

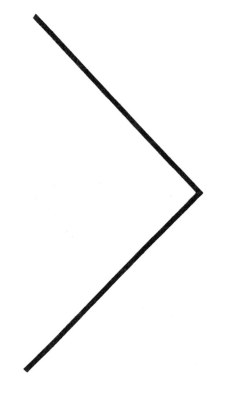

top

top

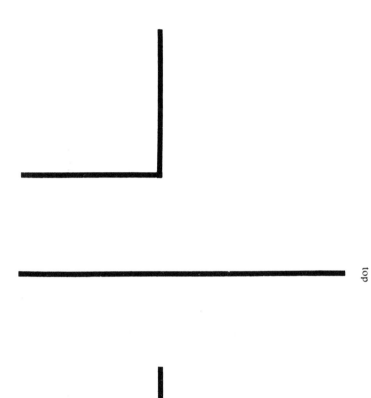

top

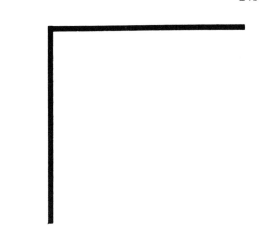

top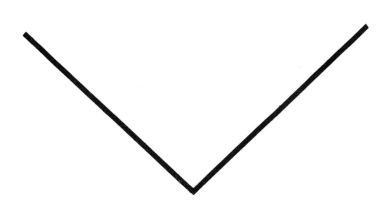

top

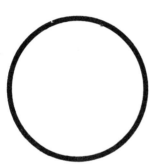

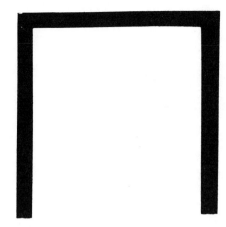

top

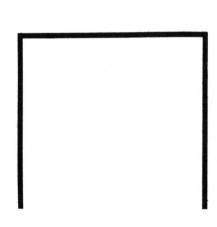

top

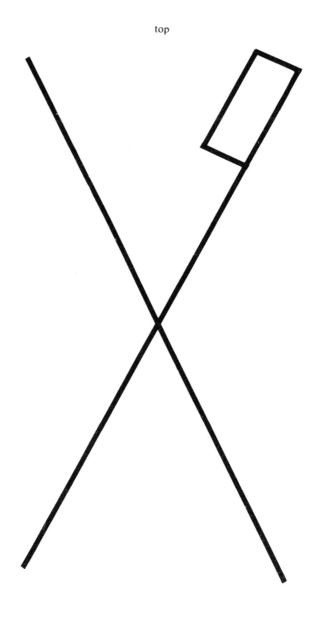

top

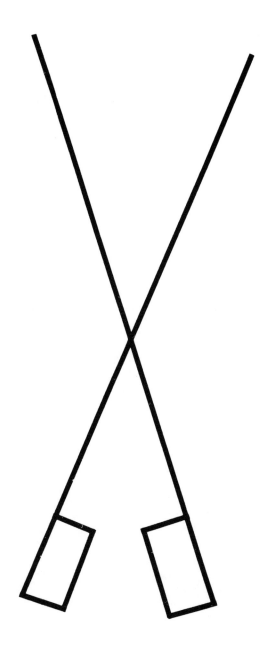

The following checklist, predominantly derived from the Peterson-Quay-Werry-Wiess-Peters Scales, consists basically of adjectives which parents and teachers will immediately recognize as descriptive of some children. The lists are loosely grouped (author's grouping) according to type. They should be read carefully and thoughtfully, not just skimmed. Some of the behavior items are found in all children at one time or another. In reviewing these lists, one must bear in mind the degree and number of items "ticked off." There is a great deal of difference between "occasionally" and "usually." Parents should also remember that what is unimportant at age 6 may be very important at age 11.

Professionals use these or similar scales for a careful and detailed analysis of a child's behavior, but parents can also use them effectively in the more general assessment regarding their decision for or against evaluation. If, for instance, a parent has to check more than four items in any two groupings, he should add this information to the results of one of the screening instruments and to conclusions reached after reading pertinent sections of this book. He should also check over the family patterns, the birth and infancy history of the child and his achievement levels in school. By then, the parent should have a fairly clear picture of whether his child is in trouble.

BEHAVIOR CHECKLIST

Group No. 1	Never	Occasionally	Usually
Disruptiveness, tendency to annoy and bother others			
Restlessness, inability to sit still			
Attention-seeking, show-off behavior			
Short attention span			
Fighting			
Temper tantrums			
Tension, inability to relax			
Disobedience, difficulty in disciplinary control			

	Never	Occasionally	Usually
Uncooperativeness in group situations			
Hyperactivity—always on the go			
Distractibility			
Destructiveness in regard to his own and/or others' property			
Profane language, swearing, cursing			
Nervousness, jitteriness, jumpiness, easily startled			
Irritability, hot-tempered, easily aroused to anger			
Excessive talking			
Requires adult supervision or attendance constantly			
Inability for quiet play			
Constantly changing activity			
Disrupts others' play			
Interrupts teacher and other children excessively			

Group No. 2	Never	Occasionally	Usually
Doesn't know how to have fun, behaves like a little adult			
Feelings of inferiority			
Crying over minor annoyances and hurts			
Preoccupation—in a world of his own			
Social withdrawal, preference for solitary activities			
Easily flustered and confused			
Reticence, secretiveness			
Hypersensitivity, feelings easily hurt			
Anxiety, chronic general fearfulness			
Excessive daydreaming			
Depression, chronic sadness			
Passivity, suggestibility, easily led by others			
Sluggishness, lethargy			
Specific fears, e.g., of dogs, of the dark, of going to sleep at night			

Group No. 3   Never   Occasionally   Usually

Dislike for school
Jealousy over attention paid other children
Prefers to play with younger children
Inattentiveness to what others say
Truancy from school
Laziness in school and in performance of
   other tasks
Irresponsibility, undependability
Negativism, tendency to do the opposite
   of what is required
Prefers to play with older children
Fluctuating performance
Socially inept behavior
Seeks parental attention excessively

Group No. 4   Never   Occasionally   Usually

Thumb sucking
Skin allergy
Headaches
Dizziness, vertigo
Difficulty in bowel control, soiling
Nausea, vomiting as associated with emotional
   stress
Masturbation
Hay fever and/or asthma
Clumsiness, awkwardness, poor muscular
   coordination
Stuttering
Drowsiness
Enuresis (bed wetting)
Stomach aches, abdominal pain of
   undefined character after illness is
   ruled out

Group No. 5   Never   Occasionally   Usually

Tics
Difficulty in settling down for sleep
Inadequate amount of sleep
Restlessness during sleep

Epilogue

There are some 209 million people in the United States. Of this number, more than 60 million are students, and about 3.5 million are teachers, supervisory, and other instructional staff. In other words, nearly one-third of our *entire* population is directly involved in some manner in the educational process.

We are currently spending more than $90 billion a year, according to the United States Office of Education, to finance this educational enterprise. By any standard, this is big business. In fact, education is second only to defense in budget expenditure if we also consider private enterprise such as publishers, manufacturers, and so forth.

This $90 billion industry is primarily financed by our tax dollars, which means, at least theoretically, that all 209 million of us own our educational system. We own it, we finance it, we work in it, and we use it.

Yet, every year, we graduate thousands of students who cannot read, cannot spell, cannot do math. Every minute of every school day, we hurt some child by not recognizing and alleviating his special needs. Each hour we turn someone, student or staff, away from the classroom.

Who is at fault? Why do we have millions of adults and

249

students who are technically or pragmatically illiterate? Why are we unable to control the quality of education if we own the system? Are we all—educators, politicians, and parents—ignorant and insensitive to the individual needs of what has been called our most vulnerable minority, our children? To blame the system is easy, but could 63.5 million people use $90 billion without a system? Without system, chaos would reign.

People plus communal money must necessarily equal system, and, unfortunately, system usually means rigidity. Rigidity, by its very nature, locks out individual needs and locks us back into the system, a full-circle pattern that must somehow be broken.

In the District of Columbia, in the 1967 case of *Hobson vs. Hansen,* the circle began to be broken. This case and other subsequent ones have been the logical progression from the initial Supreme Court's 1954 ruling on school desegregation.

Hobson vs. Hansen challenged public school classification or "tracking" practices. The cases that have followed have variously challenged the academic judgmental procedures that have excluded certain children from school, and the decisions handed down have begun to define and support the legal right children have to an education that will prepare them fully for the requirements of society. These cases have progressed from minority group's rights, to the rights of the acutely handicapped, to the rights of all individuals. The courts have begun to break the chain that limits children by labeling them.

Children who are labeled socially or academically "different" in some way at 5 or 6 years of age too often acquire a stigma that is usually irrevocable in our school systems. An academic label is highly visible because traditionally there have been only two basic forms of education—normal and special. On the basis of IQ alone, children have been funneled into one or the other of these categories. This has happened even when a child whose native language is Spanish, for instance, has been tested in English. Or the child suffering from impaired visual or auditory percepts has ended up in the back row in the classroom and been labeled unteachable.

It is practices such as these that the courts have and will cut down. Children have legal, moral, and inherent civil rights as citizens, and these rights should not be subsumed by evaluative and academic procedures that ignore the necessary components of individual cognitive processing *ab*ilities/*dis*abilities.

■

While this book is being read, thousands of children are being born who, in six years, will be expected to perform according to certain academic and cultural standards. Some of these children will have no problems in school, some will have a visible severe handicap, and some, far too many, will have a learning disability. These children will be sons and daughters, grandchildren, nephews and nieces—who become neighbors and fellow workers. These children, born today, are our tomorrow—our future. We conceive them in the "still hours" and sometimes they require that we have the courage of the still hours.

As we establish educational goals for our children and our society, we move beyond the scientific issues. We find ourselves engaged in struggles through which we express our moral and social values as well. The reader thus needs to keep in mind that we are talking about *truth* and *value*.

Rudolf Ekstein, Ph.D., and
Rocco L. Motto, M.D., 1968

Acknowledgments

Grateful acknowledgment is given to the following persons who have either offered guidance and advice or whose papers, published and unpublished, have been used as reference material for this book. Through their research, theories, and confirmed conceptualizations of the needs of learning disabled children a clinical literature has emerged that enables parents, paraprofessionals, and teachers to view and gain insight into one of the most complex childhood situations that can arise.

To cite individually every piece of literature involved with the information contained in this book would literally constitute a volume unto itself. However, the desire to give appreciative recognition has prompted this listing of those individuals whose work, and in some instances consultation, has made this book possible.

Abercrombie, M. L. J.
Abraham, H. J.
Abrahamson, E. M.
Abrams, J. C.
Abt, Jean
Ackerman, Peggy T.
Adams, J. A.
Adams, Nina

Adelman, Howard
Adler, A.
Adler, Sol
Ainsworth, Stanley
Aird, R.
Albert, J.
Alexander, D.
Allen, D. C.

Allport, F.
Allport, G. W.
Almy, Millie
Amatruda, C. S.
Amble, Bruce
Ames, H.
Ames, Louise Bates
Andersen, Ellen
Andersen, P.
Anderson, C.
Anderson, G. L.
Anderson, H. H.
Anderson, J.
Andersson, S.
Apgar, Virginia
Ardrey, Robert
Arena, John I.
Arroyo, M.
Atkinson, B.
Atkinson, R.
Atwater, S. K.
Auerbach, A.
Aug, R.
Ausubel, David P.
Axler, Morton M.
Ayers, J.

Baer, C.
Baker, Georgia
Baker, H. J.
Baker, John R.
Baldwin, Alfred L.
Ballard, P. B.
Bangs, T.
Bannatyne, Alex D.
Bannochie, Margaret N.
Barbe, Walter B.
Barnes, K.
Baron, M.
Barsch, Ray H.
Bartell, N.

Bartlett, F. C.
Bateman, Barbara D.
Battig, W. F.
Beach, Frank A.
Beberman, M.
Beck, G.
Beck, Robert H.
Becker, J.
Bee, Helen L.
Beery, K.
Belmont, I.
Bender, Lauretta
Bendinger, Richard
Bennett, E. L.
Bensberg, G. J.
Bensen, J.
Benton, Arthur L.
Benton, Curtis D., Jr.
Bentzen, F.
Berger, H.
Berkowitz, L.
Betts, E.
Bilodeau, E.
Binet, Alfred
Birch, Herbert G.
Bird, J. W.
Bishop, G. W.
Black, F. William
Bladergroen, W. J.
Blake, E.
Blankenship, M. E.
Blom, Gaston E.
Bloom, Benjamin S.
Bloomfield, Leonard
Boder, Elena
Bond, A. D.
Bond, G.
Borel-Maisonny, S.
Bosch, E.
Boshes, B.
Botel, Morton

Bousfield, W. A.
Boyle, R.
Braam, L. S.
Brabner, G.
Bracken, Dorothy K.
Bradley, C.
Brady, Joseph V.
Brain, Sir Russell
Brand, H.
Braun, H. W.
Braun, J.
Brazelton, T.
Brazier, M. A. B.
Bridge, R. Gary
Bridges, J.
Broadbent, D.
Brodal, A.
Broverman, D. M.
Brown, G.
Brown, J.
Brown, W.
Brownell, W. A.
Bruch, P.
Brueckner, L. J.
Bruce, R. W.
Bruner, Jerome S.
Brutten, Milton
Bryan, T.
Bryant, N. Dale
Bucy, P. C.
Buktenica, N.
Bunn, Hattie R.
Burgus, Roger
Burks, H.
Burtt, H. E.
Bush, Wilma J.
Butcher, H.

Cairns, H.
Call, Justin
Callantine, M. F.

Campbell, S. B.
Carey, J. E.
Carmichael, L.
Carner, Richard
Carpenter, M. B.
Carpenter, R.
Carrell, James A.
Cass, James
Castaneda, A.
Caton, R.
Cattell, Raymond B.
Cave, A. J. E.
Chalfant, James C.
Chall, Jeanne
Chappell, G.
Chang, H. T.
Chang, Thomas M. C.
Chang, Vivian A. C.
Check, J. F.
Childs, Sally B.
Chittenden, Edward
Christensen, C.
Christensen, P. R.
Cieutat, V. J.
Clements, Samuel D.
Clemmens, R. L.
Cofer, C. N.
Cohen, B. H.
Cohen, H. A.
Cohn, Robert
Cole, Edwin M.
Coleman, Howard M.
Colodny, D.
Comly, Hunter H.
Conger, John J.
Conners, C. Keith
Connolly, Christopher
Cornblath, M.
Corrigan, P. M.
Cott, Allan
Cotterell, G. C.

Coulson, J. E.
Covington, J.
Cox, J. W.
Cox, R. D.
Cratty, Bryant J.
Cravioto, J.
Crider, Blake
Critchley, MacDonald
Cruickshank, W. M.
Cukier, Lillian
Cummins, Harold
Cunningham, J. M.

Dallenbach, K. M.
D'Amato, M. F.
Damrin, Dora E.
Dart, Raymond A.
Davis, F. C.
Davis, R. A.
Day, D.
de Ajuriaguerra, J.
Dechant, Emerald V.
de Charms, R.
de Hirsch, K.
De Jong, R. N.
Delacato, Carl H.
de la Cruz, Felix
Della-Piana, G.
Demerdash, A.
Denckla, M.
Denhoff, Eric
Detambel, M. H.
Dewey, John
DeWitt, Frances B.
Diamond, I. T.
DiNola, Alfred J.
Dirks, D.
Dolch, Edward W.
Doll, Edgar A.
Dollard, J. C.
Doman, Glenn

Doman, R. J.
Donlon, Genevieve
Dörken, H.
Douglas, V. I.
Dowling, R. M.
Dozier, Paul
Drake, Charles
Dreifuss, F. E.
Drevdahl, J. E.
Drew, A. A.
Drew, A. L.
Drews, A.
Duncan, C. P.
Dunsing, Jack D.
Durbrow, Helene C.
Durell, D.
Durrell, Donald D.
Durrell, D. W.
Dworkin, Nancy
Dykman, Roscoe A.
Dykstra, R.
Dyrud, Jarl E.

Eames, T. H.
Eastman, N. J.
Eccles, J. C.
Edelman, Peter B.
Edwards, A. L.
Eeg-Olofsson, O.
Ehrhardt, A.
Eichorn, J. R.
Eikenberry, D. H.
Eisenberg, Leon
Eisenson, Jon
Ekstein, Rudolf
Eliot, J.
Ellis, M. J.
Ellis, N. R.
Engle, T. L.
English, H. B.
Epstein, L. C.

Epstein, W.
Ervin, Susan M.
Eustis, R.
Evans, J. L.

Faux, E. J.
Fawcett, H. P.
Feindel, W.
Feldhusen, J. F.
Ferinden, W.
Fernald, Grace
Ferris, F. L.
Filbin, R. L.
Fine, B. J.
Fine, M.
Fineman, Carol
Finlay, G. C.
Fishel, H. D.
Fitzgerald, D.
Flagenheimer, H.
Flathouse, Virgil E.
Foord, E. N.
Forgus, Ronald H.
Fowler, G. W.
Frame, B.
Francis, W.
Fraser, D.
Freedberg, A. S.
Freidus, Elizabeth
French, R. S.
Freud, Sigmund
Freundl, P.
Frierson, Edward C.
Fries, Charles C.
Fristoe, M.
Fromm, Erich
Frostig, Marianne
Frutchey, F. P.
Fryer, Jeane
Fuller, Gerald
Furth, Hans G.

Gaddes, W. H.
Gaines, Rosslyn
Galambos, R.
Galanter, E. H.
Gallagher, James J.
Gallagher, J. Roswell
Gallistel, E.
Galperin, P. Y.
Gann, E.
Gardner, R. W.
Garfield, S.
Garside, R. F.
Gastaut, Y.
Gates, Arthur I.
Gaudreau, J.
Gayton, William
Gerstmann, J.
Geschwind, N.
Gesell, Arnold L.
Getman, G. N.
Getzels, J. W.
Gibbs, E. L.
Gibbs, F.
Gibson, Eleanor J.
Gibson, J. J.
Giffen, M.
Giles, Marion T.
Gill, R.
Gilliland, A. R.
Gillingham, Anna
Giok, L.
Glaser, R.
Glaze, J. A.
Goetzinger, C.
Goldberg, Herman K.
Goldberger, Emanuel
Goldenson, Robert M.
Goldiamond, Israel
Goldman, R.
Goldstein, K.
Goldstein, S.

Golick, Margaret
Gomulicki, B. R.
Gonzalez, R. C.
Gooddy, William
Goodenough, D. R.
Goodenough, F.
Gordon, Ira J.
Goss, A. E.
Granit, A. R.
Gray, William S.
Green, L.
Green, Orville C.
Greenfield, Patricia
Grill, J.
Grinspoon, Lester
Gruber, J.
Guilford, J. P.
Guillemin, Roger
Gullion, M. Elizabeth
Gunderson, B.
Gustafson, Lenore M.
Guthrie, J.

Hage, D.
Hagin, Rosa R.
Hainsworth, Marian
Hainsworth, Peter
Hall, V.
Hallahan, D.
Hallgren, Bertil
Halstead, W. C.
Hammer, M.
Hammill, D.
Hamolsky, M. W.
Hanawalt, N. G.
Hanley, John
Hanson, H. B.
Hanvik, Leo J.
Harlow, H. F.
Harmon, D. B.
Harper, R.

Harris, Albert J.
Harris, D.
Harris, G.
Harris, Thomas A.
Hartlage, L.
Hartung, M. L.
Haselrud, G. M.
Hatton, D.
Havard, J.
Hebb, D. O.
Hendrickson, G.
Hegge, T. G.
Heider, F.
Heiss, Warren
Heller, T.
Hellmuth, Jerome
Henry, C.
Hermann, Knud
Herrick, C. J.
Hersh, M.
Herskowitz, Irwin J.
Hewes, G. W.
Hewett, Frank M.
Hewitt, L. E.
Hie, T.
Hildreth, G. E.
Hilgard, E. R.
Hinsey, J. C.
Hinshelwood, J.
Hinton, G.
Hintzman, D. L.
Hirshoren, A.
Hoch, Paul H.
Hodson, W.
Hoffer, Abram
Hogan, H. P.
Hohn, F. E.
Holland, J. G.
Holloway, William
Holmes, D. J.
Holzman, P. S.

Homme, L. E.
Horn, Hartmut
Horne, D.
Horne, Herman
Hornsby, Joan R.
Hornstein, Pearl
House, B. J.
Hovland, C. I.
Howard, I. P.
Howes, Davis
Hubel, D. H.
Hughes, J. A.
Hughes, John R.
Huizinga, R.
Hull, C. L.
Humphrey, James H.
Hunka, S.
Hunt, R. G.
Huttenlocher, J.
Hyden, Holgar

Ilg, Frances L.
Ingram, T. T. S.
Ingram, W.
Inhelder, Bärbel
Irvine, R. P.
Irwin, F. W.
Irwin, J. McQ.
Israel, H. E.

Jackson, Anna
Jackson, D. N.
Jackson, M.
Jackson, P. W.
Jackson, T. A.
Jaeger, E. C.
James, N. E.
James, W.
Jan, O.
Jansen, Mogens
Jansky, J.

Jarvik, Murray
Jasper, Herbert
Jastak, J. F.
Jastak, S. R.
Jenkins, J. G.
Jessup, Michael H.
Jex, J. L.
John, E. R.
Johnson, Doris J.
Johnson, G. O.
Johnson, Marjorie S.
Jones, A. W.
Jones, E. E.
Jones, J. Dean
Jones, Lewis W.
Jones, M. G.
Jones, R.
Joos, Loyal W.
Joslin, Elliott P.
Judd, C. H.

Kagan, Jerome
Kaminsky, Bernard P.
Kane, Joan
Kaplan, Barry
Karasik, Alan D.
Karpati, G.
Karpova, S. N.
Kass, Corrine E.
Katona, G.
Kaufman, J.
Kaufman, M. E.
Kawi, A. A.
Kay, H.
Keeney, A. H.
Keeney, V. T.
Keislar, E. R.
Keller, F.
Kendler, H. H.
Kennard, M.
Kenney, Helen J.

Keogh, Barbara
Kephart, Newell C.
Keppell, Francis
Kerr, James
Kershner, John
Kettner, N. W.
Kidd, B.
Kiefer, R.
Kiley, Margaret A.
Killen, James R.
Killian, C. D.
Kinsbourne, Marcel
Kirk, Samuel A.
Klare, G. R.
Klausmeier, H. J.
Klein, G. S.
Kline, C. I.
Kløve, H.
Kluever, Raymond
Kluver, H.
Knights, Robert M.
Knobel, M.
Knobloch, H.
Koffka, K.
Köhler,Wolfgang
Kooh, S.
Koons, Roberta, G.
Koontz, Elizabeth
Koppitz, E. M.
Korey, S. R.
Kraskin, Robert A.
Kratoville, E. L.
Krech, David
Kress, Roy A.
Kretch, D.
Krueger, L.
Krumboltz, J. D.
Kubany, E.
Kucera, H.
Kunst, M.
Kurlander, L.

Lacey, J.
Langford, T.
Langford, W.
Larsen, Marguerite
Lashley, K. S.
Laskey, E.
Laufer, M. W.
La Veck, Gerald D.
Lefevre, Carl
Lehmann, H. E.
Leland, Bernice
Lenneberg, E.
Lessler, K.
Levina, Rosa Ye.
Levine, Eleanor
Levy, S.
Lewis, D. J.
Lewis, R. B.
Lewis, V.
Liang, P.
Lilly, John C.
Lindsley, D.
Linhart, J.
Linton, H. B.
Lipman, I.
Lippman, Louis G.
Lipsitt, L.
Little, J. K.
Liublinskaya, A. A.
Llorens, L.
Long, Nicholas
Long, R. I.
Lorente de No, R.
Loughlin, L. J.
Lovitt, T.
Lowell, R.
Lubar, Joel F.
Luchins, A. S.
Luchins, Edith H.
Luria, A. R.
Luther, B.

Lyon, D. O.
Lytton, George J.
Mabry, J. E.
Maccoby, M.
MacGinitie, W. H.
MacRitchie, Cynthia
Madsen, Charles H.
Magendie, F.
Maginnis, G.
Magoss, M.
Magoun, H. W.
Malmquist, Eve J.
Mandler, G.
Mann, Phillip H.
Mardis, V.
Margen, Sheldon
Martin, D. M.
Martin, W.
Marx, R.
Masland, R. L.
Maslow, A.
Matthews, R. A.
McCandless, Boyd R.
McCandless, E. O.
McCann, James W., Jr.
McCarthy, D.
McCarthy, J. F.
McCarthy, J. J.
McCarthy, Jeanne McR.
McClelland, D. C.
McConnell, T. R.
McCracken, Glenn
McCrocklin, J. H.
McGeoch, G. O.
McGeoch, J. A.
McGinnis, Mildred A.
McGlannan, Frances K.
McGrady, H.
McKillop, A. S.
McLeod, John

McMahon, Audrey
McNeill, D.
Mecham, M.
Melton, A. W.
Merrifield, P. R.
Messick, S. J.
Meyer, D. R.
Meyer, Susan R.
Midlo, Charles
Miller, G. A.
Miller, N. E.
Miller, Paula
Millichap, J. G.
Milner, R.
Minami, H.
Minskoff, J. Gerald
Modiano, Nancy
Mondale, Walter F.
Money, John
Montessori, Maria
Morgan, C. T.
Morgan, W. P.
Morgenstern, G.
Morrell, F.
Mortisett, L.
Moruzzi, G.
Moser, H. E.
Mosher, F. A.
Moss, H. A.
Motto, Rocco L.
Mowrer, O. H.
Moylan, Marie C.
Munn, N. L.
Murphy, H.
Murphy, K. P.
Mussen, Paul H.
Myers, P.
Myklebust, Helmer R.

Nagge, J. W.
Nardini, J.

Natchez, Gladys
Nauta, W. J. H.
Neff, W. D.
Newcomer, P.
Newell, A.
Newman, E. B.
Nielsen, J.
Noble, C. E.
Noll, Angie
Norcross, K. J.
Norrie, Edith
Northrop, D. S.
Northway, M. L.

Oakes, W. F.
O'Donnell, P.
Oldfield, R. C.
Olds, James
Olson, D.
Olson, D. R.
Olver, Rose R.
Oppenheimer, Jess
Ort, L. L.
Orton, June L.
Orton, Samuel T.
Osgood, C. E.
Ott, John
Ozer, Mark N.

Paine, Richmond S.
Palamutlu, N.
Paley, E.
Papez, J. S.
Park, George E.
Pasamanick, B.
Passow, A. Harry
Pate, J.
Patridge, M.
Patten, C. A.
Patterson, Gerald R.
Paul, I. H.

Pauling, Linus
Paunier, L.
Pavlov, Ivan P.
Pearson, L.
Penfield, Wilder
Penrose, L. S.
Perkins, F. T.
Perlman, Suzanne M.
Peters, John E.
Petersén, I.
Peterson, L.
Peterson, M.
Peterson, W. M.
Pezet, A. W.
Phillips, W.
Piaget, Jean
Pineiro, C.
Plunkett, M. B.
Pope Pius XI
Poremba, Chester D.
Porter, A.
Porter, D.
Posner, C. M.
Postman, L.
Potter, M. C.
Potter, R.
Poulton, E. C.
Prentice, Marguerite
Pressey, S. L.
Pribram, K. H.
Pubols, B. H.

Quay, H.

Rabinovitch, M. Sam
Rabinovitch, Ralph D.
Radler, D. H.
Rampp, D.
Ranson, S. W.
Rapaport, David
Rappaport, Sheldon R.

Rasken, L.
Ratzeburg, F.
Rawson, Margaret B.
Redl, F.
Redl, H.
Reed, H. B.
Reed, L. S.
Reger, R.
Reich, Lee C.
Reid, J. F.
Reinhold, M.
Reinmuth, O. M.
Reitan, Ralph M.
Rentfrow, R.
Rice, J.
Richardson, J.
Richardson, Sylvia
Riesen, A. H.
Ringler, L.
Robbins, Lillian C.
Robbins, M. P.
Roberts, Lamar
Robinson, E.
Robinson, H. M.
Rock, I.
Rodham, Hillary
Roe, Anne
Roentgen, Wilhelm
Rogan, Laura E. Lehtinen
Rokeach, M.
Rose, Jerzy E.
Rosenthal, B. G.
Rosenzweig, M. R.
Rosman, B.
Rosner, J.
Ross, S.
Rossi, A.
Roswell, Florence
Rothschild, Gerard H.
Rubin, Eli Z.
Rudd, Augustin G.

Rudel, Rita G.
Rugel, R.
Ruis-Vestergaard, Mme.
Runkel, P. J.
Russell, D. H.
Russell, W. R.
Ryckman, D.

Sabatino, Donald A.
Sabol-Videc, Ruza
Sainz, A.
Santostefano, S.
Sassenrath, J. M.
Satz, P.
Saugstad, P.
Scheerer, M.
Schefflin, Margaret A.
Scheinfeld, Amram
Schenetzki, D.
Schiffman, Gilbert B.
Schiffrin, R. M.
Schiller, F.
Schlagenhauff, R.
Schleichkorn, J.
Schnabel, Artur
Schnitker, Max
Schpoont, S. H.
Schroeder, W. H.
Schubert, D. G.
Schulz, R. E.
Schulz, R. W.
Schwartz, L.
Schwartz, R.
Sechrest, L.
Segal, M. M.
Seidenfeld, M. A.
Selfridge, J. A.
Selldén, U.
Semel, Eleanor
Senf, G.
Sharpe, J. F.

Shaw, J. C.
Shedd, Charles L.
Sheffield, F. D.
Sheldon, Emily B.
Sheppard, Ben J.
Sherard, E.
Shields, D.
Shiffrin, R.
Shipley, W. C.
Shirley, L. P.
Shore, E.
Siegel, Ernest
Sigel, I. E.
Siipola, E. M.
Siiter, Roland
Silberberg, N.
Silberman, H. F.
Silberstein, Richard M.
Silver, Archie A.
Simon, H. A.
Sims, V. M.
Simula, V.
Singer, Susan B.
Skinner, B. F.
Skubic, V.
Slingerland, B.
Smith, B. O.
Smith, D. D.
Smith, Donald E. P.
Smith, Edwin H.
Smith, Helen K.
Smith, Henry P.
Smith, Inez
Smith, M. K.
Smith, Nila B.
Smock, C. D.
Smythe, P.
Soethe, James
Solan, H.
Solomons, Gerald
Sonstroem, A. McK.

Sotos, J.
Spache, George
Spence, D. P.
Sperry, R. W.
Spiker, C. C.
Spillane, J. D.
Spragg, S. D. S.
Sprague, R. L.
Spreen, O.
Staats, A. W.
Staats, C. K.
Stein, J. J.
Steinberg, H.
Steinhaus, A. H.
Stendler, C.
Stephens, T.
Stephens, A. L.
Sternfeld, Allan E.
Stevenson, H. W.
Stewart, L. F.
Stillman, B. W.
Stoch, M.
Stockwell, F. E.
Stolurow, L. M.
Strang, Ruth
Straug, B.
Strauss, Alfred A.
Streissguth, Ann Pytkowicz
Strich, S.
Strog, G.
Strother, Charles R.
Stroud, J. B.
Stuart, Marion F.
Suchman, J. R.
Suci, G. J.
Sullivan, Dorothy D.
Sullivan, Joanna
Sullivan, H.
Summerfield, A.
Swartz, J. D.
Swenson, C. H.

Swenson, Esther J.
Sylvester, E.
Symonds, Sir Charles

Taddonio, Robert
Taft, R.
Tannenbaum, P. H.
Tannhauser, H. T.
Tannhauser, M.
Tarnapol, L.
Tarver, S.
Taylor, C. W.
Taylor, Ian Galbraith
Taylor, W. K.
Templeton, W. B.
Thiele, C. L.
Thomas, C. J.
Thompson, Audrey A.
Thompson, L.
Thorndike, E. L.
Tinker, M.
Tobin, H.
Tolor, A.
Tomlinson, R. M.
Tonra, R.
Torrance, E. Paul
Torres, F.
Tower, D. B.
Traxler, A.
Tresselt, M. E.
Truex, R. C.
Turner, R. V.
Twining, P. E.
Tyack, D.
Tyler, R. W.
Tyrell, Sybil

Ullman, Charles
Ulmer, G.
Underwood, B. J.

Valett, R. E.
Van der Howen, T. L.
Van Ormer, E. B.
Vernon, M. D.
Vinacke, W. E.
Vogel, S.
Vygotsky, L. S.

Wagner, R.
Waites, Lucius
Walter, A. A.
Ward, A. H.
Ward, L. B.
Warren, J. M.
Warrington, Elizabeth K.
Watson, J. B.
Waugh, Kenneth W.
Wechsler, D.
Wedell, Karl
Wedell, Klaus
Wehe, R.
Weir, M. W.
Weiss, C.
Weiss, W.
Weithorn, C.
Welborn, E. L.
Welch, L.
Wellington, C. B.
Wellington, J.
Wepman, Joseph M.
Werry, John S.
Wessman, Alden E.
Wexler, D.
Whipple, J. E.
Whitcraft, C.
Whitemarsh, G. A.
Whittlesey, J. R. B.
Whitty, C. W. M.
Wiederholt, L.
Wiesel, J. M.
Wiig, E. Hemmersan

266   Acknowledgments

Williams, O.
Wilson, R. C.
Wiltbank, R. T.
Wineman, D.
Winick, M.
Withey, L.
Witkin, A. A.
Witt, P. A.
Wittrock, M. C.
Wolking, W.
Woodcock, R.
Woodrow, H.
Wooley, D. W.

Woolsey, C. N.
Wulf, F.

Yakelov, P. I.
Yamamoto, K.
Yarcozower, M.
Young, R. K.

Zach, L.
Zangwill, O. L.
Zeaman, D.
Ziegler, D. K.
Zuckerman, C. B.

Appendix A:
Service Organizations

The following organizations are vitally concerned with learning disabilities. They are the backbone of the nation's cohesive effort for learning abilities/disabilities.

ALLERGY FOUNDATION OF AMERICA
  801 Second Avenue, New York, New York 10017
AMERICAN ACADEMY OF ALLERGY
  225 East Michigan, Milwaukee, Wisconsin 53202
AMERICAN ACADEMY OF CHILD PSYCHIATRY
  Suite 904, 1800 R Street, N.W., Washington, D.C. 20009
AMERICAN ACADEMY OF NEUROLOGY
  4005 West 69 Street, Minneapolis, Minnesota 55435
AMERICAN ACADEMY OF PEDIATRICS
  1801 Hinman Avenue, Evanston, Illinois 60204
AMERICAN ASSOCIATION OF OPTHALMOLOGY
  1100–17 Street, N.W., Washington, D.C. 20036
AMERICAN EDUCATION ASSOCIATION
  1126–16 Street, N.W., Washington, D.C. 20036
AMERICAN EDUCATIONAL RESEARCH ASSOCIATION
  1126–16 Street, N.W., Washington, D.C. 20036
AMERICAN ELECTROENCEPHALOGRAPHIC SOCIETY
  36391 Maple Grove Road, Willoughby Hills, Ohio 44094
AMERICAN FEDERATION OF TEACHERS
  1012–14 Street, N.W., Washington, D.C. 20035

267

AMERICAN FOUNDATION FOR LEARNING DISABILITIES
  P.O. Box 196, Convent Station, New Jersey 07961
AMERICAN INSTITUTE OF NUTRITION
  9650 Rockville Pike, Bethesda, Maryland 20014
AMERICAN NEUROLOGICAL ASSOCIATION
  Cincinnati General Hospital, Cincinnati, Ohio 45229
AMERICAN OPTOMETRIC ASSOCIATION
  7000 Chippew Street, St. Louis, Missouri 63119
AMERICAN PSYCHOLOGICAL ASSOCIATION
  1200–17 Street, N.W., Washington, D.C. 20036
AMERICAN SOCIETY FOR ADOLESCENT PSYCHIATRY
  24 Green Valley Road, Wallingford, Pennsylvania 19086
AMERICAN SOCIETY FOR NEURO-CHEMISTRY
  McLean Hospital, Belmont, Massachusetts 02178
AMERICAN SPEECH AND HEARING ASSOCIATION
  9030 Old Georgetown Road, Washington, D.C. 20014
ASSOCIATION FOR THE ADVANCEMENT OF BEHAVIOR THERAPY
  305 East 45 Street, New York, New York 10017
ASSOCIATION FOR CHILDREN WITH LEARNING DISABILITIES (ACLD)
  5225 Grace Street, Lower Level, Pittsburgh, Pennsylvania 15236
  Note: ACLD is the largest service organization in the world. Any
  parent who has a child suffering from learning disabilities should
  contact this association. There are ACLD chapters throughout
  the United States. ACLD issues books, newsletters, and up-to-
  date information on a multidiscipline basis. Membership fees
  are nominal.
BRAIN RESEARCH FOUNDATION
  343 South Dearborn Street, Chicago, Illinois 60604
BUREAU OF EDUCATION FOR THE HANDICAPPED
  U.S. Office of Education, Division of Learning Disabilities,
  Seventh and D Streets, N.W., Washington, D.C. 20202
CALIFORNIA ASSOCIATION FOR NEUROLOGICALLY HANDICAPPED CHILDREN
  (CANHC)
  Literature Distribution Division,
  P.O. Box 1526, Vista, California 92083
CANADIAN ASSOCIATION FOR CHILDREN WITH LEARNING DISABILITIES
  (CACLD)
  Suite 316, 88 Eglinton Avenue, East Toronto 12, Ontario, Canada
    (See notation on ACLD)
CHILDREN, INC.
  P.O. Box 5381, Richmond, Virginia 23220

CLOSER LOOK
Box 1492, Washington, D.C. 20013
(A federal government project)
COUNCIL FOR EXCEPTIONAL CHILDREN (CEC)
Division for Children with Learning Disabilities (DCLD),
1920 Association Drive, Reston, Virginia 22091
Note: This is a multifaceted, interdisciplinary professional organization. CEC disseminates a wide variety of very valuable literature for both parents and professionals.
COUNCIL OF NATIONAL ORGANIZATIONS FOR CHILDREN AND YOUTH
c/o National Committee for Children and Youth,
#132, 1401 K Street, N.W., Washington, D.C. 20005
FOUNDATION FOR CHILD DEVELOPMENT
345 East 46 Street, New York, New York 10017
HEALTH, EDUCATION AND WELFARE
330 Independence Avenue, S.W., Washington, D.C. 20201
HEALTH, EDUCATION AND WELFARE
Office of Education,
400 Maryland Avenue, S.W., Washington, D.C. 20202
INTERNATIONAL FEDERATION OF LEARNING DISABILITIES
4934 East 21 Street, Indianapolis, Indiana
INTERNATIONAL READING ASSOCIATION (IRA)
800 Barksdale Road, Newark, Delaware 19711
Note: The IRA has been responsible for raising the standards of reading and literacy world-wide as well as stimulating high-level research for language arts. Also, Americans abroad should contact local chapters for help.
JEAN PIAGET SOCIETY
Box 493, Temple University, Philadelphia, Pennsylvania 19122
JOSEPH P. KENNEDY, JR. FOUNDATION
1701 K Street, N.W., Suite 205, Washington, D.C. 20006
KETTERING FOUNDATION
5335 Far Hills Avenue, Dayton, Ohio 45429
KIWANIS INTERNATIONAL
101 East Erie Street, Chicago, Illinois 60611
Note: Kiwanis is new to the efforts of the field of learning disabilities. This highly esteemed service organization is closely coordinating their work with ACLD. The Kiwanis project guide *The Younger Years* ($1.00) is valuable to parents and local governing agencies. Contact the club in your locale.

NATIONAL ASSOCIATION FOR MENTAL HEALTH
  1800 North Kent Street, Rosslyn, Virginia 22209
NATIONAL CATHOLIC EDUCATIONAL ASSOCIATION
  One DuPont Circle, N.W., Washington, D.C. 20036
NATIONAL CONGRESS OF PARENTS AND TEACHERS
  700 North Rush Street, Chicago, Illinois 60611
NATIONAL COUNCIL OF ADOPTIVE PARENTS
  P.O. Box 543, Teaneck, New Jersey 07666
NATIONAL COUNCIL OF COMMUNITY MENTAL HEALTH CENTERS
  Suite 322, Georgetown Building,
  2233 Wisconsin Avenue, N.W., Washington, D.C. 20007
  Note: Many mental health centers in the nation are performing
  evaluations and counseling at a nominal fee.
NATIONAL COUNCIL OF JEWISH WOMEN
  Community Activities Department,
  One West 47 Street, New York, New York 10036
NATIONAL EASTER SEAL SOCIETY FOR CRIPPLED CHILDREN AND ADULTS
  2023 West Ogden Avenue, Chicago, Illinois 60612
  Note: The Easter Seal Society has recognized the "crippling" effects
  of learning disabilities and now include these children under the
  broad range of services offered by this organization.
NATIONAL FOUNDATION MARCH OF DIMES
  P.O. Box 2000, White Plains, New York 10602
NATIONAL FOUNDATION FOR METABOLIC RESEARCH
  1100 Cornell Avenue, Cherry Hills, New Jersey 08304
NATIONAL HEALTH COUNCIL
  1740 Broadway, New York, New York 10019
NATIONAL INSTITUTE OF CHILD HEALTH AND HUMAN DEVELOPMENT
(NICHHD)
  9000 Rockville Pike, Bethesda, Maryland 20014
NATIONAL INSTITUTE OF MENTAL HEALTH (NIMH)
  Citizens Participation Branch,
  5600 Fishers Lane, Rockville, Maryland 20852
NATIONAL KINDERGARTEN ASSOCIATION
  23 East 16 Street, New York, New York 10016
NATIONAL ORGANIZATION ON LEGAL PROBLEMS OF EDUCATION
  825 Western Avenue, Topeka, Kansas 66606
  Note: Contact this organization for aid regarding implementation
  of the new legal rights laws.
THE ORTON SOCIETY
  8415 Bellona Lane, Towson, Maryland 21204

Note: The founder of this society was a pioneer in the field of specific learning disabilities. The society's literature and services are of high interest to parents and teachers.

PAN AMERICAN ASSOCIATION OF BIOCHEMICAL SOCIETIES
5323 Hamy Boulevard, Dallas, Texas 75235

RIGHT TO READ EFFORT
Office of Education,
400 Maryland Avenue, S.W., Washington, D.C. 20202

RURAL EDUCATION ASSOCIATION
1201–16 Street, N.W., Washington, D.C. 20036

SALK INSTITUTE FOR BIOLOGICAL STUDIES
P.O. Box 1809, San Diego, California 92112

SOCIETY OF ADOLESCENT MEDICINE
4650 Sunset Boulevard, Los Angeles, California 90027

SOCIETY FOR PEDIATRIC RESEARCH
1621 East 119 Street, Los Angeles, California 90059

SPECIAL EDUCATION INFORMATION CENTER
Box 19428, Washington, D.C. 20036

WORLD CONGRESS ON DYSLEXIA
P.O. Box 1136, Rochester, Minnesota 55901

FOR AMERICANS ABROAD

UNESCO LIAISON OFFICE AT THE UNITED NATIONS
Room 2201, U.N. Building, New York, New York 10017

U.S. COMMITTEE FOR THE WORLD HEALTH ORGANIZATION
777 United Nations Plaza, New York, New York 10017

U.S. DEPENDENT EDUCATION OFFICE
(Overseas schools for military personnel dependents)
Office of Assistant Secretary of Defense, Washington, D.C. 20301
    or
U.S. Dependent Education Office (Atlantic)
Pupil Personnel Services, Naval Air Station, Pensacola, Florida 32508
U.S. Dependent Education Office (Europe)
Pupil Personnel Services, APO New York, New York 09164
U.S. Dependent Education Office (Pacific)
Pupil Personnel Services, DOD Dependents Schools,
Pacific Area HQPACAF (DPN), APO San Francisco, California 96553
Note: For Americans abroad, even though not with the military

services, these schools can often provide local information of services available overseas. Or, in some instances, qualified teachers may be agreeable to performing private remedial tutoring.

Appendix B:
Publications

The following publications have a great deal to offer with regard to learning disabilities. Some are for parents, others for paraprofessionals, and still others for professionals only. All interested persons should feel free to contact all of these publishers; many offer supplementary material of great interest.

ACADEMIC THERAPY QUARTERLY
    1539 Fourth Street, San Rafael, California 94901
AMERICAN EDUCATION
    U.S. Office of Education (OE),
    400 Maryland Avenue, S.W., Washington, D.C. 20202
AMERICAN JOURNAL OF ORTHOPSYCHIATRY
    1790 Broadway, New York, New York 10019
AMERICAN MOTHERS-TO-BE
    10 East 52nd Street, New York, New York 10022
AMERICAN TEACHER
    1012–14 Street, N.W., Washington, D.C. 20005
BEHAVIORAL SCIENCES NEWSLETTER
    10605 Concord Street, Kensington, Maryland 20795
BULLETIN OF THE ORTON SOCIETY
    8415 Bellona Lane, Towson, Maryland 21204
CHANGING EDUCATION
    1012–14 Street, N.W., Washington, D.C. 20005

CHILD AND FAMILY
    Box 508, Oak Park, Illinois 60303
CHILDHOOD EDUCATION
    3615 Wisconsin Avenue, N.W., Washington, D.C. 20016
CHILDREN TODAY
    P.O. Box 1182, Washington, D.C. 20013
COMPACT
    1860 Lincoln Street, Denver, Colorado 80203
DEVELOPMENTAL PSYCHOLOGY
    1200–17 Street, N.W., Washington, D.C. 20036
DIRECTORY OF FACILITIES FOR THE LEARNING-DISABLED AND
HANDICAPPED
    Harper & Row, Publishers
    10 East 53 Street, New York, New York 10022
EARLY YEARS
    P.O. Box 1223, Darien, Connecticut 06820
EDUCATION RECAPS
    Princeton, New Jersey 08540
EDUCATION SUMMARY
    100 Garfield Avenue, New London, Connecticut 06320
ERIC DOCUMENT REPRODUCTION SERVICE
    c/o National Cash Register Co.,
    4936 Fairmont Avenue, Bethesda, Maryland 20014
FAMILY HEALTH
    1271 Avenue of the Americas, New York, New York 10020
GRADE TEACHER
    22 West Putnam Avenue, Greenwich, Connecticut 06830
HEALTH CARE MAGAZINE
    P.O. Box 251, Madison Square Station, New York, New York
    10010
JOURNAL OF APPLIED BEHAVIORAL SCIENCE
    N.I.A.B.S., 1201–16 Street, N.W., Washington, D.C. 20036
JOURNAL OF LEARNING DISABILITIES
    101 East Ontario Street, Chicago, Illinois 60611
JOURNAL OF OPTOMETRIC VISION THERAPY
    Box 285, Chula Vista, California 92012
JOURNAL OF PERSONALITY
    6697 College Station, Durham, North Carolina 27708
LANGUAGE, SPEECH AND HEARING SERVICES IN SCHOOLS
    9030 Old Georgetown Road, Bethesda, Maryland 20014

NEA RESEARCH BULLETIN
1201–16 Street, N.W., Washington, D.C. 20036
NEWS RELEASES
Department of HEW, Washington, D.C. 20201
NUTRITION TODAY
1140 Connecticut Avenue, N.W., Washington, D.C. 20036
PERCEPTUAL COGNITIVE DEVELOPMENT
Box 35336, Preuss Station, Los Angeles, California 90035
PARENTS MAGAZINE
52 Vanderbilt Avenue, New York, New York 10017
PSYCHOLOGY TODAY
Del Mar, California 92014
READING RESEARCH QUARTERLY
800 Barksdale Road, Newark, Delaware 19711
READING TEACHER
800 Barksdale Road, Newark, Delaware 19711
REHABILITATION LITERATURE
2023 West Ogden Avenue, Chicago, Illinois 60612
REVIEW OF EDUCATIONAL RESEARCH
1126–16 Street, N.W., Washington, D.C. 20036
SCHOOL AND SOCIETY
1860 Broadway, New York, New York 10023
TODAY'S EDUCATION
1201–16 Street, N.W., Washington, D.C. 20036
TODAY'S HEALTH
535 North Dearborn Street, Chicago, Illinois 60610
YOUNG CHILDREN
1834 Connecticut Avenue, N.W., Washington, D.C. 20009
XEROX CORPORATION NEW RELEASES
280 Park Avenue, New York, New York 10017

Index